in search of modern ireland

In Search of Modern Ireland

An American Traveler's Odyssey

Bryce Webster

Dodd, Mead & Company • New York

The recipe for Guinness Cake and The Guinness Diet are reprinted with permission of Arthur Guinness & Son Co. Ltd. Passages from *Georgian Dublin* by Harold Clarke reprinted with permission of Harold Clarke. Bailey's Ice Cream recipe reprinted with permission of Daniel Mullane and Tim Gibbons of The Mustard Seed, Adare, Co. Limerick, Ireland.

Published by Dodd, Mead & Company, Inc.
79 Madison Avenue, New York, N.Y. 10016
Distributed in Canada by
McClelland and Stewart Limited, Toronto
Manufactured in the United States of America
Designed by Erich Hobbing

First Edition

Library of Congress Cataloging-in-Publication Data

Webster, Bryce.
In search of modern Ireland.

Includes index.
1. Ireland—Description and travel—1981–
2. Ireland—Civilization—20th century. 3. Northern Ireland—Description and travel—1981–
4. Webster, Bryce—Journeys—Ireland. I. Title.
DA978.2.W43 1986 914.15'04824 86-6326
ISBN 0-396-08695-0 (pbk.)

1 2 3 4 5 6 7 8 9 10

TO PATRICE COBB COOPER, who has been in the forefront of the raking of the new fire and keeping of the flame of Ireland—past, present, and future.

contents

acknowledgments

I thank my editor, Jerry Gross, for understanding when the manuscript was late that I was having trouble digesting the rich Irish meal I had just had and needed time to let it settle a bit before I used it as fuel.

I thank my agent, Charles Neighbors, for his eons of help and understanding—and for working closely with both Jerry and me on this book.

I thank my mother, Louise Box, for accompanying me on part of my voyage of discovery; she helped me to rediscover a familiar land through her stranger's eyes.

I thank many friends, all Irish in fact or in spirit, for the inestimable help they've rendered by being who they are. Thanks, then, to Jane and Tom Lydon; Frank Madden; Hiroko Tamaki Byers and David Byers; Mary Jane Holland; Mercia and Patrick Byrne; Lenora and Sam Hern.

I thank most profoundly the many real people whose names appear in this book. Without them, the Emerald Isle would be pale indeed. And I thank also the many Irish men and women who appear nameless in the book; their contributions are certainly to be congratulated all the same.

Finally, I thank the Industrial Development Authority of Ireland. Without their help—which has been generous to a fault—I might have missed industrial Ireland. I further thank them for their evenhandedness and professionalism. They are by far, as they have been to me for eight years, the most pleasant group of men and women a journalist could meet, in that country or any other.

PROLOGUE

One of the most difficult things in the world is to write about a place that's been written about before, and to do so in a fresh new way. Simply coping with the reams and reams of information, the memorable phrases of the earlier authors, the expectations of editors and readers alike, not to mention one's own, becomes a task that strikes dark fear and trembling into the journalist's breast. At the same time, one is infused with the excitement of the hunt for a new insight, and—dare one hope it?—a new place among the travel classics.

It is impossible for me to judge how well I have done this, sitting as I am in a warm climate some months after the last of my chilly journeys through the Emerald Isle was complete. It pleases me to think, now, that emeralds are not only green, as Ireland is, but hard and cold—and immensely valuable. These qualities, too, it is possible to find in Ireland. The people are hard—in a characteristically soft way. They have endured much and have gained strength through it, but it's hidden well under the soft folds of their Gaelic English speech, in the comforting offering of hospitality all over the nation, from humble hotels to the boardrooms of international businesses perched on the rocky island for their swoop into Europe.

And there's no doubt Ireland is cold. Not a week ago, I had dinner with a young visitor from Dublin who said, "No one goes to Ireland for the weather."

There are those who say emeralds are fiery stones—and this quality, too, is not to be denied Ireland. Fractious and opinionated to this day, there is a wild streak in the Irish breast that cleaves the progress of Irish life into a thousand glimmering facets.

Ireland offers the world much, as well. It has given the United States some of its most famous dynastic families. It has exported literature and art for centuries; it was a candle flickering in the sea of ignorance in the Dark Ages, its monks copying and carrying abroad the Good Word. Subsequently, of course, Ireland fell into its own dark times, the plunder-bumpkins of the Norse, the puppets and poppets of centuries of British domination. Today, however, it is getting its own back, entering the postindustrial world with a vengeance, and very often besting its European neighbors in attracting the new gold—high-tech industry—to its shores.

Did I mention Ireland is a hard land? Indeed I did. But I failed to fully expound on that. Ireland is an impossible land to understand, to reduce to a series of thoughts logically connected, grammatically set forth. It is a bundle of irreconcilable opposites, and yet, it certainly attracts. Even as I write, I can feel the blood rise in my veins, the beginnings of frustration stir in my heart, the potential for a splitting headache laid on as I grind the nuggets of all that is Ireland in the hopper of my brain. Like emeralds, these nuggets are very difficult, almost impossible, to crush. Far better to set them in a way that seems most pleasing. And that, in this book, is what I have tried to accomplish.

I have more or less followed the path taken by the great British travel writer H.V. Morton in his 1930 book about his jaunt around Ireland called *In Search of Ireland*. He traveled to the country by ferry; I went by jet plane. He traveled through the land by car and sometimes donkey cart. I saw some carts, indeed some still in use occasionally in Dublin, but I didn't have need of them, thank goodness.

Morton circumnavigated Ireland, only once or twice venturing inland, and then not very far. I penetrated the place more deeply. Indeed, some of my favorite stories are born of the country's lush middle. On the other hand, my personal favorite places are all at the edge of the land, pounded by the eternal sea.

Morton liked Cork best, or so it seems. I found it less interesting than almost anywhere else. Morton hit all the tourist high spots and wrote on them extensively. I did not. To be sure, I visited some, many of those Morton did. But these days they are overrun with tourists and set about with people hawking wares. I quickly decided that I'd do better finding out about Ireland if I visited Ireland, not Fantasy Ireland. Morton wrote from the vantage point of being a British citizen and a man. I am an American woman; this alone would point out subtle differences in the book. Indeed, it is literally impossible that we would have similar experiences, indeed unlikely that we would be innately drawn to the same persons, places, and things. Not only our nationalities and genders demand this, of course, but also the genetic makeup each of us was born with. Nonetheless, he was with me all the way.

There is one highly significant area, too, where Morton and I see eye to eye. Ireland is well worth a visit. It is endlessly fascinating, endlessly vexing. It is, I have lately decided, an addiction. Beware. Once you've stuck the needle under your skin, the only way to beat the habit is cold turkey—total abstention. So violent is the fever that, if I want to avoid spending my vacation money there again, I must store my Irish records in the attic for months ahead, resolutely send to cold storage the winter clothes I have bought there (including the last of the *real* fishermen's knit sweaters I snagged on my very first visit), and ignore calls from all friends named Lydon or Byrne or Ahearn or Donlon or anyone with a "Mc" or "O' " in their names. I give wide berth to the Aer Lingus counter in international airports, lest I take out my plastic money and impulsively book a flight.

This, too, differs from Morton. He spent twelve weeks in Ireland at one time. I split my journey into two six-week segments. Morton, in that earlier, more leisurely era, could easily take himself off, as they say, for a long traipse. I could not. I had other pressing needs, family and business. Nephews to cosset, a widowed mother to attend to, a husband who was loath to have me leave for such a time. There were other books to be written, articles prepared. And, unlike Morton, I had been to Ireland before—eight times, in fact, beginning in 1977. Some of these trips were for pleasure, others for business, one or two a combination. At times, I have used notes from those earlier visits, most notably one with my mother in 1983, to expand on a point I had tripped over again. The bulk of this book is drawn from my two most recent trips with my husband. It helped, in fact, to have these other experiences to draw on. I doubled my insight power; things that happened to others might never have happened to me. I have since developed it as a theory that, if you want to truly know about a place, you would do well first to visit it on your own, and then bring along a neophyte, lest your observations get hidebound and stilted.

There is, in fact, one person who traveled through Ireland with me and never shows up in the book. Indeed, he was my silent partner all along, my late father. He was the Irish member of our clan, and even then, he was only half Irish on his mother's side.

Besides, he never wanted to be Irish. As far back as I can remember, he avoided the Irish relations. He took us, my brother and I, to grow up in a sterile, WASPish environment on Long Island, assiduously avoiding the rich stew of Irish-American life our cousins were boiled up in in Brooklyn.

On all my trips before my father died, which were many, he never once expressed a desire to go along, though I'd gladly have taken him. I thought, as I always had, that he didn't want to be Irish.

Alas, I was mistaken. The year of his death, I took my mother, who is French and English, with me. I thought she needed a change, and I wasn't ready to tackle Paris with her; it wasn't yet familiar enough to me. But Ireland was. "You know," she said the day we visited the site of the Pope's visit to Phoenix Park, "your father had decided he did want to see Ireland after all. I guess I'm seeing it for him."

When the opportunity came to write this book, I began to think about dedications. Should I dedicate it to my father? I had dedicated an earlier book to him, but might this not be more fitting? Should I dedicate it to my father, who never visited the land of his birthright because, by that very birthright, he was too stubborn to admit of a change of heart? My father, who had raised me to the best of his ability, whom I miss still, though he was a fractious person to say the least? My father, tall and dark with flashing eyes, almost Spanish-looking, a true representative of the famed "black Irish"? My father, the gentle man who had held me in his arms and, in best Irish tradition, though I didn't know it then, told me fractured fairy tales—The Princess and the Billy Goat's Gruff, Prince Jack and the Pea, The Twelve Dancing Little Shoemakers—and hundreds more? (To this day, I have to wonder what the real stories are about.)

I decided not to. A book is a poor thing to dedicate to one's father. Indeed, there is nothing fitting, save a lifetime of love and memory.

Should I dedicate it to my husband, who has been relentlessly helpful for the twelve years of our marriage, who is my soulmate and heartmate and meets and bests and spars with my mind, and about whom it is impossible for me to speak without sounding like the writer of a potboiler romance? (He understands.) No, he comes more or less under the same heading as a father, maybe more so.

Should I dedicate it to those who have been so helpful with my writing trips to Ireland? The dozens of men and women on both sides of the Atlantic, "the pond," who set up appointments for me, gave me their insights or their hospitality or both? Should I dedicate it to the editor who pushed through this project, at last letting me get off my chest the crushing weight of my relationship with this most complicated of countries? (Of course, he is—as am I—interested in the literary value as well.)

Perhaps I should make no dedication, I began to think. But then, in true Irish fashion, leaping perilously on the waves of a tall glass of Jameson's Irish Whiskey, the solution came to me. The lady in question knows all about the whiskey. She it was who plied me with it at a dinner-dance for one of her favorite charities. She it is who, at the age of seventy-six, runs the rest of us in the Society of Ireland, which she founded, completely into the ground. She it is who will be angry with me when she reads this because I have left the state out of the society's name. (Calm down, Patrice. I'll tell you why later.)

But I won't give the dedication again here. You've read it already. Unlike the Irish, I don't like to repeat myself at all, at all.

In Search of Modern Ireland

1. Dublin

I fly to Dublin, am warmly received, and begin my search for cultural heroes. I meet an old Republican of a different sort, the son of a peer, and some friendly brothers not my own. I drink "the black stuff," go househunting, and seek some gaiety.

Although not my first flight "across the pond" to Europe, this most recent one, in May 1985, may have been the one I most enjoyed, I thought as we approached Dublin airport after a brief off-loading and on-loading at Shannon. I had booked Aer Lingus' executive class; the seats were large and reclined and had footrests. Beyond that, the cabin crew had provided ample blankets and pillows; free champagne, although the plane had taken off on time; a minimum of interruptions; a toiletry kit that I had just used to very pleasant effect; and a pair of blue socks with a green shamrock that were, if you ask me, the best part of the service. Until this trip, I have never flown without having my feet freeze, especially in the window seats I prefer. The socks enabled me to kick off my shoes and curl up—and still trek to the lavatories without squeezing flight-swollen feet into stiff, cold leather.

Shortly after taking off on this leg of the journey (which takes just over half an hour, the plane never reaching anything like cruising altitude), one of the cabin crew came up and sat on the arm of the seat next to me, to talk. "We knew, of course, that we had an author on the flight," she told me, "who was writing a book about Ireland. But, you know, we had some trouble in the back early in the trip." That much had been obvious to me; I was dying to know what it had been. I had seen the captain trek back there somewhere over Maine or Newfoundland.

"A man got on drunk in New York and we weren't aware of his condition until he had had a couple more on board and got abusive. Unfortunately, it was a full flight, so we'd nowhere to put him where he wouldn't cause more trouble. If the captain going back and speaking firmly to him hadn't worked, I'm afraid we were going to put down in Canada and get him off." I breathed a sigh of relief. "He did finally just go to sleep," she said.

The flight attendant was named Eleanor Lynch, and she was just the sort of long-legged Nordic blond type of Irishwoman my husband admires greatly—and on Aer Lingus, not from very far, as the cabin crews are always particularly attentive to him.

By that time, we were landing in Dublin, and Eleanor Lynch went to buckle herself into her seat belt. I didn't see her when we disembarked; she was tending to clean up business in the galley. My baggage came through in record time. I passed easily through the "green" customs line for those with nothing to declare and waltzed right into my rental car. And not a moment too soon. Although I'm glad not to have to endure an ocean-surface crossing, as Morton did for his visit when he crossed the Irish Sea from England, a particularly capricious body of water, the night flight from New York is taxing. Although I had caught an hour's sleep on the plane, I had lost the other seven and was suffering from jet lag and weather change as well.

Morton, I recalled, had been fortunate on his crossing, too. It was June and the waters were dead calm. To hear him tell it, the turbulence we had *over* the ocean was worse than he had on it, and we had little at all. Like me, Morton had chosen to travel in a better section; indeed, he explored steerage on his journey, as I might have explored the tourist section. But, while I'd have found the drunken American causing all the trouble, he found only drinking Irish lads, in high spirits but not particularly high.

Morton was fascinated by this floating bit of Ireland. My flying bit of Ireland was not the same at all, at all. First, there were very few Irish on the plane. And such few as there were certainly were not domestic servants. Ireland's exported workers these days tend to be scientists or oil-rig roughnecks. I had met one of the latter on a plane once, only he wasn't coming from America but from Australia. And he wasn't on holiday. He was going to the funeral of his brother, who had died in Northern Ireland. His brother hadn't died in the modern-day Troubles, but in an industrial accident.

Like Morton, on his boat, I found priests and nuns on the plane—mainly Americans of Irish descent. None of these were in executive class. Rather, the cabin was filled with executives—Americans and "Returned Yanks." Returned Yanks are Irish men and women who have gone to the United States to begin a career. Later, highly trained and highly prized, they return to their homeland bearing the priceless gifts needed by a country planning to leap straight from the agrarian age to the computer age. And doing a creditable job of it, I would find.

Getting to my hotel was easy enough and took only about twenty minutes. I was at first amazed by the amount of traffic; I was, after all, on a holiday of sorts. But, of course, the Irish were not. I had landed on a Thursday morning, about 8 A.M. By now, the Irish were on their way to work, or driving their trucks to deliver goods, or setting out shopping—in short, doing all the things any modern society does at nine in the morning in its cars and trucks. And, most amazingly of all, they were doing it on the "wrong" side of the road. It took me quite a time to adjust my judgment with any accuracy; luckily, I had only two minor incidents. In one, hurrying out to Malahide, a posh Dublin suburb, I nicked a tire on a marble curb while passing too wide. In another, I twirled my mirror on the side of a bus. The bus was not harmed, and mirrors on Irish cars are made to twirl. Could it be, I thought later, that most people have trouble with left-side driving, even those for whom it is "normal"? I don't know for sure, or with any scientific evidence. But I am absolutely certain the turning radius on the cars is not as good as ours, due to the position of the wheel and drive train, and so on.

I had decided to stay in Glasnevin, a section of the city renowned for being several things, but not posh. Glasnevin is a working-class area, with a few small family-run hotels. The one I stayed in is called Egan's House, and it is, in effect, an extension of the Egan family. John Egan is a former champion Irish soccer player. Mrs. Egan was a nurse. They started a family and a hotel, and, at breakfast during the school year, you can see the young Egans eating their porridge all togged out in the school uniforms. Before long, Mrs. Egan will hurry them out and dash out the front door, car keys in hand, to deliver one or more of them to a before-school activity—sports and such. At night, you can hear the faint yips of the small family dog, happily running back and forth between family quarters and the front desk. And as often as not, if you need to make a phone call, it is the teenage daughter who rings it for you.

Glasnevin is on a very useful main route into Dublin's center from the north. Coming from the airport, you pass Prospect Cemetery, where many gallant souls of the Irish "Troubles" are buried, including Charles Stewart Parnell. The only other major attraction to recommend the area is the Botanic Gardens. Originally, these were lands surrounding the house of Addison, an essayist who came to Ireland in 1714 as secretary to the Earl of Sutherland. The Royal Dublin Society purchased the gardens from his successor in about 1740; since 1901, they have been administered by the Department of Agriculture. The gardens sport lily ponds, a rock garden with pygmy pine trees, and a cast-iron house. All this is perched on the Tolka River, a small stream hardly larger than the Grand Canal slightly to the south. Flowing as it does through several parks and parklike areas, it has, however, avoided the Grand Canal's fate. While the Tolka hardly runs wild and free, the Grand Canal is the Irish answer to Brooklyn's Gowanus Canal—a great, green, greasy body of sluggish water, sooted upon by both barges and nearby trains, surrounded by factories both past and present, and ignored by all but the occasional wanderer off the beaten track, such as cats, small boys with stones to throw, and hoboes. And me.

Indeed, it was on a short walk the afternoon of my arrival that I found both the Grand Canal as it passes through Glasnevin, and specifically Iona Park, and a Republican of different color. In Ireland, when you say "Republican," it is assumed you are talking about an elderly person who took the separatist part, or at least side, in Ireland's fight for political independence from Great Britain.

On my walk to the Canal, I wandered in the cool spring drizzle past blocks of neat and quite substantial Victorian and Edwardian houses, the same sort as Egan's House, though theirs had been a double house to begin with and had been much expanded. Many of the houses, most in fact, still had their original trimming of small leaded-glass windows in odd places, the original wrought-iron fences and gates, and ornate doors, many with a central octagonal doorknob. In this neighborhood, the way things are these days, many also had burglar-alarm boxes attached under the eaves. Many of the Irish claim that Ireland is still a very moral society. An equal number claim it is not, that all the "high morality" talk is hypocrisy. Whatever the truth is (and I tend to side with the group believing that the bulk of the Irish are more moral than the bulk of the people in the U.S.), petty crime is on the increase. In Glasnevin, which is experiencing both decline and "gentrification," this is certainly true.

The economic shift in Glasnevin is not from down to up, nor up to down exactly. Never a posh area, neither was it of the wretched tenements James Joyce glorified. Solid and working-class, with some rough edges, perhaps. Now, it is partly that. But on the streets at five o'clock, there seem to be a great number of young and trendy-looking working men and women, the Irish version of the Yuppie—a Gaelic Upwardly Mobile Professional. Guppie, they might be called. The shops are beginning to cater to them: the hair salons are showing posters of European styling; there are fruit markets of the sort admired by this group the Western world over—glossy local fruit and vegetables, preferably displayed in the open air, and supplemented by exotics like kiwis, star fruit and the like, and gourmet and health-food items.

It is not this influx doing the thievery, apparently. But the glossy lifestyle is attractive to thieves, who figure there is something to steal. Still, most of these young people live in flats created out of the rambling houses; more traffic seems to engender more break-ins in any country.

In any case, as I rounded a corner I saw an elderly man with wild white hair mowing his tiny front lawn—hardly more than a grass patch—with a hand mower. I noticed two things right off. The man, who must have been in his late seventies, was wearing a white shirt, suspenders, and a tie to mow his yard. That formality over a simple chore impressed me as part of the man's strength of character, about which I soon learned more.

Second, and more important, the yard boasted the most spectacular display of tulips I had ever seen outside of a botanic garden, and in a space not more than thirty square feet. There were many colors, yellows and reds and whites, and many multicolored ones. The white tulips that seem to drip with pink or red stripes I particularly admired. And, like most growing things in Ireland, they were enormous, some as much as two feet tall, well past my knee. The petals of the overblown blooms spread larger than a pianist's hand.

I walked up to the gate and said loudly so the man could hear me above the clippity noise of his mower, "Those are very beautiful tulips."

The man stopped and turned. He took out a handkerchief and wiped his face as he sauntered over to the gate. "Aye, they're not that much. They're about done. They have to come out next week." He had that air of modesty I have come to appreciate and enjoy in the Irish.

But I refused to take his modesty seriously and praised his flowers again. This time, he recognized my American accent and asked, "Well, now, are you from the States?" I said yes, and he asked me where I was from and, for a moment, we made small talk about his relatives in the States and my travels in Ireland. The man was about my height, and had the face of a weathered cherub. He vaguely resembled a happy Robert Frost.

Then, to my surprise, because the Irish tend not to ask strangers questions about the "SRP" unmentionables (sex, race, and politics) in polite company, he asked, "What do you think of Reagan?" (he pronounced it "Ree-gan"). I made noncommittal noises about my personal feelings toward our President. But he launched into an excited speech about the President and said he was a staunch supporter of Reagan's defense policies. "You can't show weakness to the Russians. A strong hand is all they understand," he concluded.

He continued in this vein for a couple of minutes. I mention it only because of the reaction I got when I asked some Irish friends of mine about this unsolicited support of President Reagan. In Ireland, although Reagan is personally very popular, many of his policies, especially defense spending, détente, South Africa, and Central America, are actively opposed. Their reaction was, "Oh, he probably didn't really feel that way. You know, many Irish people will only say what they think you want to hear."

But I think differently, certainly in this case. I didn't solicit the man's views; he solicited mine. Although I was noncommittal, he was very definite in his views. Perhaps he had been a soldier during World War II (or even World War I, for that matter). Or perhaps he had been in the Irish Army. I don't know. I do know that the Irish are very polite and are loath to criticize or even disagree with a stranger. But I also know the Irish love politics and a good argument. Although they are subtle about it, when the Irish disagree with a stranger, they usually change the subject or disagree through the back door with an "Aye, well, yes that may be true, but don't you know that . . ." sort of approach.

As I was to learn several times during my trip, the Irish are often quick to criticize what I consider their strengths as a people, especially their politeness and manners, and slow to appreciate these customs, practiced far less often in the United States.

In any case, after my pleasant interlude with the old man, I walked away, warmed by his civility, his energy, and his directness of conversation.

I went on from there to the Canal. I climbed the black iron stairs and looked down from the overpass into the water; it was black and glassy as a mirror, and in my weakened condition, I didn't stay long. I turned and watched instead as a cat in a kitchen garden stalked a bird. It was a huge cat and a small bird, but the cat missed. He did not, I surmised, get so fat on a diet he caught for himself. Nor did I. Despite my filling breakfast (two actually, both the one on the plane and one Egan's provided when I checked in), I was hungry. I had missed my lunch in favor of some sleep. The sun was going down, but very gradually. I knew it wouldn't be down—and it wouldn't be dinnertime—until at least 8 P.M. But I could go to The Maples, a nearby small hotel with full bar and restaurant, and have a glass of something warm to prepare myself for dinner.

I had very badly misjudged the need for woolens. When I left New York in May, it had been warm, definitely weather for a silk or cotton blouse under a lightweight wool suit. I assumed a trench coat over that would take care of Ireland in May. Although May can be quite warm in the Emerald Isle, this year I was wrong. I needed some woolen turtlenecks and hadn't any along. And even a pair of gloves would have been welcome at night. Luckily, the country still boasts fireplaces in dining rooms, and The Maples had a good one. The hostess/waitress (there was only one, as high season had not really begun) must have noticed my shivering, for she cleared and set immediately a table next to the fire.

This was the first of my huge dinners, the beginning of the end of my figure for at least a time. I have found it difficult, when traveling, to be careful of how much I eat and how often. So often, it is not under one's own control—when one is a houseguest, for example. Ordinarily true that you can choose what you want in a restaurant, where you're paying for the privilege, it is not true in Ireland. Leaving food on the plate will bring, as often as not, a query from the cook as to its quality. "Did you not enjoy your meal, then?" the waitress will ask. The country had been poor for a long time, and no one visited it to eat. Indeed, in stories from relatives who traveled there in the early 1950s, it was apparently hard to get a steak. When you did, it would be meager and it might be boiled. Today, they make absolutely sure that you've had enough, and then some.

There are still complaints about the food, and it is true that the country does not have a gourmet tradition. One of the country's most famous cooks, who runs an Irish restaurant in Paris partly at the behest of the Irish government, admits the best of Irish food is the simple hearty fare of the North Atlantic islands, the beef roasts, carrots, potatoes, custard puddings, berry-filled pies.

Like Morton, I arrived at my Dublin Zoo appointment in a most ancient of taxicabs; after a few excursions over the weekend, I decided I would leave the car parked as much as possible in Dublin, a most confusing city. Unlike Morton, I did not get to attend one of the famous breakfasts. Indeed, they are open only by very special invitation, not to the public. But they do still continue, both the breakfasts of the board of directors and, more recently, monthly Strawberry Breakfasts for zoo members. The members' breakfasts, which take place on Saturday mornings, are served in the restaurant, built in 1898 with a view to the future. Because I couldn't make it to a breakfast, I ate lunch there. Like Irish public midday meals the country over, it was substantial and served with a multitude of plates and cups and glasses and implements—a far cry from the American snack-bar type of feeding for zoogoers. But, like a U.S. zoo, the dining-room menu took advantage of the local favorites—not hamburgers and hot dogs, but consommé, fish fillets, boiled potatoes, carrots, good Irish bread, and a sweet—jam tart with cream or Black Forest gateau.

The board of directors' breakfasts also offer local favorites—among them porridge, eaten standing up. "Why?" I asked the recently retired director, Dr. E. T. Murphy, who is writing a book about the Dublin Zoo. "I'm not sure anyone knows, really," he said. "I would suspect, however, that it was because the first director was Scottish. As you know, porridge—or oatmeal—is the thing the Scots eat for breakfast, and I've no doubt it was considered heartier or more workmanlike to eat it while standing."

My walk round the gardens was conducted by Gregory Forde, a tall, dark, handsome, and rather new employee of the zoo, and one of the new, highly educated type of zoo keeper. Forde had recently received his doctorate in zoology and had spent the previous summer in the Arctic, studying the habits of the Brent Goose, which summers there and winters in Ireland.

Mr. Forde has charge of training new zoo guides, so every visitor to the zoo might experience something of the same lighthearted tour as I did. I remarked at one point on the flamingos.

"We feed them special food to turn their feathers flamingo color," he said. "Otherwise, their feathers would be white. Then they'd really live up to their name—Chilly-an flamingos," he added. Chilean flamingos indeed!

No stranger to strangeness, Forde gamely brought me round to a cage full of monkeys of a sort. "These are lion-tailed macaques," he explained, and silently went up to the cage, where he made a frightful face at the largest male. The macaque made a similar face back. "He loves to play like that," Forde said. And so, apparently, does Forde.

The monkeys are so abundant, in fact, that some of the females have already been moved in preparation for beginning a second troop. Natives of the southern tip of India, the macaques nonetheless thrive in Ireland's colder climate.

Tommy, too, is thriving in Ireland, as he has for forty-eight of his sixty years. Tommy is believed to be the oldest crocodile in captivity. Maybe, says Forde, it can be attributed to his lean diet; he is fed only on Fridays, and only horsemeat. "If something splashes into his pond, though, he gets confused," says Forde, "although he does basically seem to know when Friday is. These creatures are smarter than we give them credit for. When he is annoyed, he rears back up, opens his lower jaw, fills it with water, and snaps it shut. It really clears the kids out," he laughs.

Giraffes are the Dublin Zoo's most spectacular—or, at any rate, largest—breeding success these days. "They're six feet, six inches tall when they're born. They seem to have no problem breeding. In fact, we've recently moved a herd of them to Fota House." Fota House is an historic house and wildlife sanctuary near Cork.

The two most popular residents of the zoo—one with the public and one with the staff—are quite a bit smaller. Leonie, a young orangutan, is, to say the least, a curmudgeon. "This animal has been on TV and can behave herself quite nicely," Forde said. "But every now and then, maybe when she's annoyed at being stared at, she begins a game with the public. She scouts the crowd, chooses a victim, picks up a piece of her dung, and flings it, usually with deadly accuracy."

My Saint Francis complex was beginning to get the best of me. I'd never met an animal I didn't like, nor one who didn't like me. There, out of the corner of my eye, I could see Leonie scouting us. She had a choice: me, Forde, three schoolchildren, an elderly woman, and a young couple. There seemed to be a naughty gleam, though, whenever her big black eyes glanced my way. I eased us out.

Finally, there was the Mad Bird. This, said Forde, is a favorite with the staff, though it's not really exotic, and they didn't get it in the usual way. "There was a little old lady somewhere around here who had the bird for years. The story goes that she left town for a few days, and it didn't like whoever was taking care of it and went off its trolley. The old lady couldn't put up with the bird any longer and called the zoo." The bird, which is a female, is called Lothar. Maybe it learned its name and didn't like it. Or maybe it caught sight of itself in a mirror; it's beyond ugly duckling in appearance. In any case, it now has a comfy cage, Forde lets it chew on a stick he holds for it every now and then, and it can squawk and carry on to its heart's content. What kind of bird is it? Can't recall. I was busy snapping a photo of Forde and Lothar and it was quite chilly and the bird broke the pencil I was using anyway . . .

Before I left, I was taken to the Gate Lodge, a charming three-room, half-timbered structure just up the hill from the present gate. Built within two years of the zoo's founding, this little structure appears in numerous early photographs of the zoo.

When it was built, in about 1820, the zoo contained twenty-three animals: two wapiti deer, two sambur deer, one nylghai, two emus, two ostriches, two red-and-yellow macaws, two cockatoos, one coatimundi, one falcon, one African dove, two passenger pigeons, a hunting panther, a fox, a raccoon, a bear, and a wild boar.

The population soared, however, both through acquisition and breeding; today the zoo counts at least 690 animals, 153 of them homegrown. From its great stock, the zoo loans animals to other zoos—the Glasgow and Zurich zoos most recently. Indeed, the Dublin Zoo is the third oldest in the world, after London and Paris. But, while venerable, it is not creaky. The layout is mainly "environmental," and the animals appear as content as the strolling families who come year round, seven days a week, to marvel at their antics. I have been in zoos all over the Western world, and

I have identified two favorites. One is a small zoo in Evansville, Indiana. The other is the Dublin Zoo. Definitely a world-class zoo in its specimens and its arrangement, it was praised even in the early days. *The Dublin Penny Journal* published this zoo review in 1832:

> Look at the grounds, ye that have travelled to London and Paris, and say, could a better spot be selected. As we enter the grounds, can we not fancy ourselves in Paradise and see Adam and Eve walking in innocence amongst the creatures while they sported and frisked about them? In this delightful spot, possessing natural advantages which the wealth of London or the munificence of the French Government could not purchase, animals from every quarter of the World are brought together. So genial is our climate to their general constitutions that there is not a collection in Europe, in which the animals generally are in such fine condition or in which the proportion of death is so small.

Though the zoo has expanded from the original five and a half acres of 1832 to its present thirty, it is still charming and manageable and full of laughter and happiness. It is a peculiar blend of science and amusement that the Irish were almost bound to be good at. And it sports the amenities the Irish take for granted as well—good snacks and restaurant, adequate toilets, no "hard sell" of the souvenirs (as I have most thoroughly detested at our own National Zoo in Washington, D.C.), a friendly staff, and a low admission price, the equivalent of less than two dollars.

Morton found it worth mentioning fifty-five years ago that it was ironic that the Dublin Zoo was renowned for breeding that most English of symbols, the lion. The zoo is still famous for cat-breeding, but no one mentions that the capital of Ireland is breeding the symbol of England. Now that they are two sovereign nations, it is no more paradoxical than the fact that U.S. zoos breed China's giant panda. And in any case, the animals themselves have never waved a flag.

The very first person I met during a visit to the Guinness brewery was named Billy Porter. "Of course, we don't make porter anymore, just stout, but naturally my name does cause comment," he admitted. And probably often, as he is the public affairs director. "There are a couple of lawyers in Sligo," he pointed out, "whose names are the equal of mine. The firm is called Argue & Phibb."

(You never know when the Irish are pulling your leg, so I looked up Argue & Phibb in the Irish telephone directory—two volumes cover the whole country—and sure enough, there they were.)

Founded in 1759, the Guinness brewery was the largest in the world by 1914; it is still the largest in Europe. The central brewhouse, at St. James's Gate, is designed to produce two and a half million pints a day. This is, of course, a new brewhouse; it opened in 1977. Today, Guinness also has satellite breweries in Britain, Nigeria, Malaysia, Cameroun, Ghana, and Jamaica. Fifteen other countries produce Guinness under license.

Dublin's Guinness plant is also its largest employer and very likely covers the most ground. On sixty acres today, it covered only four when it was founded. The lease signed then by Arthur Guinness did, however, guarantee him the land for nine thousand years—at £45 per year. Needless to say, he expected to be in business for a while, and he has been. The spirit of Arthur Guinness is everywhere, from the Georgian house he built for himself on the grounds, to the modern boardrooms, where one of his descendants carries on the family concern. After only five others since its founding, the current chairman of the board is Benjamin Guinness, the Earl of Iveagh. Having been born in 1937, he still has some years to be the king of beers. As to the land lease—also needless to say—there have been some changes in the arrangements along the way.

Rising like gray mountains above the River Liffey, the gargantuan Guinness complex of old and new buildings sits on both sides of the road. To enter anywhere, you've got to pass a gatekeeper. To find the right entrance for your purpose, you'll likely encounter several, as I did. When I found the right one, a very policemanlike gentleman, he ushered me into a stunning Georgian waiting room in one of the older buildings while he rang Billy Porter. It used to be that even a casual visitor could have a tour right around the factory itself. Today, there is too much heavy machinery, not to mention health codes, to permit that. In response, Guinness is building a new model visitors' center; when I visited, it was not yet completed and visitors were shown a very informative film, followed by a free tasting. There, in the Guinness "pub," I had my first sip of the deep-brown syrupy brew, with its "whipped cream" head. And I had a talk with the curator of the Guinness Museum, Peter Walsh. "We do intend to bring back the tours in a couple of years," he said, "after we've added some safety features. Meanwhile, we've redone the old hop store into a visitors' center and an extensive art gallery."

During our discussion, over my half-pint, Walsh pointed out some of the familiar Guinness advertising slogans, the most famous being "Guinness Is Good for You."

"It is?" I asked.

"It is. At least, doctors are said to prescribe it for nursing mothers and the sickly. Maybe it is the vitamin and mineral content." I told him that my own brother took it, self-prescribed, for his ulcer. "There you are," Walsh agreed. "But I do know of one creature it wasn't so good for."

Walsh briefly left the room, returning with a brown grocery bag. "We found this at the bottom of an elevator shaft when we began redoing the hop store," Walsh said, dragging from the bag a perfectly mummified, entirely whole cat. If he'd been found in a processing part of the plant, rather than the storage building for raw materials, he might have died another way—by being gassed.

Morton also regaled his readers with a favorite Guinness brewery joke. When Morton visited, the factory made a substance called Foreign Extra Stout. The joke? Give a man two bottles—then watch him walk to the gate. I wasn't so impaired after my mere half-pint of the "black stuff," but it did nicely fill out the lunch I'd had a couple hours before at Malahide Castle.

You'd almost think I was on a diet. And, drinking Guinness, I could have been. Indeed, the company puts out an attractive brochure, complete with bikini-clad sylph, to prove it. "Welcome to the Guinness Diet (the one that won't reduce you to tears)," says the copy. "It's a seven-day diet, complete with menus for three meals every day."

It also tells you when to drink your Guinness, and how much. And it provides recipes. It looks quite tasty; I wonder how much weight you could lose by leaving out the Guinness? Or perhaps it's meant to add vitamins and minerals; it does contain some.

In any case, here's a sample—Thursday's menu—that adds up to twelve hundred calories, including the "black stuff."

> **Breakfast** 1 banana mashed with 1 tablsp. cream off "top of milk," topped with 1 tablesp. crushed cornflakes and sprinkled with cinnamon. Lemon tea or black coffee. [Lemon tea is merely tea with lemon, as opposed to tea with milk. White coffee is coffee with cream.]

Lunch ½-pint Guinness. Blue cheese salad—chicory, lettuce, raw cauliflower, raw mushroom, cucumber (chopped finely). Top with crumbled Danish blue cheese. Serve with tomato dressing (tomato juice, dash Worcester sauce, vinegar, salt, pepper and mustard.)

Mid-afternoon Tea or coffee. 1 pear.

Evening meal ½-pint Guinness. 1 portion Sweet and Sour Lamb. Broccoli. Black cherry jam omelette (1 dessert tsp. jam, 2 eggs).

I'd love to try it, especially the "cream off top of milk" part—but alas, U.S. milk doesn't come that way anymore. Irish milk does. Just that morning, as I left my hotel, the milk truck drove up. An open-air affair, with only the cab enclosed, it carried metal cartons of glass bottles of pasteurized, but not homogenized, milk. The bottles were left off at the door by a boy—really a boy. One presumed the bills were sent later.

Finally, though, I decided to skip the diet, in favor of bringing back a nondiet recipe. And besides, this recipe, I noticed, has a "mañana" quality quite in keeping with the way things are done in Ireland.

The recipe is from a Guinness brochure and is reprinted with their permission.

Guinness Cake

8 oz. butter
8 oz. soft brown sugar
4 eggs (lightly beaten)
10 oz. plain flour and 2 level teasp. of mixed spice sieved together
8 oz. seedless raisins
8 oz. sultanas
4 oz. mixed peel
8–12 tablesp. of Guinness
4 oz. walnuts

Cream butter and sugar together until light and creamy. Gradually beat in the eggs. Fold in the flour and mixed spice. Then add the raisins, sultanas, mixed peel and walnuts. Mix well together. Stir 4 tablespoons of Guinness into the mixture. Mix to a soft dropping consistency. Turn into a prepared 7 inch cake tin. Bake in a very moderate oven: Gas mark 2—325°F. for 1 hour. Then reduce heat to a cool oven: Gas mark 2—300°F. and cook for another 1½ hours.

Allow it to become cold. Remove from cake tin. Prick the base of the cake with a skewer and spoon over the remaining 4–8 tablesp. of Guinness. Keep the cake for 1 week before eating.

If you can.

I like Guinness, both the stout and the company. They are, it seems to me, worthy keepers of the flame, both for hops beverages and Irish tradition. It can be said, of course, that they are keepers of the Anglo-Irish tradition. After all, there are no indigenous Irish noble titles. All the same, the Anglo-Irish were often in the forefront of separatism, from the earliest days. They are, it has been said by more than one, more Irish than the Irish. And it is undoubtedly true: they have the zeal of the convert. And they also—virtually all of them, I would say—have Celtic blood flowing in their veins. Perhaps more Celtic blood than the Celtic Irish, who had, after all, intermarried with the Vikings.

When I first set foot in Dublin Airport, my first impression was "My word, all these people look *Irish*!" It seems a foolish statement, except that in a U.S. airport, all the people *don't* look American: some are Greek-looking, some Nordic, some Irish, some Oriental, some Spanish, some black, some Slavic, and on and on.

There are races in Ireland; it's just that Ireland's melting pot was cooked up so long ago that, because of gene pooling and cultural transfer, by now they seem all to look, well, Irish. And this is true even when the tableau you're looking at contains the red-haired Celtic type; the pale blond Viking type; the "black Irish" (rumored to be descended from intermarrying between Spaniards from the Armada and Celts, producing black hair and blue eyes); the long-nosed Normans (who make up much of the Anglo-Irish stock); or the short, dark-eyed genetic inheritors of Ireland's first population, the Firbolgs, about whose culture little is said or known.

It was on the way to Malahide, to lunch with Miriam Logan, an Irish Tourist Board food specialist, that I had nicked the tire. The castle itself is not now one of the restored ancient strongholds meant to keep invading tribes or Anglo-Saxons or anyone else at bay. Rather, it is dandified, having been added onto by its owners, the Talbots of Malahide, from 1185 until 1976, when it became publicly owned. Today it houses a great many fine paintings from the National Portrait collection, as well as a gift shop, a restaurant, and some officials of the Irish Tourist Board. For years, the Boswell Papers, insightful eighteenth-century travel writings from the famous James, were hidden here in a croquet box lying about the place.

Miriam Logan's job, I thought, would be tasting food all over Ireland for the Tourist Board. But it is not so. "We don't do that sort of thing at all," she said. "After all, everyone's taste is his own, isn't it? Rather, we inspect the restaurants to be sure they fulfill health and fire standards before we allow them to be listed in any of our publications. But it is important for them to be included: visitors and business people use them, and, if your restaurant isn't in it, you won't do very well out of those sources of custom."

Still, she had some personal insights from her professional, as well as private, tastings. "I'd say the Irish membership in the EEC has had an effect on our cooking. It's had at least an effect on what we call things. We call *aubergines* what you call *eggplants*; likewise, we use the French word *courgettes* instead of *zucchini*. And we've gotten used to some delicacies we didn't have before—avocados and limes, for two. It seems to have freed our cuisine a bit, even to the point where people are returning to traditional foods they once shunned. For example, mussels are becoming very popular. For a long time, they were considered peasant food, food of starvation. But now, they're trendy."

We discussed this over a creditable chicken curry and some white wine turned out by Malahide's "tourist kitchen." Not haute cuisine, by any means, it was filling and tasty, and the company was good. Having been called by an Irish government employee a "go-ahead woman" myself just a few years ago, I was interested to meet Miriam Logan, a go-ahead woman if ever there was one—poised and professional, but with the inevitable Irish hospitality that demanded she go to my car with me to see if the nicked tire was serious, and make sure I'd get back to Dublin all right.

Parson's Book Store had been recommended to me by a dear friend. "It's a real bookstore," he had said, "where the owner is there and the assistants know every book in the building and most of the customers, and they sell pens and stationery as well, in case you want to write up a journal of your own." Well, I certainly did intend to write up a journal. So, one morning early, I stopped in.

Hanging at the back, over a stack of books and not really well hidden from view, though not leaping out either, was a lovely charcoal-and-sepia portrait of a woman of mature years. A few steps away, I saw the very woman wrapping a book at the counter.

"That's a lovely portrait of you," I said.

"Aye, 'tis that. But I'll tell you, the first one wasn't. I didn't really want to have my portrait done, but it was a gift, you see, and I felt that the artist's income was dependent on my accepting the gift and going to sit for my portrait; it was the giver who'd pay him, you see.

"The first one he did I didn't like at all. 'It looks just like my grandmother,' I told him. 'And she was not a nice woman.' Well, of course, I do look something like my grandmother, but it did look like her, not me, so he did it again, and that time he did what you see there."

Portrait of Miss O'Flaherty, proprietor of Parson's, by Owen Walsh, is indeed a masterful and precious small work. The shock of white hair leaping over a high forehead, the bridge of an aristocratic nose creating a needed respite between the bright and all-seeing eyes, the high cheekbones and blushing color of this woman, a lady at any age—these are the features that stay with the viewer. Between them, artist and subject have created a memorable piece, one that was made more memorable still when Miss O'Flaherty had her way.

"If you're looking for the cultural life of Dublin, you've come to the right place," she said. "Owen Walsh is what I'd call one of the real artists. He's eccentric, you know, and lives just a terrace or two from here. Wait 'til I get you his address—he hasn't a phone—and you can go and see him. But I warn you, one day he may be glad to see you, another he may just tell you to get out."

I was game, so I waited while Miss O'Flaherty and her assistants searched various little black books for his address. "Well, I can't find it right now, but I can tell you the house. It's just up on the next terrace and it's across from the Bank of Ireland, and the windows are very dirty. They haven't been washed for ages because the landlord wants to sell the building and Mr. Walsh doesn't want to leave. Oh, and there's no buzzer, so you'll have to knock loud and long to get him to hear you on the top floor. Loud and long, remember."

As I was about to leave, wondering whether I'd actually "knock up" Owen Walsh, Miss O'Flaherty asked, "Will you be in Dublin for a few days? Good. Then come back tomorrow and I'll have his address for you."

After a few days in Dublin, I was beginning to be turned in circles, and I was dying for a glimpse of something other than buildings and pavement and roads that run out or turn into something else without warning. Even the cab drivers get lost in Dublin. So, one evening I drove south to the sea at Dun Laoghaire. There, beside the splendid Victorian houses and the honky-tonk seafront resort amusements, was Joyce's Tower in Sandycove. Although James Joyce merely stayed in it for a weekend with Gogarty, it ended up in *Ulysses* rather than in Gogarty's *As I Walked Down Sackville Street*. The claim of the literary lion won, and so, though Gogarty lived there and Joyce merely freeloaded, it is *Joyce's* Tower. Today, it contains a museum of Joycean memorabilia, but I didn't bother to look. I had come down to escape, for an hour, the convolutions of Dublin and had no need to be reminded of them through glimpses of Joyce's convoluted life, no doubt a contributor to his convoluted prose.

I stood looking at the sea, devouring the fresh, salty, and sunshot early-evening mists, munching on a full-cream Cadbury bar. Irish chocolate is not elegant like the Belgian, nor chunky like the Swiss, nor nondescript like ours. It is creamy, semichunky, filled with delicious things like rum and butter, and I was beginning to eat lots of it. The only other place I've seen such an abundance of candy at level eight on a fineness scale of one to ten is in Salt Lake City. There, it seems to be the inhabitants' single vice, since they basically lack booze and coffee and the like. Dubliners, naturally, do have the other civilized vices. But when it comes to the old saying "Candy is dandy but liquor is quicker," they take the first part as gospel, the second as a challenge. After all, who wants a pleasurable vice to be quick?

(Lest the acronyms, from MADD to AA, or Ireland's own Pioneers come after me, I hasten to add that Ireland's per-capita liquor consumption is lower than England's. It would be far better to view Ireland's fondness for the "black stuff" and the "uisce beatha"—water of life, or whiskey—in much the same way French or Italian or Spanish wine-bibbing is viewed—as a cultural norm. And in fact, Ireland is not a nation with an alcohol problem on the order of the Scandinavian countries. Of course, neither are the Irish saints.)

The next day, I thought I'd better pop into the Tourist Board and see if they had dug up any exciting cultural heroes for me to meet. As I waited for the man in charge, I commented on the rather nice watercolors hung around the reception area. The receptionist liked them, too. And, as I was waiting on "Irish time," in which today is forever and tomorrow may never come, we had time to chat.

"You flew from New York?" she asked. "Aren't you afraid to be there? I saw a program on the telly the other night about that man who shot the teenagers on the subway. Gosh, I'd be afraid to be in New York—all those poor black people and everyone getting shot."

"Well, those incidents are about the same as the occasional bombing in Northern Ireland; sometimes it takes an innocent life, but the incidents are really rather rare. And, as in visiting Northern Ireland, you just don't go to certain areas and then you're all right," I said. "You know, Americans are often afraid to come here because of the way the bombings up north are treated in our press."

That was news to her—news I shouldn't have thought anyone working at the Tourist Board should have been surprised at. But it seems naiveté about press distortion is similar the world over. I had run into attitudes like hers in Paris. Though I've been through Northern Ireland more than once and have spent time during troubled periods in the Republic, remaining unscathed because I don't tend to "tour" a country's slums, my own family still breathes a sigh of relief whenever I tell them I'm safely at the airport and on the way home.

But the Tourist Board had no cultural luminaries lined up. Well, I thought, maybe Miss O'Flaherty will produce Owen Walsh for me. Meanwhile, I had been invited to dinner by the Honourable Desmond Guinness and Mrs. Guinness at their home near Dublin—Leixlip Castle in County Kildare. The castle is a straight shot out the Liffey past the Guinness brewery, which is run by a different branch of the family. Desmond Guinness is the son of Lord Moyne, and founded the Irish Georgian Society in 1958. Born in 1931, he is a graduate of Oxford University, having "read"

French and Italian. He is an author as well, having published *Georgian Dublin, Irish Houses & Castles,* and *The White House,* as well as three collaborative books. This is not surprising: Lord Moyne is a poet and novelist, and Mr. Guinness's mother, Lady Mosley, also writes. Lady Mosley, Diana, is the sister of Nancy and Jessica Mitford.

Leixlip Castle, like most castles, sits on a hill. I drove up and saw I had a choice of two doors. I tried one and, getting no response (maybe I had to rap loud and long here, too?), I was walking through the chill night air of May to the other when another car drove up. "Hullo!" the driver called. "Anyone in?"

"I don't know. I hope so."

"Me, too. I'm a little early, but they should be here, I think. I'm Denis McCarthy," he said.

Finally, walking back to the first door I'd tried, we were greeted by Mrs. Guinness. "So sorry. Were you out here long? I was busy in the kitchen and didn't hear you right away."

We went into the cozy drawing room. "I'm afraid Desmond will be a little late. We've just got a new tractor, you see, and he's out playing on it. Can I get you something to drink?"

She did, and disappeared to where the wonderful aromas were coming from. We all pulled up around the roaring fires: castles are chilly even in May, and we had been warned to dress warmly, as the central heating was off and awaiting a new part.

Denis is a professor of English, Irish, and American literature at Trinity College half the year and New York University the other half, giving him the best of both worlds, the warm months in Ireland and the height of the cultural, academic, and social season in New York. Before Desmond arrived, we engaged in small talk and discovered, to my delight, but certainly not astonishment, that Denis and I had not only frequented, but practically worshipped at, the same Greenwich Village Italian restaurant. During my travels, I never cease to be amazed at what a small world Americans and the Irish share. Time and again, whether at table with a professor or across a fence in the countryside, people I meet always seem to know people I know, either in America or Ireland or even elsewhere in the world.

Two other guests arrived: Julian Lloyd, manager of the famous Airlie Stud Farm, and his wife. I had begun to love the faces of Ireland, and this crowd was especially fascinating. Desmond himself has a most pronounced and preppy Anglo-Saxon nose, and water-blue eyes. He is full of smiles, but his innate intelligence is everywhere pronounced. Mrs. Guinness, Penny, is more earthy, and more Anglo-Saxon, perhaps not having been Irish for so long. Her hair, falling to her shoulders, is the marvelous mix of innocent colors found only on all Caucasian babies and grown Englishwomen everywhere. Denis is long and lean, with the cherubic face of a monk, high-cheekboned, and slightly pointed of chin. He has the long fingers of an artist. And the strong ranginess of a James Stewart.

The Lloyds might themselves have stepped out of the television show *The Irish R.M.* He is slight and quiet and even-tempered and sandy-colored. She is wispy and gay and auburn-haired. She has high cheekbones and good coloring and pronounced that "Wearing a hat always makes one look elegant and important, don't you think?" to compliments on her race-day attire from the week before. No doubt she had turned a lot of heads.

The conversation was fun, but, in a serious moment, I learned a serious lesson about the subtleties of the Troubles between Northern Ireland and the Republic. I don't know how the topic of the North came up, but it did, as topics do during a dinner party. Denis pointed out to me that the Irish government is in a peculiar—at least to American minds—bind. Elected officials of the Irish government are sworn, in their oath of allegiance and by the Irish Constitution, to seek the reunification of the North and South. If an elected Irish politician should suggest the North and South need not or should not be reunified, he or she could be impeached. I was shocked to hear this: it seemed to me like requiring our President to swear to try to unify the United States and Canada. But then, we in the States hear very little about such serious political and legal problems as finding a solution to the division of Northern Ireland and the Republic. I was to learn much more during the rest of my trip.

The conversation ranged over many topics until late in the evening. Desmond's passion for Georgian Ireland, and his extensive knowledge of Washington, D.C. and the White House—after all, an Irishman designed the latter and helped lay out the former. My amateur's interest in Irish megalithic monuments. The success of Desmond's family and their manager in breeding Irish racehorses. A conference in Los Angeles, at which Desmond and Denis were to be the featured speakers. And so on.

We also discussed fine furnishings: I had mentioned a commission to do an article about faux finishes, and it turned out Desmond was chairing a dinner in New York City, not two weeks later, to raise funds for a U.S. group devoted to decorative finishes—faux marbre, onyx, gilding, and the like. All in all, it was exhilarating conversation and stimulating company.

The food, which tasted as good as it smelled, was actually leftovers; it was the staff's night out, and they'd had to work hard entertaining various visiting groups concerned with restoration work, the Honourable Desmond Guinness's consuming passion in life (besides family and home, of course). The repast was a traditional Sunday supper buffet. The seven of us speared our own sliced ham and turkey, scooped our own delicious scalloped potatoes au gratin, and, for dessert, shared Desmond's leftover birthday cake. I ate more of a scrumptious Anglo-Irish dish called Raspberry Fool than I care to admit. What made this simple, yet delicious, Sunday buffet an unforgettable experience was the ambience of the room: roaring flames in a centuries-old marble fireplace, the focal point of a perfect Georgian dining room with authentic furnishings and oil paintings.

Before the end of the evening, Desmond had invited me to another gathering, this one a cocktail party for a visiting historical society. "It will be held in the Friendly Brothers Club, 22 St. Stephen's Green," he said. "Do come. It's a marvelous Georgian building."

My quest for modern literary Dublin took me, one sunny Tuesday afternoon when I felt I should be out taking photos in the all-too-rare sunshine this particular May was giving me, to the offices of Harold Clarke, chairman of Eason's, Ireland's largest bookstores and publishers. Mr. Clarke, whose office was across the Liffey from the journalistic hurly-burly of Fleet Street, is an author, as well. And he has taken the liberty of writing the *Georgian Dublin* booklet for Eason's Irish Heritage Series. I will take the liberty of extensively quoting him; though I have grown very fond of Dublin indeed, Mr. Clarke lives there, in a house he lovingly restored with his own hands.

"In Dublin's streets there is an uncanny skill in the combination of the curve and the straight line in flowing patterns avoiding both monotony and absurdity. There is an eloquent grace in the unfailing variety from one street to the next," he writes.

Part of the reason for this is that Dublin enjoyed the very first official town-planning authority, the Wide Streets Commissioners, established in 1757. Because of it, Dublin's O'Connell Street is 154 feet wide and provides a major conduit into and out of the north side of the city, as well as the city's most sweeping span across the Liffey. Upper Merrion Street and Baggot Street, both entirely south of the Liffey, are 102 and 100 feet wide, respectively.

O'Connell Street sports huge movie houses, second-floor Chinese restaurants, Clery's (Dublin's largest department store), offices of various sorts, fast-food restaurants, and the front door of a huge Eason's bookstore. Like the rest of Dublin, the bookstore is civilized. It sells not only books, as ours do, but pens and pencils and paper of many sorts, from fine engraved types to bulk typing paper, newspapers, and, best of all, candy. It seems so sensible to me. Often, I have wandered to a park bench to read a book. Often, I've had to go first to the bookstore to get the book, and then to a stationer's if I wanted to take notes. If I wanted something to munch on, it meant another stop at a deli or candy store. In the United States, we tend to compartmentalize. We specialize. We are puritans. When we read, we seem to think, we should not also be enjoying a snack.

The Irish have no such preconceptions. They'd as likely enjoy a block of chocolate (candy bar), or a cigarette and a draft beer, or a cup of tea with their reading. They are great readers, virtually everyone in the country being literate. They read their own writers, and they read ours. They even read England's.

They take books from lending libraries, or they buy them, and often pass them around until a whole group of people has read the same one. Then they can discuss it. And they'll discuss anything, from Hans Küng to Stephen King. They'll have a good time doing it, too, unlike Americans, who feel that unless we have "studied" a thing, we've no license to express a thought about it.

Eason's is not, however, a Georgian delight, but a functional modern store with good lighting and miles of books. On its shelves, one will find, among other things, the works of Brian Cleeve.

"He was quite a popular, mainstream writer for a number of years," Clarke said. "And his books sold well."

I had run into Cleeve, I explained, one early morning in Parson's Book Store. "Oh, here's a real writer for you now," said Miss O'Flaherty. "Brian Cleeve. See, we've his books right over on the table." And indeed they did.

Cleeve is overpoweringly tall, with a wild, Zorba-like mane of yellow-white hair. His hawk's nose splits a face animated by Celtic blue eyes, and his retrograde front teeth give him all the more the appearance of a great bird perched to swoop on some delightful morsel—in this case, some more reading material from Parson's. When I met him, his brown-gray trousers were nondescript. But he was one of the few Irishmen I have ever seen wearing green, in the form of a woolen fisherman's smock—no doubt useful against this season's unwelcome and unexpected chill and for stashing "pocket" books or candy bars for his rambles. On his feet he wore sandals.

"Yes, that sounds like Brian Cleeve these days," Harold Clarke agreed. "He has become quite a bit more ascetic in his writing, for whatever reasons, and I believe he may have taken a religious turn as well."

At Parson's, they had displayed copies of Dr. Cleeve's book *A View of the Irish.* As I write this, his new book, *A Biographic Dictionary of Irish Writers,* is being published in Ireland, and will be distributed in the United States by St. Martin's Press. I wished he had done it a year before, so I could have used it in my search for modern Irish literary figures.

But, said Clarke, there didn't seem to be a lot of innovation in that regard just now. Sean O'Faolain was still popular, of course. Many of the British and U.S. expatriate writers who inhabited Ireland for a time seem to have departed for other shores. Why? I asked. "Well, this is a small, closed society," Clarke explained. "I'd say that for most of them there just isn't the cosmopolitan stimulation they're used to in other places. There may be a drying-up of inspiration when they discover it takes their intellectual equals a long while to reach them in their country homes, no matter how charming. So, they move on so that their inspiration will continue."

We chatted a few more minutes, when Harold Clarke explained he had a little business to take care of and then would be off to a cocktail reception on St. Stephen's Green. "At the Friendly Brothers Club?" I asked. Yes, he said, it was, and would I be there, too?

Harold Clarke is an old friend of Desmond Guinness, and I was a new one—and Dublin is, socially, a very small place.

Mrs. Guinness was in the doorway, receiving the guests when I arrived, and Harold Clarke was there already. In the course of the next forty-five minutes—for I had to leave early to see Peter Bowles in a play at the Gaiety—I met a local optometrist who was a Georgianophile, a young architect of the same bent, an archivist in the government's architectural library, and a woman from the midwest.

"What part of Dublin do you live in?" she asked me.

"I'm staying in Glasnevin," I replied. "I don't live here at all, though I might try it someday." This seemed to fluster her.

"Oh, I knew you weren't part of our group [a visiting historical society, for whom the party was being put on], and you looked like you belonged here," she said, which was the nicest "apology" I'd ever gotten. Miss O'Flaherty had assumed, at first, that I was a Dubliner, too. It's easy to perpetrate this ruse. Simply dress as you would in New York or Paris, except warmer for an equivalent season, and don't wear Kelly green—or, for that matter, unless you're a kid, any bright color. You can even get on this way after you've spoken, as long as you betray no drawl, no twang, no piercing consonants, no flat vowels, no nasality, and no obscenities. Luckily, my family background represents every American regional and ethnic group, almost, so I end up with very neutral speech patterns—when I want them.

But it wasn't just for play that I had begun passing for Irish; it was very practical. It was far and away the best way to be treated politely; in many of the more tourist-laden areas, U.S. tourists are likely to be gently twitted, and deservedly so. Most seem to forget that the Irish *live* there. It isn't a quaint place to them, and they hardly like being patronized by Americans on package tours. Nor do they deserve it. In some quarters, when it was thought I was British (because of my neutral accent and Anglo-European outfits), I was treated too politely, a little coldly in some cases, and that didn't seem to augur well for getting on with this book. No, I wanted people to treat me as their neighbor, not as an exotic of any sort, if I were to discover the true bases of their attitudes and lifestyles.

The Friendly Brothers Club is part of an almost extinct Irish lifestyle, except for the few active people like Desmond Guinness who keep it alive. The Club was founded after William III ascended the British throne in the 1690s, when dueling to settle arguments was proper and popular. There were numbers of deaths because of it, and some bright fellow in Dublin got the idea of starting a club to combat dueling, and called it the Friendly Brothers Club. There were, for a long time, affiliates in all other major urban areas, like Cork and Galway, where dueling might have been the "peacemaker" of choice. The last affiliate, Galway, has just recently been absorbed into the Dublin father house; it seems dueling has fallen out of fashion, along with the desire to belong to a man's club. But the Dublin club, housed as it is on St. Stephen's Green in a spectacular Georgian town house, still lives.

Aside from the architecture, the house is filled with ceremonial furnishings, seemingly indestructible and carved with gargoyles of numerous ilks. It is not, however, as spectacular as another of Guinness's haunts, Castletown, as described by Harold Clarke in his small book, *Georgian Dublin*.

> Although twelve miles from the city in Celbridge in County Kildare, no study of Dublin eighteenth century building would be complete which excluded Castletown House. Since it was purchased by the Hon. Desmond Guinness, founder of the Irish Georgian Society, in 1967, the house has become the headquarters of the Society. Members worked over several years on its preservation and decoration so that it might be saved for posterity. On summer evenings and at weekends, musical performances and entertainments attract large audiences to "the finest house Ireland ever saw."
>
> The long drawn-out task of building and decoration began in 1722 for "Speaker" Conolly, so called because he was the speaker of the Irish House of Commons, and the architect was an Italian, Alessandro Galilei, whose best known work is the facade of St. John Lateran in Rome. The house was designed with a central block linked to wings by curved colonnades. The plan had been used earlier at Santry and was copied and adapted in country houses, large and small, all over Ireland. The wings and curtain walls were sometimes used to make a modest house more impressive. The chief glory of Castletown is the Long Gallery decorated in the Pompeian manner by Thomas Reilly who was a pupil of Reynolds, in 1775. . . .
>
> From the windows, there is a fine two-mile vista to the Conolly Folly, an obelisk 140 feet high built in 1740 by the widow of Speaker Conolly, to alleviate distress following a very severe winter.

Alleviating long winters was often done by the English landlords in Ireland. Not at all is it true that they all, to a man, starved the Irish; many were generous to the point of their own ruination. But as in any society, it is not the good eggs, but the bad apples, that get all the press coverage. (Though I didn't know it then, I was later on the journey to sleep in a magnificent Georgian boudoir that gave onto a famine wall. These structures generally served only one good purpose: to provide employment for local people and so keep them in porridge and cabbage, at least, during hard times. This early enlightenment, it seems to me, is no different, and possibly better due to local control, than the make-work our own government instituted during our own Great Depression.)

Castletown would have been, in Georgian times, the seat of many a glittering house party, with carriages arriving laden with beautiful ladies, trunks of clothing, and jolly gentlemen from the terraces of Dublin.

Of course, the "terrace" houses in Dublin, while not as large, were equally luxurious. Oscar Wilde was born in such a house on the corner of Lower Merrion Street. Daniel O'Connell lived in No. 58; from its balcony, the patriot addressed the crowd upon his release from Richmond Prison. Leinster House, which now houses Parliament, is in Merrion Square as well. Today, these are well-preserved, with the delicate fanlights intact, and colonnaded doorways still often sporting the original brass fittings or excellent copies. Many such buildings now house societies like the Friendly Brothers Club or commercial offices, rather than the families they sheltered when they were built. Alternative usage does save buildings, if not lifestyles.

"My wife and I lived in part of one of the old houses," Tom Waters, an official with the Industrial Development Authority, told me. "It was charming, all right. But to tell you the truth, there's no room in them, the way they're subdivided now, to have a bicycle or a dog, much less children." Waters and company—wife, child, and dog—have thus moved into more modern digs. But there is an endless stream of young people and young couples in the youngest population in Europe to inhabit them, each for a few years. It may be enough to help save the houses. And I was soon to meet one who fervently hopes so.

Arnold White is a house agent, or what we would call a realtor. Principal in one of the most venerable of Dublin firms, he is nonetheless accessible, as willing to show a modest home as a temple of commerce.

Mr. White was born in Scotland, and the traces of that brogue underlie his Dublin accent. A connoisseur of fine buildings, he is also a connoisseur of fine paintings, with a special interest in the French Impressionists. All this I found out as we drove out to see a Victorian gatehouse on the edge of a newer subdivision. I toyed with buying it. It had a view of Dublin's harbor and yet was secluded behind the remains of the once-upon-a-time estate's great walls. It was a wreck, and yet the charm was there for the asking—and buckets of paper and paint and cleaning and elbow grease. And if I bought it, I knew, I would come to Dublin year after year forever, which seemed a pleasant prospect.

"It's a shame, really, what they've done with some of the old buildings, simply tearing them down and putting up these horrible new glass things in their place," Mr. White lamented. "I love the old buildings, and I wish there was more being done to save them. A lot of us do. But then, it's the large commercial interests that can pay for the land under the old buildings, and if they need the space, they just tear them down."

One of the great tragedies, he explained, had to do with a site even older than the Georgian row houses—a Viking fortification/village unearthed several years ago on the banks of the Liffey. "It could have been of enormous value to historians and archaeologists," White said. "And they could have made an excellent tourist attraction of it as well. After all, so many people come to Ireland for the history. But they decided to put up a government office building—and a very undistinguished one at that—on the site. They gave the researchers a few months to have a look, then paved it over. And built that ghastly building on it."

He was right; the building is ghastly. It is undifferentiated gray concrete, rising nine stories, and unrelieved by a single window. I had noticed the building before I knew what it was. It was a monument to poor taste, of that I was sure upon sight. Now I also considered it a monument to grossly negligent judgment.

In the end, I didn't buy the house. No doubt Mr. White was right; it was a bargain, just the sort of thing a young family would love to have and redo. And there would be a place for a dog and bikes and kids, though the three bedrooms were tiny.

But I've got Mr. White forever. He is a gentleman of a type not found anymore anywhere. It didn't faze him that I was a go-ahead woman; he simply treated me as he had no doubt treated ladies all his already quite long life, and it was a joy. He spoke of his wife in matter-of-fact but equally romantic terms—and one knew he had been a faithful husband in all ways, and she a faithful wife. It seemed as if they had an equality born of affection, not insurrection. It was highly attractive, as was he. I have promised to send him catalogs from museum shows for his collection. And I will be glad to.

While the Abbey Theatre is known internationally for its fine performances of very literate plays, the Gaiety also lives up to its name. On the Tuesday evening of my Friendly Brothers visit, I went there to see Peter Bowles in an uproariously funny French drawing-room comedy, adapted for the Irish stage by the author of *Da,* Hugh Leonard. *Some of My Best Friends Are Husbands* is a very free adaptation of *Celimare, Le Bien-Aime* by Eugene Labiche, and depends on an amplitude of French double-entendre, none of which was lost on the Irish audience, nor on me. But the owner of my hotel refused to see the play, making a face when I agreed that it was, indeed, the Peter Bowles thing. There is, in some wards, a bit of anti-British feeling, I observed. But then, in this instance, there was an extremely unflattering and, I think unnecessary, line in the playbill copy. Of Hugh Leonard, who was "born in Dublin in 1926 and admits to being 38," the program also says, "His hobbies are travel, vintage movies, French canals and getting out of Ireland." John Andrew, the very Anglican rector of St. Thomas Church in Manhattan, once told me, "It is often not as important what you are doing as what you are perceived to be doing, and that's where one must be careful." In this case, I believe the Irish—or at least one Irishman, for his own good—might take a small hint from the British.

Still, this crassness in the program did not prevent my enjoyment of the play, or of the whole experience. Sitting in the dress circle, I had a wondrous view of all the ornate gilding and gewgawgery that embellish this venerable comedy house, one of only two of these opulent buildings that still survive. (The other is the Olympia.) When they were first built, these palaces played works by the then popular and now revered Dion Boucicault, who, besides writing for the Irish theater, became a popular actor in the United States. He wrote on American themes, including *The Octaroon* (1859), said to be the earliest play to seriously discuss the "Negro question." But his greatest triumph in Ireland was his trilogy, *The Colleen Bawn, Arrah na Pogue,* and *The Shaugran,* all composed of sentimental Irish patriotism and rustic humor. *Some of My Best Friends Are Husbands* was hardly that.

2. Dublin, continued

I meet some very old Dubliners. I search for the future at venerable Trinity College, and find industry. I trace my roots and find a checkered past of sorts.

Dublin, while whimsical, is more cosmopolitan in its musical tastes than the rest of the country. It has its share of pubs with rustic fiddle-players, to be sure. But there, it seems, they are much like New York City's Lone Star Café, with its country and western music. There's room for a bit of this music, for the hard-core fan, but it's not part of the pulse of life. The music of Dublin is more orchestral. Indeed, it has long been; Handel gave the very first performance of his *Messiah* there in 1743.

The premiere of the opus is recorded to have been at Mr. Neal's New Musick Hall in Fishamble Street; but it is a strong tradition that Handel himself played it shortly later, for a discerning crowd, at St. Michan's Church.

St. Michan's, though still a popular tourist site, is no longer the fashionable house of prayer it once was. Today, St. Michan's stands in one of Dublin's most unprepossessing streets, across the street from some Council Houses—public housing erected, as in the rest of Ireland, by the town council. Up the street are small stores selling cheap goods, and one of the city's two McDonald's (the other being on O'Connell Street, which has the flavor of Broadway, in any case). Down the street are factories and warehouses and vacant lots and, finally, the Liffey, in one of its most unpicturesque stretches.

But the church is ancient. Built in 1095 over the probable site of an earlier Danish church, it also probably lies over the body of Samuel O'Haingli, an Irish-Danish bishop who died in 1121. All this is merely probable because there were no written records that far back. The church is probably named after a Danish saint. It is, however, still part of the Church of Ireland, as it was when it was founded, rather than a church of Ireland's dominant Roman Catholic faith. For centuries, it was the only church north of the Liffey, which was then the best part of town.

The church itself, remodeled in 1686, is not spectacular, except for its organ. This magnificent creature—for it lives and breathes, and has lived and breathed at the hands of Handel—was built by J. Baptist de Couville of Dublin, a famous organ builder, in 1724. Cost? Eight hundred fifty pounds. As an embellishment, for an additional eight pounds, a wood carving of various orchestral instruments and ribbons was added in the organ gallery; today, an etching of this piece graces the back of Irish pound notes.

This was not sufficient to draw me to St. Michan's; it hadn't been enough to draw Morton, either. What did entice is the fact that St. Michan's has some fashionable communicants who decided, at one time or another, never to leave it. It contains, in vaults below its hallowed floor, a band of Irish mummies.

There are four bodies to view. Guided by the church sexton, Mr. Saul, I dutifully viewed them, as Morton had. To get to them, one crawls down a stone stairway that is very nearly a ladder. Once we were below, Mr. Saul secured the huge clanking metal doors to a stanchion with a stout stainless-steel lock and chain—lest anyone take a notion to create some new mummies.

Being in the vault is less alarming than getting there. It does not smell; indeed, the air is quite the most breathable in Dublin, a city that still heats with peat and coal and has breweries and rendering houses and all the other more odiferous enterprises of modern life.

The mummies are quite young as mummies go, the youngest having been entombed a mere 150 years ago or so. The ones on view are all "orphan" mummies. One is a child. One is a very tall man, said to have been a Crusader. Another man may have been a convict. And the female mummy is said to have been a nun who had been tortured and mutilated, her feet and right hand amputated. In any case, the skin remains intact on all the bodies. The fingernails are as they were at the time of death. In one or two, where skin has stretched away, organs, turned a dark gray-brown, like a darker version of the dun-colored skin itself, are visible.

In fact, there are more mummies, but they belong to living families and are in vaults not open to the public.

In Morton's day, no one knew exactly why people entombed at St. Michan's become mummified. Obviously, lots of wealthy people wanted to live on in this way; there are dozens of very old, richly embellished caskets among the bodies. (The wooden caskets originally holding the mummies have, amazingly, rotted, baring the contents to public view.) But as far as is known, no special Egyptian-style preparation of the bodies was done. Though they may or may not have died of natural causes, natural causes seem to be preserving them.

In 1964, A. T. Lucas, Director of the National Museum of Ireland, stated: "The church stands on formerly marshy ground and there is a relatively high methane content in the air of the vaults which acts as a preservative." It has also been suggested that the preservation is caused by the current peculiar dryness of the air, or the fact that there was an ancient oak forest nearby. In ancient Celtic belief, oak forests were inhabited by all sorts of spirits; indeed, sacred wells were often located in copses of oak, and the supreme of the Celtic deities, the mother goddess, lived in an oak wood. Morton was aware of this possibility, though he ignored the supernatural portion of it.

There were five of us on the tour that Saturday morning, three women and two men. None of us fainted; indeed, there was nothing to faint about. When Mr. Saul brought us back up, he relocked the door and matter-of-factly had a short conversation with an elderly parishioner who was preparing the altar flowers for the following day—as if there were not something very unusual in the basement.

St. Michan's above and below ground are both worth a visit; students of the Irish Troubles relish it because it is the place from which Charles Stewart Parnell—a Republican but a Protestant—was taken to his final rest in Prospect Cemetery.

Whether you're writing a book or not, it's nice to have introductions to real people in foreign countries. I had one to a lady named Ellen Lynch Heggarty, who had proposed afternoon tea for my "St. Michan's Saturday"—I had planned recovery time—at the Westbury Hotel in Dublin.

The Westbury is a new hotel, with huge slabs of marble for floors and some modernist art hung around. It's plunked down next to a newly created shopping area, a sort of indoor/outdoor mall called Powerscourt Centre, off Dublin's famous Grafton Street. Tea is served there in a huge lobby one floor off the ground, furnished traditionally with sitting areas for four, six, ten, and so on, floating on Oriental rug islands in an ocean of russet marble. The high-ceilinged room—a hall, really—offers views of the street below, a small alley giving onto Grafton. And it provides, like many newer Dublin buildings, a view of the sky as well. Although Dublin acquires more skyscrapers daily, there seems to be a plan afoot—or maybe it is just the natural Celtic fabric of things—that keeps them from being placed cheek to cheek and creating the sort of drab canyons city dwellers elsewhere take for granted. Maybe the spirit of the Wide Streets Commission still lives, in the form of some sort of Well-gapped Skyscrapers Authority or the like.

In the late afternoon, the sky over Dublin, on a rare sunny day as this one was, is breathtaking. It is not just the blue, the blue of a sky-color Crayola, that takes you. It is the sky and the roofs, most of a deep terra cotta seemingly flecked with gold. Together, they set up a vibration of color that makes the air shimmer with light and life. Chimney pots, still used and still as charming as they were when Dickens lived, tie the magnificent to the mundane with wispy ribbons of turf smoke, or coal soot.

Watching Dublin's sky had become a daily delight to me, and I didn't mind at all that I arrived first. I took a seat with my back to the far wall, facing the room and the windows both, and waited until I saw someone who looked as if she were looking for someone else. We had never met, and we didn't even have descriptions to go by.

But I had assumed rightly that the receptionist would know Mrs. Heggarty and had also let her know I had arrived and whom I was waiting for. Mrs. Heggarty is a well-known publicist with her own firm, and was formerly with the Bank of Ireland. She had, I surmised, taken people to tea here more than once before. And to the Irish, knowing people and their names is not only important but a normal part of polite living.

Mrs. Heggarty ordered a full tea for us, not only the milky liquid the Irish prefer, but finger sandwiches and half a dozen sorts of pastries. All this came on a serving tray, three tiers high, that was placed on the table so we could help ourselves.

The introduction to Mrs. Heggarty had come from my banker, a woman with whom she had been friends in Dublin when they were both just starting out in business. Both seem to me to be go-ahead women; both are fashionable, well-educated, savvy, and cosmopolitan. Luckily, I am dependent on Irish time as I write this, for I have yet to thank either of them for their helpfulness to me. Mrs. Heggarty, despite a heavy work schedule and a family illness, checked up frequently with me about my progress on the book. And she was to be the last person in Ireland I spoke with before I left for home—again over an abundant tea. Meanwhile, she wanted to be sure I met knowledgeable experts, and pointed me in more than one good direction.

"Who have you met?" she asked. I had met Dr. Vincent McBrierty, Dean of Science at Trinity College, the day before. "He's one of my best friends!" she said. And he turned out to be one of my best sources.

Dr. McBrierty, a tall man of medium build with eyes that pierce you with an intelligent, accomplished glance, epitomizes the best of Ireland's little-appreciated academic prowess. Just as Irish monks traveled throughout Europe to keep the light of learning burning during the early Middle Ages, Irish academics such as Dr. McBrierty travel the world advancing technical knowledge today. Dr. McBrierty is not only Dean of Science at Trinity College, he is also professor of polymer physics, and works on both sides of "the pond"—the Atlantic Ocean—to find new ways to use polymers, the building blocks of plastics. His specialty is research into using polymers to make semiconductors and integrated circuits, the ubiquitous computer "chips" that are having such a dramatic and positive impact on the world.

Dr. McBrierty has been a consultant for Bell Laboratories in New Jersey for eighteen years, and he could command an enormous salary, a very comfortable lifestyle, and even more widespread academic recognition. But, like many Irish academics and intellectuals I have met, he prefers to live, teach, and raise his family near Dublin. I thought this unusual, and I asked him why he didn't choose the "good life" in the States.

"I know this may sound like flag-waving PR, but I am a committed scientist with a sense of responsibility to my country," he explained. "And I like to live here. There is something about Trinity College, its age, the feel of walking through the halls and seeing the Book of Kells from A.D. 900, and the Irish harp from the 1500s, that really hits you. Trinity is more than four hundred years old, and the original building from that time is still standing. Edmund Burke, the famous eighteenth-century political philosopher, and Oliver Goldsmith, the poet and novelist (*She Stoops to Conquer* and *The Vicar of Wakefield*), for example, attended Trinity at the same time.

"Yet, today, with four centuries of tradition in literature, the arts, philosophy, and politics, Trinity is the leading generator of government-sponsored research and receiver of competitive research grants in key technological areas in Europe. A new, ultramodern microfabrication facility and between 10 and 12 percent of the total college budget is set aside for technical research and development. Trinity plays a critical role in the development of modern Ireland, and I am very pleased to be part of it." (For the uninitiated, a microfabrication facility is a place where sophisticated computer chips are made.)

The current emphasis in Ireland on advanced technological development and attracting high-technology firms in all fields from around the world—especially the States—is a dramatic departure from Ireland's past. Until the late 1950s, and even until Ireland joined the European Economic Community (EEC), or Common Market, in 1973, Ireland was an agricultural backwater. Since the late Middle Ages, almost all of its commerce had been with England. And Irish agriculture and industry were severely restricted, if not prohibited, by English Penal Laws and prohibitions. After the Irish Free State was formed in 1922, the Irish government followed an extreme protectionist policy designed to make Ireland self-sufficient. After the Irish Constitution was established during the 1930s, Prime Minister (and national hero) Eamon de Valera wanted Ireland to be close to the land, "close to the simple, country life," as McBrierty noted.

De Valera is often quoted as saying his fondest sight was that of barefoot Irish children playing in the doorway of a humble Irish thatched cottage. This is the Ireland Morton saw during his trip in 1930, very pastoral and bucolic, with practically no industry outside of Belfast and Dublin. As McBrierty charitably said, this rural image is very attractive, but unrealistic in the modern world. Yet, Irish government policy made this inward-looking agrarianism a fact for almost thirty years. By the end of that time, Ireland was desperately poor. Moreover, and distressingly, England or English companies continued to control more than two-thirds of its commerce.

Recently, however, a wave of industrial investment and support from the EEC has rapidly reduced Ireland's dependence on England's "beneficence," an Irish goal for almost eight hundred years. Despite greater economic independence than at any time in its history, the Irish still feel—and well they should—caught between forces beyond their control. It remains a tiny country, and, as McBrierty noted, "We do not have our own destiny. We cannot use our ability to develop as we want. The strength of the U.S. dollar can wipe out our aspirations. The material wealth, yet popular unrest, in the Third World makes it a strong force influencing Ireland. These and other external forces are so strong and so integrated into the world economy that Ireland must inevitably sway with the tide."

Yet McBrierty also spoke of how much influence, if not control and domination, the Irish can have in the world. Consider that, as a neutral Western nation, it sent peacekeeping forces to Lebanon, yet also maintains a thriving trade in butter, milk, food, personnel, and technology with Saudi Arabia. In a land where the sun is a rare commodity, a small company has developed a sophisticated solar energy system it is selling in Australia, the Middle East, and Africa.

In Europe, McBrierty emphasized, "On EEC committees, Irish play critical roles as mediators. The Big Three or Four countries [United Kingdom, France, West Germany, and Italy] may be suspicious of each other. So, of the English-speaking countries, inevitably Ireland has the most efficient language capability and ability to run meetings and smooth the path to get things done."

McBrierty's observation is very accurate. During the week, the lobbies and restaurants of Dublin's hotels are filled with European businesspeople and Common Market bureaucrats. Many times, I saw people of several nationalities huddled over coffee or a meal earnestly discussing whatever business or political situation was at hand. Thus, he said, "Ireland has an input into European politics far beyond our population of three and a half million, about one-twentieth of the U.K.'s."

One of the most entertaining international meetings I saw was not, however, European, but Japanese. In addition to the huge American investment in Ireland, there is a very substantial Japanese one. Partly to serve the Japanese officials and employees, partly because Dublin is more and more becoming a world city, there is a Japanese restaurant—complete with sushi and the ritual Friday-night Japanese-businessman drinking party. I witnessed one, at which two Japanese were hosting two visibly bewildered Irish businessmen. Although the Irish eat a lot of fish, they had never considered eating it raw. Or spicy. Or washed down with fiery sake. But eat they did. And drink. And, finally, valiantly, they sang. By that time, the Irish, always resourceful and at least as polite as the Japanese in their own way, had caught up. The already raucous table let fly a huge belly laugh when the Irishmen handed their Japanese hosts printed copies of "Danny Boy"—and insisted it be sung. Until you've heard "Danny Boy" sung without accompaniment by two slightly drunken Japanese executives saving face, you don't know what fun is. Morton, who regarded "Danny Boy" as the greatest song ever written in English, might have been appalled. Or maybe he would have taken note, as I did, that his favorite ballad had become a friendship token between two cultures that, at first sight, could not be more divergent. In fact, there are ample and cogent reasons for the Irish and Japanese to prosper together, but I'll deal with that later on.

Ireland's role in the future appears to be to do for modern industry and science what it did for learning and the Christian religion during the early Middle Ages: to contribute brainpower and talented and well-educated people to the world stage. "Ireland doesn't have natural resources. We have the personnel to make expert contributions to the EEC. Because of our troubled past, you find in the Irish good judgment of character. To survive, the Irish have had to develop an innate awareness of the individual. And this serves the IDA, in its search for industry, very well. I would say that Ireland's past has given us a sense of involved maturity that holds us in good stead," McBrierty said.

Yet Ireland's impact as a nation, and not just as a people, is just beginning. For a country with a five-thousand-year history of civilization, it is remarkably young as a nation. More than half of the population is under the age of twenty-five. All through my travels, I was continuously amazed at the number of young people I saw. Every weekday morning, as I left my hotel, I saw dozens, if not hundreds, of children of all ages walking, riding bicycles, cramming double-decker buses in the city, or packing to the windows the dull orange-and-black-striped "scoile buses" (school buses) in the countryside. The girls were almost invariably wearing white blouses and skirts in the blue or burgundy or deep green of their schools. The boys wore white shirts, ties, dark pants, and jackets with the school emblem on the pocket. They traveled in sex-segregated straggles, right through high-school age. I have wondered if there is any such thing in Ireland as a kindergartner "in love." Probably not. Andrew Greeley, the American priest who writes popular novels of the tormented

Catholic Irish-Americans of his background, theorizes, in more than one volume, that Irish women act as if they are always right—but only because they always are. This would be a little offputting to males of any age, I imagine, if it's true. Certainly, there is a nugget of truth in it.

As an American, I am more used to seeing legions of elderly people wherever I go. In Ireland, there are far fewer, proportionately. In Dublin, it looks as if the young people must outnumber the middle-aged and elderly by at least three or four to one. Walking down Grafton Street, closed off to traffic to become an "instant" pedestrian mall on that very sunny Saturday, I saw a scene reminiscent of the 1960s in the States. Irish hippie types, mixed with 1980s punk rockers, dotted the crowd. Most of the shoppers, though, were stylishly dressed young people, imitating the latest rock stars and movie idols, enjoying the normal pleasures of a warm, sunny day. And they seemed to really enjoy themselves, taking their pleasure in the sun as intensely as the Irish take everything else.

These young Irish are also the best educated in Europe. A formal education is highly prized in Ireland, largely because, for two hundred years, the English prevented the Catholic Irish from attending secondary school and college. Irish parents and their support of the organization of the educational system around strict Catholic and national practices ensure that Irish children learn to read, write, do math, and have a basic grasp of many other subjects. In Ireland, the leaving certificate ("leaving cert," as it's called) signifies an Irish student has passed a tough course and a very tough test in each subject. Obtaining a leaving certificate in a variety of subjects is much harder than receiving a high-school diploma in the States. The leaving cert test for each subject takes all morning or afternoon, and students must take several of them within a few days.

To enter a university or institute of higher education, a student must have high marks—the equivalent of A's and B+'s in the States—on five or six leaving certificates in math, science, English, a foreign language, and similar subjects.

At the universities, institutes, and colleges, students work according to the English system of "reading" subjects. They attend few classes or lectures, and work on their own far more often than college students in the States. They work with tutors, and they rarely have the same distractions—football, basketball, etc.—students in the States have.

When I had heard how well educated Irish young people were, I also thought about the very high unemployment rate—a startling 18 percent in mid-1985. I asked Dr. McBrierty and numerous industrial-development officials about this problem and its impact on the young people and Ireland as a whole. Dr. McBrierty was very upbeat, saying, "Ireland's greatest asset is its young population. Current thinking among the young is attuned to high technology, lasers, 'Star Wars,' and the like. High technology holds no mental block for them. They take it for granted. Our large young population should be considered in the context of our European partners. Germany's single greatest concern is its *lack* of youth. Other countries have very low birth rates and similar concerns.

"So, we can marry our young, highly trained young people with the needs of Europe. We are emphasizing our ability to speak foreign languages, so our young people can become the feedstock for the future development of Europe. In the interim, of course, we will face a very difficult period with social problems similar to those the United States experienced during the 1960s and 1970s."

To make those days pass more quickly, McBrierty added, the government, through the IDA, the universities, and various agencies, is encouraging "third-level linkups" between industry and academia. "We have demonstrated that we can succeed in agriculture and in the assembly and manufacturing of goods. The next step in this logical development is to demonstrate that we can accomplish the concept of a whole autonomous company. The big drive is to use the know-how and backup technical support in the academic world to develop indigenous Irish high-technology companies.

"Academics are essential to that, and Ireland has plenty of Ph.D.s and masters of science. This massive investment in brainpower, coupled with capital investment, can produce a significant multiplier effect in terms of jobs and economic growth."

At Trinity alone, academic-industrial couplings have led to work in advanced materials development, biotechnology (to help Ireland's large dairy, beef, and grain industries), and informatics—the science of information processing. And Dr. McBrierty says the research is of the highest order, and has gained respect in Belgium and France and from MIT and Bell Labs.

This very high-level research is only one aspect of Ireland's drive to become and remain an educational and technological leader. In the late 1970s, it established the NIHE in Limerick. During my trip, I also visited with Dr. John McGinn, Director of Cooperative Education at NIHE, Limerick, and Dr. Joseph A. Watson, Assistant Secretary, Industrial Liaison, University College—Galway.

At NIHE Limerick, for example, each year more than seven hundred students graduate in engineering, scientific, and business careers. Unfortunately, many of these seven hundred cannot find jobs, and either accept lesser jobs or emigrate to the U.K., the States, Australia, the Middle East, Africa, or the Continent. Ireland suffers from brain drain—it has too many brains for the available jobs under the economic conditions of the mid-1980s. But the Irish are unwilling refugees. Almost all of the graduates would stay in Ireland, if they could find jobs.

But the Industrial Development Authority is trying to help change this sad situation. During the late 1970s and early 1980s, the IDA was made aware that encouraging the building of large factories employing hundreds or thousands of workers would be difficult in a European and world economy in recession or growing slowly. And the IDA tended, from various social and political pressures, to overpromise the impact of the large projects. At one time, it set a goal of bringing in twenty-five thousand new jobs a year; it actually encouraged only three thousand. Clearly, a reexamination was in order.

During the mid-1980s, says Barry McConnell, Director of Marketing and Promotion for the IDA, the IDA has reoriented its drive from large factories, where assembly work dominates, toward high technology and international service firms. These types of businesses can "soak up" some of this surplus brainpower pouring out of Ireland's universities, institutes, and technical schools. Until 1984, the IDA had offered an attractive package of financial incentives and tax breaks only to manufacturing firms. But in that year, McConnell said, the incentives and tax breaks were expanded to eleven types of international service firms, including computer software development; technical and consulting services; research and development centers; health-care services and training; international financial services; commercial testing labs; administrative headquarters; data processing firms; and more. Currently, the largest IBM software facility in Europe is in Dublin.

The IDA wants firms that can employ fifty to a hundred people to locate in Ireland, to take advantage of the incentives and use the country as its "nerve center" for Europe and world markets. With its reoriented direction, the IDA is emphasizing the indirect effects of job creation. Admittedly, the IDA is under political pressure because the current government's main thrust is to capture the vote of the large young voting population. Now, instead of boasting that a new plant will create so many hundreds of jobs, the IDA weighs the "value-added" effects of the new industry's wages, profits retained in Ireland, local purchases, and financial and legal services purchases. The IDA's target for the next decade is to double output, with a 7.5-percent-a-year average growth rate—three thousand new jobs created directly and fifteen thousand new jobs created indirectly. McConnell said, "During 1984, the net contribution of foreign investment in Ireland was two billion Irish pounds [about $2 billion], while the IDA spent only eighty million Irish pounds [about $80 million] in grants to industry."

In another push to help the large youth population, the IDA is encouraging entrepreneurship and has established programs for young managers and engineers to set up their own companies. I have noticed during my travels that the Irish generally do not appreciate go-ahead men and women. I know several successful Irish entrepreneurs, and they tend to be resented by their countrymen. Perhaps this is left over from the many years of oppression by landlords and foreign agents, but I also believe it goes back to the days of the Celtic tribes. In those days, Irish "kings" were little more than managers who led the tribe according to a consensus of the men and women of the tribe. Ireland never had a long history of absolute monarchy as did England and France, nor did it develop a history of republican or parliamentary rule until modern times. So, for many reasons, the Irish tend to be slightly suspicious of self-made men and women, trusting more in cooperative efforts.

They also have tended to be very job-security–conscious. McConnell noted that for the past sixty years, the best jobs have been jobs with the Irish government, banking, or semistate agencies. The emphasis in the education system and universities has been to get a secure position upon graduation and stay there.

I do hope the IDA succeeds in its drive to encourage young people to set up and run their own businesses. "We are making more effort at the secondary-school level to highlight entrepreneurship, to show them how to take risks with their own companies and succeed. A number of agencies offer programs in entrepreneurship—AnCO (the state job-training agency), the Youth Employment Service, the IDA Student Enterprise Award, and bank-sponsored seed-capital programs," McConnell added.

But the Irish tax system—with a 60-percent income tax that starts at a very low income level compared to that in the U.S. tax code—penalizes entrepreneurship. And until 1983, the Irish tax code did not allow for the use of venture capital. Most businesses in the United States, most notably the microcomputer industry, get started with money from venture capitalists. In Ireland, venture capital is limited to a maximum of twenty-five thousand Irish pounds of equity in a start-up company, and strict limits are placed on its use.

It appeared to me that the IDA has a long way to go before its aim to encourage entrepreneurship will become a reality. U.S. entrepreneurs I know want to make money, and lots of it, but the Irish system is not designed to allow or encourage creating large fortunes—no matter how many auxiliary fortunes and good jobs it creates as well.

But for established firms seeking a location for a European facility, Ireland is tops. During my trip, I visited factories of all kinds all over the country, from Dublin to Cork, and from Limerick to Dundalk and many places in between. I met many forward-looking and successful Returned Yank managers. I met some indigenous Irish managers who had never temporarily exported their own expertise. And I met a few strictly foreign managers. I saw apparel manufacturing at Farah (the El Paso, Texas giant) and china-making (at small Irish Royal Tara China) in Galway. I saw sophisticated minicomputers being made by teams of bright, young engineers. I saw computer chips being assembled by dozens of young "school leavers" and heard that, sadly, 140 of a total of 550 of them had been laid off the day after my visit. This was a testimony to McBrierty's comments about Ireland's not being in control of its own destiny. The world semiconductor market was being battered, and the parent company, Mostek of Dallas, Texas, laid off hundreds of its workers in its plants all over the world.

I saw huge, advanced process-control machinery being built on a factory sitting next to a thousand-year-old "souterrain," an underground dwelling where the Celts hid from Viking invaders. This was at Accuray, a forward-looking Ohio company that opened its plant in Ireland to build its process-control equipment for European industries. I saw Irish crystal being made in the small Clarenbridge factory near Galway and the huge factory in Waterford where two thousand craftsmen cut the famous designs.

I saw many kinds of industry, both Irish and American, and I was most impressed by the quality of the management at the successful firms. Truly, I believe the success of Irish industry depends largely on how enlightened management works with the characteristics that make the Irish what they are. Someone told me the Irish, despite the myth of laziness, are a very intense people. They work and play and argue and live and love and believe with great intensity. They do not respond well at all to overbearing or superior attitudes. And they practice "lateral thinking"; that is, they do not think in straight lines. Their minds tend to roam over many subjects, and they tend to be interested in many things at once. They are a very literate and politically alert people, reading several newspapers a day and being well-informed on many subjects. Successful businesses recognize these traits and try to constantly challenge their employees. Floating Point Systems, located in the Dublin suburb of Swords near a twelfth-century castle, enjoys great success with work teams in which each person is responsible for many activities related to making and quality-testing a minicomputer.

In addition, successful firms recognize the Irish commitment to home and hearth and their leisure time. Liebert, Inc., an Ohio company, brought a similar attitude to Ireland, and has gained a firm commitment from its more than two hundred employees by encouraging employees' families to get involved with the company's activities. It, too, encourages a team effort and discourages prima donnas, says Managing Director Raymond Geaney, himself another Returned Yank.

The future of Irish industrial development rests partially with the competitiveness of the IDA's incentives and grants. The IDA must compete with similar authorities in England, Scotland, Wales, France, the Netherlands, and many other countries. The IDA offers a range of incentives, including, in brief:

- A 10-percent maximum income tax on manufacturing and service-firm income until the year 2000 (and most likely beyond).
- Grants for capital expenses of up to 60 percent of the cost of fixed assets for a new facility.
- Grants of up to 100 percent of the cost of training employees in Ireland or anywhere else.
- Low-cost purchase or lease of prebuilt advance factories, or factories custom-built for a new industry.
- Low-cost loans arranged with Irish banks.

Ultimately, the success of Ireland in a postindustrial world of high-technology companies and service firms depends on the willingness of its young people to grow out of their jobs with these companies and establish independent Irish companies, and the willingness of the Irish government to encourage, rather than hamper, their efforts.

I was mightily impressed by the rapid changes in Ireland since my first visit in 1977, and the proliferation of many new businesses around the country. Much more needs to be done to employ the many young people I described earlier. There may very well be some of the sort of social unrest we experienced in the States during the 1960s, but I would guess that Ireland will emerge a stronger, more vibrant nation for it.

There is never any lack of things to do in Dublin. I had been trying for days to schedule myself a shopping trip, and a lunch at Brown-Thomas department store on Grafton Street. One Thursday, I finally made it. I had a cabbie let me out at the top of Dawson Street, which parallels Grafton. I started down it at Stephen's Green, and was shortly charmed by a small shop on a corner with a sign that read RAINBOW ANTIQUES. In the window, there were abundant silver serving pieces and Victorian and Edwardian jewelry. Inside, there were a few fine chairs, some paintings, a game board or two, and other bric-a-brac of a bygone era. I went in. "Can you show me some early Irish silver?" I asked. They could and did: two caddy spoons with very crudely done saints atop the handles. They weren't to my taste. But a silver-and-amethyst necklace and a small gold-and-emerald ring were. I looked at them. I bought them, or, at least, I agreed to a price with the owner, a tall red-haired Lorelei whose name, I later learned, was June Murphy. I hadn't the cash with me, and was to come back the next day and finish the transaction.

When I arrived, Mrs. Murphy was not about, but a tall young man was. "Oh, yes. The necklace and the little ring, wasn't it? Just let me ring my mother and see where she might have put them safe for you."

As he wrapped them, another young man came to the door. "Don't let him in," said the proprietor as I offered to. "He's dangerous." Then he began to laugh. The man outside was his friend, come about arranging a tennis match before his brother went off to America for the summer to work. "There aren't any jobs here," he said. "Luckily, we've an uncle there who can get him a good-paying job, probably in construction, so he'll have some money for school next year. And he'll get to see some of America, too, and won't have any housing costs."

One topic led to another, and shortly we were on the subject of police protection. Just that week, I had read that the Gardai were no longer permitted to go on motorcycle patrol in Dublin. It seemed that "cop-bashing" had become the sport of the hour, and several policemen had been seriously hurt. (Ireland has a national, rather than local, police force, called the Garda Siochana. An individual policeman is called a "gard." Plural is "gardai," pronounced "gar-dee.")

The newspaper pundits had been putting the "sport" down to troubled economics, disadvantaged youth, and the like. I mentioned this to the two young men. "That's not an excuse, then, is it?" answered the store's young co-owner, James Csunihan. "There are lots of us who don't have lots of things we might want, and we don't go round hurting people and bashing things up because of it." I had to agree with him; it sounded as lame applied to the Irish as anywhere else. Not even Midas had all he wanted, and there's no evidence he first beat up the people he turned to gold—or anyone, for that matter—before he got the golden touch. Of course, the knee-jerk sociologist in me later pointed out that we were discussing this from the vantage point of selling and buying fairly expensive baubles, and talking of tennis matches. But we were also talking of working darned hard for it: the friend's brother going off halfway around the world to find the work that would permit him to remain in school; the young man spending his Saturday morning minding the store while others lay about; I collecting information for a book it would yet take me months to complete, after the months of labor setting up the project with no guarantee of success in the first place. We had all had to be clever and work hard for what we wanted; we'd none of us have been in that store if we'd resorted to the mindless brutality of cop-bashing to cope with our frustrations. "It's all a matter of discipline, isn't it?" Mr. Csunihan said. Yes, it was, and yes, it is.

I was in a buying mood, and I'd been on a short leash throughout my stay, what with finding people and things and the real Dublin. But shopping is most assuredly the real Dublin as well. Each day, they close off Grafton Street to make it an instant shopping mall. On Saturday, you can barely tell where the sidewalk ends and cobblestones begin, until you've fallen off the curbing, to be carried along without breaking stride or an ankle by the world-class shoppers meandering shoulder to shoulder, bad weather or no. I finished up at Rainbow and went on down to Anne Street, which runs between Dawson and Grafton, and is world-famous for silver. I made the mistake of going in to Danker's, but it's a mistake I'd gladly repeat. I wanted some formal shirt studs for my husband; he was getting sick of the tacky button strip that came with the shirt from Brooks.

"I'm sorry, I don't seem to know just what it is you want," the young boy said as he pulled out tray after tray of things that were not shirt studs. "We close early today, and I'm here alone, but if you'll come back on Monday, someone can surely help you then."

It was a stunning day, and I decided to do that, and spend the rest of the afternoon strolling in Stephen's Green. A central city layout of formal gardens, Stephen's Green sports duck ponds and gazebos and, this day, a couple of small boys who had lost control of a Labrador retriever. The dog wanted one of those ducks, and badly. I sat down on a bench to watch. The dog had splashed in at a shallow point where there was no fence, but had swum over to the "wilderness" side, where there was a fence the boys couldn't get over. The ducks were the smartest of all; the adults played decoy, spelling each other, to keep the frenzied dog away from the ducklings. It worked time and again.

The dog was a mess of mud and wet grasses stuck in its dewclaws, but it had that hunter's gleam in its eye, and I was convinced the boys would have to go home to their dinner without the animal (would it become a stray? would I conduct a trans-Atlantic rescue mission?) if it kept up. But miraculously, and very suddenly, it tired of the game—just as the boys figured out how to help one of their number over the fence to fetch the dog. At that precise moment, out flopped the dog at the shallow end, racing off with the other three boys and leaving the fence-climber behind to wade or climb out as best he could. I wondered if it was all planned from the beginning. Was the dog in on it? Or did the other boys just take the main chance when it presented itself to play a joke on their friend? No time to reflect, however, because a Yuppie couple arrived with a bag of bread trimmings and a baby, whom they were teaching to feed the ducks. After another quarter hour of this innocent scene, I got up to stretch my legs. The sun was setting, in any case, and I was beginning to be chilled. I walked over one of the stone bridges. On it there was a bearded man painting a watercolor of the marshy area at the bottom of the duck pond. He was pretty good, but I didn't stop to chat. He looked standoffish, not something common in Dublin, but something to be respected, obviously, when it appears.

When I came out the other side of the park, there were a fat gypsy woman and her two ragamuffins washing the dirt off their faces in a horse trough. Dublin no longer has the horses, but Stephen's Green still has water for them, and hitching rings. It also has diagonal parking and meters. And "parkers," as I shall call them for want of a better name.

On weekdays the spaces cost ten pence per hour, to be put in the meters. It's tough to find a space, as it's true that Dublin, like all cities, has parking space at a premium. On Saturdays, when shopping is in season and the meters officially are not, it has parkers. These are somewhat elderly men, each of whom takes a side of the park and walks up and down it, looking for people leaving, directing newcomers into the about-to-be-vacated spaces. They wear brimmed hats, the ubiquitous black balmacaan raincoat of the working-class Dubliner. And they accept tips. I have the idea, maybe fanciful, that if the tip is large enough they'll sort of keep an eye on your car for you and make sure it isn't one that gets swiped, or sideswiped. I have seen them direct the parking of the unsure. And I'm sure they must have stage-managed the parking of an enormous 1960-vintage American Chevy I saw at the Baggot Street end of the Green one day.

On Monday, I duly returned to Danker's, and the young woman who helped me, a Danker daughter named Joy, did indeed know what I wanted. But they had none. We had a lovely chat, and I admired her speech. It was a fascinating mixture of Dubliner and European Yiddish, and her manner was a fascinating mixture as well: very upper-crust, but with a warmth that could only have come from a more earthy ethnic background. And she was quite handsome, with curly dark hair, a high aquiline nose, and bright light eyes. She was also knowledgeable about antique silver, and sensitive to what an American who wasn't explaining herself very well might want. After over an hour in the store, during which she had had numbers of things out on trays for me to look at, I was ready to buy. Mr. Danker offered me a cup of tea; Mrs. Danker polished up what I'd bought; Joy told me about her husband, who is an accountant. I told her about the book; for some reason, I also told her about one of my other endeavors, portrait painting. She said she'd very much like for me to paint her, God willing, when I'm next in Dublin.

"God willing" was a phrase I hadn't heard often, nor from anyone so young. It was so Old World. Indeed, though Joy is a thoroughly modern Irish young woman, she hearkens to something very European, very charming, and very worth saving in Ireland. She spoke of much with a pronounced reverence, and I got the feeling that in naming her Joy her parents had tapped some primeval wellspring of names to come up with precisely that which fit the energies of this offspring. I would love to paint her someday. God willing.

I had met so many people in Dublin already. I liked all of them, but then, in that respect, I'm somewhat like Will Rogers. In Joy, I'd found someone with whom I would like to be friends, if I lived in Dublin. But none of the people I had met so far had been politicians; unlike Will Rogers, I hadn't been sorely tested yet. But at lunch in Brown-Thomas, I very nearly was.

"We're very busy right now, and I haven't a table for one. Would you mind sharing?" the hostess asked.

No, indeed, I would admire it, I said. She led me to a table for four that held a young woman and her two daughters. Sharing a table with people you don't know is a concept unheard of in the United States—or, at least, I had never heard of it, save one fast health-food restaurant in Manhattan where it seemed to be the norm. This particular restaurant was Israeli-owned, however, and I assumed the habit to be something imported from the kibbutzes of Israel. Ireland has some of the same background: contended borders, insufficient space, roaring inflation at times, precarious economics, a society split between the agrarian and the intellectual. In short, it didn't surprise me, the more I thought about it, that it is permissible in Ireland to share tables with strangers rather than stand around and wait—to be alone. And there's the added Celtic adaptation: you might meet someone worth talking to. You might even have some good crack (a few laughs, to us) which is valued even more highly.

One of the little girls was quite shy, but the other kept looking at me in fascination, I think because I ordered the same thing they were having—sausages and chips (or french fries, as we call them). It seems it is mostly a kids' lunch food, like our burgers and fries, and my ordering it amused them quite a bit. But I love the stuff.

The children's mother was a doctor who taught medicine at Trinity. They were on school holiday and she was taking them to buy summer clothes before quality clothes disappeared from the racks. She was good friends with Gemma Hussey, the Irish minister of education, and it seems both Mrs. Hussey and the doctor had been early members, in the 1970s, of a burgeoning women's political caucus in Ireland. I had an introduction to Mrs. Hussey, too, from a friend in America who was Irish by birth and still consulted for Irish government agencies. Unfortunately, Hussey was out of the country when I was in it.

Still, the doctor was a good mirror of the life of the upper-middle class in Ireland. In Ireland, the taxes are more burdensome than ours, and, though the school systems are excellent, producing an entire nation of literate people, the middle class still likes to send its offspring to private schools, which are expensive. "Their school costs a thousand pounds," the doctor told me. "It doesn't sound like much to you, of course, especially at the exchange rate now [at the time, a pound was roughly equal to a dollar, making Ireland a cheap vacation for millions of Americans, and America out of the question for vacations for the Irish], but it is quite a sum to us."

Both the little girls went to project-oriented schools, where they learned all about a particular subject before going on to another. The government schools, naturally, hit heavily on the three Rs. But, said the doctor, that was slowly changing and progressive education was arriving. I had all I could do to keep from groaning. It would be nice if Ireland could maintain its astounding literacy; in the U.S., we have finally learned we've got to get back to the three Rs to get it back.

I had remaining only two more "musts" before I left Dublin: finding something out about my Irish heritage, and meeting Owen Walsh.

I was to meet Tom Lindert, founder and president of Hibernian Research Limited, for tea at the Kilkenny Design Workshop. I was quite early, so I browsed. The design shop is Dublin's answer to Conran's, The Door Store, or almost any modern "habilitation" outlet you can name. It is crammed with very modern-looking fabrics and furnishings and tableware and sweaters and jewelry. The floors are covered in de rigueur modern gray rubber floor covering, the stuff with quarter-size round raised places. The columns supporting the glass-and-steel structure are plain and white. The salespeople are young and trendy. The colors are—this year—the muted pastels of preference in international design. Next year, next month perhaps, they'll change to whatever is au courant. But upstairs, in the restaurant, all is Irish and as usual. The coffee comes with demarrara sugar; there are pastries galore to go with it. The service, although cafeteria-style, sports the Celtic adaptation of an employee bringing plates to you if, for instance, you asked for your apple tart heated before the thick double cream was applied.

Tom Lindert looked an unlikely candidate to be an expatriate. He didn't, for one, look Irish, though he assured me there were some McLoughlins in his heritage. He fell into Hibernian Research almost by chance. But he's gotten it on its feet, and now it's of invaluable help to people looking for their Irish roots.

"For most people, it's not possible to go any further back in their Irish heritage than 1817. Before that, there really was no system of record-keeping in the parishes, and certainly none by the government. That's as far back as we were able to go for President Reagan," he said. If, however, you're from a noble family, either Irish or Anglo-Irish, it is likely you can trace your ancestry further. It may be written in a family document. And, for the noble and famous families, says Lindert, there are ways of tracing a family through historical and cultural documents, like legislation or history books of an era, and so on.

"Of course, to Americans, 1800 is a long way away," he adds.

"Most people just want to know about their grandparents and great-grandparents." Most of his clients come from two age groups, those over sixty and young marrieds in their late twenties and early thirties. He doesn't know why. Other searchers are checking on land that might have been left to them, or tracing family for other estate purposes. Bord Failte, the Irish Tourist Board, sometimes commissions a search. "All four of John McEnroe's grandparents were born in Ireland," Lindert says. "So, for the Davis Cup finals, Bord Failte presented him with a family history, and his family was delighted."

Although Ireland speaks a common tongue, and government records are written in English, there are obstacles to tracing roots in Ireland. "The worst of these is being able to make sense of the church registers, most of which were written in Latin. And sometimes the priest didn't stick strictly to the facts."

In addition, many government records were destroyed in the 1922 Rising; reconstruction is possible through different sources, but difficult.

Of course, there's also the problem of getting accurate recent information to begin with. My own family sports one Irish-born ancestor. All I knew about her was the town she grew up in, her name (although Irish names are not always what they seem), and her parents' professions. I thought. As I would be in the country several more weeks, I commissioned Lindert to do a search. Customarily, two weeks will do. When I received his packet at my hotel the day before I left, it was jammed with interesting information about three different families. It seems, after poring over what Lindert provided, that my grandmother was a liar. We had always been told her parents were schoolteachers. But if that were true, then her real name was Rose. But her name was Nora. And—if she were Rose—she was twenty-nine when she emigrated, not fourteen. "It would have been highly unusual," Lindert had told me, "for the fourteen-year-old daughter of a schoolteacher to emigrate." But it wouldn't have been unusual for a farmer's daughter. Now, the second family—the farmer's family—contained a child named Nora, who would have been fourteen or so when she emigrated. And they were cousins to the schoolteachers.

"Well," my mother said when I called to discuss the probabilities. "I think we're safe in assuming Grandma lied. She did have some cousins who came to the U.S. later, in 1935 or so, who seemed much better educated than she, and they were well-spoken. She probably just 'borrowed' the more distinguished parents." When my mother had told me the names of these cousins, I realized they indeed matched the names of the schoolteacher's children.

"One of the ways we decide which family is the right one, if a group in the same area have the same name, which is common—is by the Christian names," Lindert had said. "They tend to be repeated." Indeed, to this day, my family is filled with Jameses and Johns and Margarets; there are no Bernards and Roses.

I'll excuse my grandmother her deception. After all, it probably enabled her to marry my grandfather, a contractor who built her several houses and a nice nest egg. He enabled her to send money home, where she is still remembered for her generosity. And she was one tough old bird; I both admired and loved her. And she could still do a jig at eighty. I think I'll attribute the deception to her "lateral" thinking; I realize others might uncharitably call her a liar.

I had a definite appointment to see Owen Walsh at 1 P.M. "Remember, knock loud and long," Miss O'Flaherty had impressed on me when she gave me a slip of paper with his address.

The morning was bright and lovely and warm, after several drear ones, as I set out down Baggot Street toward Walsh's apartment. I was overdressed for this weather, with a jacket and raincoat and scarf, and carrying briefcase and camera, and wearing high heels. I'd spent weeks being fed and plied with drink. I hadn't refused much of it. And I was exhausted, as only a traveler can get. I had gotten to the point of knowing all my clothes were a bit soiled; I knew it would be another week until I landed at a hotel equipped to deal with that. My hair needed trimming. My legs were sore. I wanted to slump during a meal—not possible in a hotel dining room. I wanted, so to speak, my own rubber ducky in the tub when I got in to soak at night. I wanted to see someone I knew very well—and let my hair down. I missed my dogs. I had just been to the bank—and I knew that traveling was a lot more costly than in Morton's day. What with the trappings of modern life—hair dryers and extra camera lenses and toiletries of two dozen sorts and piles of notebooks and bags of film and emergency candy bars and address books to check off as each postcard home had been sent and gifts for those left behind—it was more difficult. I wanted to lie down. Or sit down. So, as I passed the taxi rank at the Shelbourne, I hopped into a cab. I gave the address.

"Sure, you'll not be wanting to spend the money for such a short ride. You can walk it in five minutes," the driver said. Yes, I did want to spend the money for a short ride. Well, no I didn't. I had just been to the bank, again, after all. But I was so tired. In any case, the driver didn't seem to want to brook an argument, having leaped out of his seat to open the door for me. He had been reading the paper when I got in. No doubt, finishing the first of the day's papers—or maybe the second or third—was more worthwhile than a small fare. As I have explained before, the Irish are highly literate. And highly political. And not highly motivated, in our Puritan ethic way, for money.

So I continued walking. But it was hot. And I was overdressed. . . .

Two short blocks before I got there, I turned around, trudged to the nearest taxi rank, and got a cab back to my hotel. I never met Owen Walsh. I doubt I'd have had the energy to knock loud and long. And I was certainly in no condition, or mood, for one of his artistic tantrums. I was having one of my own, after all.

But I'll meet Owen Walsh someday, I expect. Maybe I'll be his neighbor. Eight years ago, a business contact asked me if I thought I could live in Dublin full-time. I didn't think so. And yet, I came whisper close to buying a house there this trip. But no, just now I'm still a traveler in Ireland. And there's a lot left to explore.

3 Wicklow

Wicklow, the place where the English dared not go during the Troubles to chase the rebels, nor for hundreds of years before that. Wild, beautiful, and still, as always, free. I visit Glendalough, Wicklow City, and ride over the wicked hills to Blessington, meeting a horse on the way.

My hotel was the Inn of the Downs, located, fittingly, in Glen of the Downs, an area about an hour south of Dublin. It's a two-hour drive from the airport, which is northeast of the city. On a previous trip, I had made that jet-lagged drive on top of the inevitable wait at Kennedy Airport for the Aer Lingus night flight on the day that Bobby Sands had died. That death had led to a few minor traffic snarls, and some not inconsiderable discoveries during the next few weeks about the modern revolutionary "heroes."

It had surprised me, at first, that there was so little fuss. On his hunger strike for weeks, and getting much media attention in the United States, amazingly little was said on the radio about Sands. Less still was heard from the ordinary people. Although the American press had led me to believe the Irish would be crying in their Guinness for a week, if there was a single tear shed into a pint anywhere in the country, the evidence didn't pass my eyes. In fact, not a word was mentioned about it by the hotel staff when I checked in, nor by the waitress who served me fried plaice (flounder) for my lunch, nor by the shopkeeper who sold me a hair dryer in Bray (the nearby large suburban town), nor at the bank, where I cashed a draft on my bank in New York.

Later, I learned that Bobby Sands was not held in the same regard as the true revolutionary heroes—Michael Collins, Charles Stewart Parnell, Eamon de Valera. He was considered, by many Irish men and women, to be a "t'ug," the Irish *h*-less word for thug. Indeed, a few of "the boys" had tried to strongarm some shops into closing for a vigil. On the TV news that night, those interviewed had declined to close, despite threats of violence, because they believed Sands to have been a misfit who had latched on to the cause for purposes of his own—to die a hero rather than a felon. They were having none of it, beyond a prayer or two for a lost soul. The real Irish heroes, it seems, are long gone. Or, at least, the nation awaits a man of superior intellect, wit, power, and luck to find a solution—rather than tawdry gestures—to the Irish partition.

Checking into the quiet, spectacularly sited Inn of the Downs, after a delightful stay in Dublin, brought me only pleasure. The hotel was more than adequate: it was clean and cheerful, and, in the Irish tradition of politesse, no one asked questions when I requested a pot of boiling water, cream, demarrara sugar, a sharp knife, a cup, and a salad plate on the morning after my arrival. The previous afternoon in Bray, I had bought the most excellent pears of a type unknown in the States, and I wanted them for breakfast with some herbal tea that had crossed the Atlantic with me. This, of course, is heresy, for an Irish breakfast is one of the most wondrous culinary inventions in the world. But to slough off some of Dublin's excesses, I intended to follow a vegetarian regime, for a time, as much as possible. But even then, my resolve was weakening.

How could I pass up those delicate, two-inch-long, pink sausages, perfectly roasted to a russet blush? The rashers of bacon, sporting no marbling of lard or dripping of fat, nor curling into little snippets as ours do, but lying rose-colored and succulent the width of the plate and then some, with one outer film only of fat and rind? The sweet fresh eggs tenderly coddled? The brown-flecked bread spread with local (and therefore fresh-as-morn) butter and tangy marmalade? The coffee, always in a silver pot, always served hot and not the least bitter, with cream and demarrara sugar? I do not know. Nor do I know how I passed up even the prunes stewed with lemon rind, anathema to many but ambrosia to me.

There are other things one *might* have for an Irish breakfast. There's porridge—but I've never had it. It is one of the oldest of Irish traditional foods, though, having reached the island nation with the early Celts. There are broiled tomatoes (an English breakfast food), another I've also ignored wherever it rears its watery head. And cold white toast, another abominable legacy from the British—and worse, in my opinion, than the primogeniture laws and other horrors. (Not literally, of course. The primogeniture laws stated that for an oldest son to inherit his father's land, he had to become a Protestant and disown the family. This caused severe interfamilial strife and served to separate many an Irishman from his farm and some from their families. Still others lost life and limb over it all.)

Still, the cold toast, to an American, is pretty dreadful. And it's followed closely by the juice.

Although Ireland has had access to the most wonderful European and North African fruits and vegetables, especially since joining the EEC, the Valencias of Spain have never so much as been introduced to an Irish breakfast cloth. The juice in Ireland, whether grapefruit, orange, or tomato, comes almost entirely out of "tins" from New Zealand or Australia and is a second cousin to battery acid. Its redeeming value is that it can, quicker than you can say "Ballyjamesduff," snatch the coat from a reveler's tongue after a night of stout or Jameson's or even Paddy's.

My odd (they actually would have said "queer") tray was delivered by a "girl." In Ireland, "girl" still denotes any unmarried woman, almost. I'm not sure at what age a girl would pass, without marriage, to "woman." Possibly she'd go right to spinster at some arbitrary age. Or maybe she'd become a nun. In point of fact, it is still true that marriage is the goal of a female in Ireland. And if she doesn't get that white net veil in good time, it's likely to be the black veil of a nun instead. Even now, there are not many go-ahead women in the rural areas, making their own way in life. By way of illustration, I'll digress from breakfast to a massage I had at Lisdoonvarna a few years ago.

Lisdoonvarna, on the other coast and north of Bray, is the place where the Irish take the waters, as it offers sulphurous springs bubbling up from the ground. There, a "girl" who gave me a massage illuminated Ireland's attitude toward "girls" and how the "girls" still live in Ireland.

The masseuse, whom I judged to be about twenty-two, was quite pretty with auburn hair, pale skin, blue eyes, and a pert figure. She asked me if I was married.

"Oh, yes. In fact, my husband is going to have a massage after me."

"How long have you been married, then?"

"Nine years."

"Are your children with you on holiday?"

"We don't have any children."

After this, there was a long silence. In fact, the subject didn't come up until two days later, during my third massage.

"If you don't mind my asking, I wonder, is it that you didn't want any children or that you couldn't have any?" the girl shyly asked.

I told her the truth: We didn't want any, and, in fact, having never wanted any, had never tried, and thus didn't know whether or not we also couldn't.

This was a brand-new thought to her. She followed it with a comment that she wasn't going to get married for several years yet, and hadn't even begun looking for a man. She wasn't keen on children either, but assumed they were as inevitable in marriage as white hair in old age.

(The Dail passed, in 1985, a law allowing birth control, so women may achieve some sexual freedom, if not full gender equality. Abortion is still prohibited by the Irish Constitution.)

While the young women of Dublin and Galway and Cork and even Sligo may be sophisticated, even to the point of visiting England every so often for abortions, the idea of not wanting children—within marriage—is a foreign one in Ireland indeed. In fact, it has been a policy not only of the dominant Catholic Church, but of the government, to encourage children. The population of Ireland before the potato famine of the 1840s was nine million; today, after the Irish diaspora, it is only a little more than a third of that.

But back to the tray. I finished the breakfast at a table by the window, with a view of the hotel's garden, terraced down the hill to the road, and watched the morning mist rise and burn off in a rare fine day—full sun and only a gentle breeze.

I drove south to the turning for Glendalough. Glendalough is at the head of a valley from which there's only one road in and out. In Utah, it would have been called a blind canyon, and arrowheads and musket bullets would doubtless have been found within it. In Ireland, such a valley—this valley in particular—is far more sacred, this one being the site of more than one early Christian church. Rumor and tradition have it that there are seven churches here, but there is no evidence to support that claim.

The founder of Glendalough is thought to be Saint Kevin, who arrived in the year 520 to be a hermit—which wouldn't have been hard. His place of prayer is high on the valley wall, once reached only by climbing through forest, now by steep trails up the hillside, after rounding a large lake.

On reaching Glendalough, I parked near the hotel, which advertised a salad for lunch; my vegetarian eyes delighted. I walked into the historic site with just a few other visitors in the early part of high season, May. In the fifty years or more since it first became a popular attraction, little has changed. The paths are wider, but maybe that's due to the crush of Yank feet over them. No longer must one be rowed across the lake to climb to Saint Kevin's bed. You can walk around on a cow path. In fact, one is likely to share it with cows, as I did. They were placid creatures who let me walk right by them, flicking their long lashes like ingenues.

The view of the valley from Saint Kevin's bed, an easy climb, is stunning. I was alone at the top, the few other tourists having made the trip first. (Being a city slicker from America, I took pictures of the loose cows; as native Irish men and women, with all the loose cows they can handle, the others didn't.)

The silence was profound. There were no planes overhead. In the heat of noon (all of 68°F!) the creatures—birds and bees and rabbits—were all drowsy and silent. Cars crawling along the road, on the far side of the valley from my perch, seemed to be gliding on waves of shimmering heat, not trundling along on internal combustion. Puffs and tails of light gray smoke rose from the few turf-heated cottages across the lake, which gleamed white in the rare full sun. They had bright blue or red doors, a dun-colored thatched roof or dark slate, and a dooryard full of roses or a mini Minor almost-toy car. The men were at work. (This was Saturday, but only the factory workers, and there would be few in this rural area, would not be at their jobs.) The women baked or washed or marketed, the children played soccer or other games or did farm work or fished. The dogs lay by the steps; if there was work for them, it would be bringing in the animals at teatime. Until then, they could take their "aise" (ease). Could I see all this from a valley distant? No. But the imagining was there, and experience, prior and subsequent, told me it was true. Could a person choose a less stressful existence, or one more healthful? Probably not.

And I'm certain that someday, before my hair turns gray, I will choose it for a year or two.

Lunchtime in Ireland is never before 1 P.M. and never ends before two-thirty. It was "just on one" when I got back to the hotel car park. I flung my camera into the back seat, locked up, and fairly sprinted to the hotel for the salad. My mouth watered at the very thought of piles of lettuce or spinach, or both.

Inside the dining room, the manager seated me at a table overlooking a brook that flowed from the lake. I could see the round tower I had just passed by and the chapel building that now housed a gift shop. It was a very fine view.

Unfortunately, the salad was on a lesser scale. It consisted of a few leaves of lettuce, some cole slaw, pickled beets, and a couple of hard-cooked eggs. It was served with a huge basket of brown bread, some scones and butter, and buckets of tea with sugar and milk. Naturally, there was a "sweet" for dessert—a jam tart, I think. I was satisfied with the meal, but a serious dieter—for whose delight it was supposedly meant—would have had a hard time keeping the girth down on that feed. Amazingly, excess weight seems to be a matter of little concern to the Irish. I've rarely seen a fat person, despite the butter mountains and cream lakes the Irish both produce and consume. Not, mind, that the whole country is emaciated. The women, generally, are well filled out, and the men still hard-muscled. And all this without any apparent occurrence of Jane Fonda/Jack La Lanne syndrome. It comes, I rather think, from enjoying life, not worrying, eating abundant and natural (that is, unprocessed) foods from birth to death, and having an ancient history of culture and beauty behind one.

I took a leisurely drive back to Bray, getting caught on the way by a small horse. He was white and brown, unshod, and was standing in the road as I came over a rise. He had no intention of moving, so I slowed down. As I did, he came over to the car and pushed his muzzle into the driver's side. It seemed as if he were looking for someone. I leaped out, camera in hand, and caught him in several engaging views. He nuzzled my hand eventually, and I knew he wanted a treat. But I had none, and my apologies in English didn't impress him. (For all I knew, in the Wicklow hills, he might have responded only to Gaelic.) Eventually, he ambled off. When I next drove that track a few days later, I had provisioned myself with some Jacob's Digestive Creams—a sort of Irish granola cookie—but the horse was nowhere to be seen.

On yet another jaunt through the Wicklows, as I came to the summit of a windy rise, I saw two enormous yellow Labrador retrievers galloping toward a red station wagon that was half on and half off the road. Always a soft touch for a canine—and having my Jacob's biscuits along—I pulled off behind.

"Do you mind if I pet your dogs?" I asked the young man standing, now, at the rear door of the wagon.

"Not at all. But mind, they're wet and sloppy. You'll not be wanting their wet paws on your jumper," he said.

It was an old jumper—sweater—brought along for just such lazy outdoor days. Shortly, the young man's wife returned, followed by an older couple. The dogs, it seemed, belonged to the second pair.

"Do you always bring them out with you?" I asked.

"Well, we let them run up here as often as we can bear it. They love it, of course. But they're an awful mess to be bringing into the house when we get home," the woman answered.

The dogs chased off, having eaten me out of provisions. But by that time we all had a good chat going, and on it went.

"I'm glad you don't want to take our pictures," the elder man said.

"Aye, aye," his wife agreed. "We'd enough of that yesterday."

The foursome fell about laughing, as they used to say.

"We've only just leased this land, you see," the woman said. "We'd never any of us cut bog a day in our lives before yesterday. But sure enough, didn't a group of Norwegian tourists come along and ask if they could snap our photo? And all of us from right in Dublin, to boot."

The wind had picked up. I was getting quite chilly, and there were fierce rain clouds on the horizon. I wished aloud for a sweater that would turn into a slicker when needed.

"Well, you'll just have to find a gap in the market and fill it," the woman laughed. The others laughed, too.

"There's a saying popping up in the newspapers now—it's supposed to be telling us all how to be prosperous, I guess—'Find a gap in the market and fill it!' " she explained.

This phrase had the same effect on them as some of our own

political catchwords have had in years past. What American doesn't recall the repeated ad nauseam phrase "I am not a crook"? Anyone who made a political cartoon of that in the early 1970s was almost guaranteed a good chuckle. I got the impression that "Find a gap in the market and fill it" had, in fact, found a gap in the market and filled it.

There was a storm brewing. So, I said my good-byes to the entertaining lot and drove on. It was one of several times I have been entertained by "just folks," have liked them and wanted to see them again. But in Ireland, it's not always so easy to exchange names and addresses. Sometimes it's possible for everyone to be friendly and even entertaining—and then, like the famous, return to hiding in plain sight.

There's a saying in Ireland that, if you don't like the weather, wait ten minutes and it will change. True to form, my second morning at the Inn of the Downs dawned even brighter than the one before. By the time I was on the road, headed deep into the hills and over them to Blessington, however, it was pouring. But it was spectacular.

"We can feel the beauty of a magnificent landscape, perhaps, but we can describe a leg of mutton and turnips better," says Thackeray in his *Irish Sketch Book*. Perhaps Thackeray didn't find beauty in the storms; they are every bit as flavorful as a leg of mutton.

To begin with, of course, the gray day was disappointing after the previous day's brilliance. The day before, my bare forearms had even picked up the Irish equivalent of a tan.

As the little car—a Ford Escort, continental-size—leaped up the mountains and the rain washed in waves over the car as if it were a ship, I was afraid. Despite being small and highly civilized, Ireland has a fair amount of utterly wild terrain, lurking as close as five miles from the nearest town, or two or three from the nearest isolated farm. But it is as if, in wild weather especially, a traveler through the Wicklows has been transported to the craters of the moon, or some other fantastical planet. The magic of the place is such that one can imagine being set upon by brigands and highwaymen. It is easy to feel one is alone in a dangerous place at the top of the world.

But this is fancy; the crime rate in Ireland (there are no brigands and highwaymen) is so incredibly low as to be not worth mentioning. And if one's car conks out, the next car that passes, even if it is two hours later, will provide help. And when the sun comes out, if you've got a Cadbury bar with you and munch it to fill the void the fear has made in your stomach, all will be well again with the world, and Ireland will be beautiful.

From the top of the hill, the vista, even in the rain, was fully detailed. In the glare of full sun, I think, I would not have seen so clearly the other dun-colored hills (and this in a green land), with valleys in purple shadow, and yellow-gray pregnant clouds hanging over them. I could see the air moving, the huge systems of weather pushed by the Gulf Stream, passing so close to the tiny rock island on its western edge, knocked back by the arctic air not very far from the country's northern edge, pulled into Europe by the systems created by age-old mountains and warm Mediterranean waters.

And I could see, at road's edge, the black-walled cuts of turf. I could see the turf-cutters huddled in their cars to await the passing of the storm, some having left a spade stuck in the earth or even a jacket or cap forgotten on its shovel-handle hanger in the mad rush from the deluge. The flagged stakes that separated one man's turf from another's shuddered in the wind. The thin layer of bedraggled flora wavered across the turf face. Thousands of roiling rivulets filled the base of the bog with water that would percolate into the dark, menacing earth. In time, this creates still more turf, the peat much of Ireland still burns in fireplaces to keep warm. There would be more generations of men cutting and drying it, as there had always been.

I rattled down from the top of the hill, stopping at a lay-by near a stream, now swollen within an inch of its banks. Nearby was a large car filled with a family waiting for its picnic to begin again. I watched the stream with them for a while, then got back on the road to Blessington.

By the time I arrived at the outskirts of the town, the scenery had become civilized again. Green hedgerows were punctuated by winding tree-lined driveways leading to neat houses. There were street signs and, in the distance, a stoplight. In the town proper, there were clean rows of modern shops with non-neon signs, angle parking on the main street, and that most civilized of Irish amenities—public toilets. These were charmingly situated behind a fountain and statue erected to the honor of the English lord of the town a century ago. It has not, like Nelson's Column in O'Connell Street, Dublin, been blown up.

It wasn't too odd to me by then that such artwork should grace such humble facilities. In Ireland, they have no cutesy epithets for toilets. They don't say "little boys' room," lavatory, powder room, or such things. The doors to them are generally marked FIR (Men) or MNA (Women), or, rarely, GENTS and LADIES. But when you're asking where they are, it's "Where's the toilet?" plain and simple.

I went from there to the hotel, as it was teatime. I had lunched on cheese and Cadbury chocolate bars—fruit & nut—and fruit at the "laotabh," a lay-by or roadside picnic area. There are, of course, tea shops in Ireland, and rare coffee houses like Bewley's in Dublin. But if you're not having tea at home or in one of the department-store cafés, then a large hotel is the place to go.

Blessington's chief hotel is a rambling, comfortable place, with Navan cabbage-rose carpeting and comfortable leather chairs in the lobby. I mentioned at the desk that I'd like tea.

"The girl will be with you in a minute," said the girl at the desk. And it wasn't much more.

"Tea for one, is it?" she asked. Yes, I said, and biscuits as well.

The tea was hot and strong, and the biscuits ample for two.

The manageress, at the side of the lobby interviewing another girl for a summer job, sounded quite British in her speech—but then, Blessington, despite its location across the Wicklows, has acquired and retained a very British flavor, from the noble's monument to the neat hedgerows to the hotel manageress's accents. Geographically, however, Blessington is indeed "Beyond the Pale"—the term for that area around Dublin the English thought safe for them to live.

"Do I know your mother?" the manageress asked the girl. This, then, was the Irish showing through. It was important that the girl be neat and clean, which she was. But equally, the manageress wanted to know what family the girl was from. And more, she wanted the girl to know that, if anything ran amiss, the doom would fall not on the girl alone but on the family's reputation. The way Palm Beach does social business, Ireland does family business. But the saying "The branch doesn't fall far from the tree" is a verbal sword that cuts both ways in Ireland, with both the branch and the tree demanding the best of each other.

After tea, I had just time to make a quick stop at a Georgian house open for show. I caught the last tour that day of Russborough House, and was treated to a great collection of British and Irish portraiture and to some of the most magnificent Georgian plasterwork in the country. The main stairwell was embellished with the usual garlands and cupids, but also with portraits of the original owners of the house. Most was in mint condition; only small parts of it had been restored, but it had been so painstakingly done that it could not be told from the original work.

The tour over, I went back outside—to brilliant sunshine, in which I drove back to Glen of the Downs.

That night, I treated myself to some nonrural entertainment. I drove in to Bray, looking for a restaurant where I could get something less filling than a hotel full-meal, and then to a movie. I found a Chinese restaurant.

Amazingly, it was quite crowded, and the food was good, although it had a distinctly Irish-Chinese flavor. For example, instead of the hot-and-sour dishes so popular in the United States, the curries—made with Irish cream and Dublin Bay prawns, among other things—were far more popular than the more vegetable-filled courses Americans favor. And hearing English spoken by an Oriental with an Irish accent is one of the true linguistic delights of the world. "Tea, is it?" asked a chrysanthemum-colored waitress, her long black hair falling over crisp linen, when I was done. "And fortune cookies?"

She was a sweet girl. And she wanted to move to the States, she said. Or, at least, she hoped to visit New York, because she had heard there were very many Oriental people there. She herself had gotten to Ireland from Hong Kong by way of England.

At the movies, on a second floor over a shopping arcade, the show was just starting when I got there. I bought some—what else?—Cadbury bars and went hunting a seat, to find the only one remaining was in the front row. And I also found that there are no sections set aside for smoking in Irish movie houses; the whole place is a smoking section, with ashtrays built into the backs of the wide and unbelievably comfortable seats. As a nonsmoker, I was lucky to be in the front row: no one was smoking in front of me, and the nicotine from beside me wafted rearward. The movie, an American comedy, was made doubly enjoyable by the fact that Irish audiences like to roar and will actually still burst into applause, the fact that the celluloid actors cannot hear them notwithstanding. Though they're extremely civilized and in many ways continentally sophisticated, the people of the Emerald Isle, I discovered, are anything but jaded.

4. Kilkenny

I follow an Alpine scenic route. I visit an American in a famous author's house. I find a small crystal factory, a horse show, and a little village of which fond memories are made.

Just south of the wild Wicklows lies an area much beloved by many American tourists—the Vale of Avoca. I decided to travel through it on my way to Kilkenny. It was a gray day, not soft at all but lashing rain over the green landscape. Going through this vale was, too, the long way to Kilkenny, and I had a dinner invitation south of there. Still, I thought it would be worth the risk of delay and the lengthening drive to bring back an impression of this famous valley. It was not.

There was nothing particularly scenic about the first part of the route; indeed, with tall trees pressing close on either side of the narrow road, there wasn't much to see at all. I'd seen taller trees elsewhere—not in Ireland, of course, because the primeval forests had long since been shipped to England as fuel for that nation's industrial revolution. As a curiosity, perhaps this large expanse of hardwoods was worth a short note—but the drive into the forest and back out was tiring. Boggy earth, made boggier still by the constant dripping of the sodden leaves, made for soft "margins," or shoulders, and I hoped I'd not have a puncture here. It is easier, in a foreign English-speaking country, to adopt their idiom than to expect them to adopt yours. Thus, I had already begun thinking of tyres (tires), punctures (flat tyres), petrol (gas), bonnets (hoods), and boots (trunks). This last was to prove quite fortunate when I crossed the border to Northern Ireland; but more on that later.

I like to use the Irish idiom, both when I'm there and when I'm writing about the place. It is, after all, characteristic of the land I explored. And using it, I'm fairly certain, also helps me pass as Irish.

Finally, the woods opened out and I caught a glimpse of the Avonbeg River. I was, by then, running low on petrol, and began looking for a station. I found one, in a quarrylike clearing, all raw earth looking at me from behind the cement-and-glass building and the canopied pumps. It was desolate, but not in the same exciting way as the Wicklows. It looked poor, hardscrabble—the way almost–ghost towns have appeared to me in Wyoming, the way made-up way stations in New York's Adirondack Preserve look. But there was a boy pumping gas, and his dog was helping him. I had a nice moment with the dog, who appreciated a few of the biscuits I carry for such occasions.

Back on the road for me, I decided, and no more stops until Kilkenny. But I had forgotten about the Dunmore Caves, and I pulled off, still in the rain, to tour them.

It is not true by any means that the English were the only people, or even the most savage ones, to take advantage of Ireland's native population. Though regarded as poor through much of the last two centuries, the island nation has been a rich prize for plunderers of many ages, including the fierce Vikings. Indeed, the place became poor primarily because of the repeated pillages.

The caves are do-it-yourself touring. Stout shoes are needed for wending down uneven stairs deep into the dripping earth, I cannot recall how far. And a couple of extra sweaters wouldn't hurt. So dank and eerie were even the first hundred feet, I wondered how people lived in the descending grottoes, for they did live here, more or less continuously, for many decades. I wondered less how they died, for the agonies of the doomed seem still to penetrate the mists. If places do indeed retain some of the energies of events that happen in them, then Dunmore will cause tingling spines for a long, long time to come. In the caves, the Vikings slew more than a thousand Irish in a single raid.

Kilkenny itself rises from the surrounding countryside like a sleepy elephant, awakening among the green brush, pointing its great head skyward. An ancient city, and a stronghold, it was the seat where Irish and Anglo-Normans formed a confederation in 1642 to ward off Cromwell. Paved, and in many cases built, of black Kilkenny marble, the old center of the city appears today as it must have in Cromwell's time.

Today, still, the town center is dominated by Kilkenny Castle, lived in until 1935 by the Butler family. Now, it is open to the public and forms the vista for the family of crafts workers and designers who make up the Kilkenny Design Centre across the street, housed in the castle's former outbuildings—courtyards and stable, coach-houses, dairy, and smithy. Mainly young, and greatly influenced by Scandinavian motifs introduced by the international designers who founded the center in the mid-1960s as well as by their own Celtic background, these artists are designing everything from dinnerware to typescripts, from high-fashion clothing to toilet pulls.

Toilet pulls? I asked. Indeed, yes. Ireland has, as I had noted by then, a half-dozen or more different ways to flush a toilet. Some toilets have a handle on the side of the tank, some on the front like ours. Some have chains, while others work from a foot pedal in the floor. Still others offer a triangular metal lever located at shoulder height in the wall; this you "palm" to make the water descend. At Kilkenny, they had done something very bright: they had created a simple metal plunger in the middle of the tank cover, right over the hole to the bowl. You simply pull up on it to let water into the bowl and push it back down to stop the flush. It seemed to me a most sensible cure for the problems caused by jumbles of rusting chains, slime-covered plastic balls, hissing tubes, and cheap, jangling handles. It was brilliantly simple. It worked. And I am therefore confident that it will not replace Ireland's other flushing methods. After all, this is a country where the people prefer the word toilet to lavatory or ladies room or water closet or any other Western euphemism. So matter-of-fact is their approach that I can't imagine their being concerned with the niceties of flushing; a good 60 to 70 percent of the toilets I used on the trip, save those in my own room (and even some of those), were unheated.

"Don't take the road to Callan. When you come out of the city, take the road straight south. There really are no big towns between here and there," Mrs. Griffith said when I called her, at last, from my hotel in Kilkenny. With my stops and meanderings, the trip had taken a lot longer than I expected; I was expected by Mrs. Griffith—for dinner—in ten minutes. I had yet to clean up and change. Her house, in the little town of Kilmaganny, was seventeen miles away over an almost completely unsignposted country road. "I expect to be about half an hour late," I told her.

She gasped. "I've never made that trip in less than thirty-five minutes, and I know the road," she said. But she didn't know my driving.

Mrs. Griffith was an acquaintance from the States. I had met her and her husband once in Florida, while I was being regaled with Irish tales by an Irish friend at a museum dinner-dance. The Griffiths, Christina and Walter, maintain a home in Florida for the winter.

I expected to make it. There are virtually no speeding violations given in Ireland; the Garda does not make a habit of lying in wait under overpasses and under bushes for the unwary motorist. And there probably aren't a hundred miles of four-lane road in the whole country, so there is a limit to one's speed, naturally. And if you have an accident due to excessive speed, you can expect to be dealt with harshly. (For drunken driving, there is only one punishment. Your license is revoked. And that's that.)

Nonetheless, I expected to make it. I flung on the standard, all-occasion black-skirted suit with a white blouse, a couple of pearl earrings, and black pumps. I dabbed on some lipstick and ran a comb through my mist-dampened and -curled hair as I passed the front desk.

Luckily, there was no traffic whatever in Kilkenny at a quarter past seven on a Saturday night. It is a little early for the Irish; they tend not to go out until nine o'clock or even later. I was on the other side of town in no time. And, sure enough, there was no sign to Kilmaganny. Still, the sun was setting, so picking the road (there were three) that went due south wasn't difficult, and I leaned on the gas.

I passed a crossroads with a few houses. Still no sign, or at least not one I needed. The single one I passed pointed to Callan, so I avoided that. I went on. Finally, with just the last twinkle of light left in the sky, I came to a bona fide town. It was seven-thirty. I hoped it was Kilmaganny, but there was no way to tell. Rural Ireland sports no house numbers to help a visitor; in fact, there are no street names. But I knew I was looking for Rossenarra House, which I supposed would be a substantial one. Only the big ones are named.

At the town's single intersection, a woman was hurrying across the street. "Can you tell me how to get to Rossenarra House?" I called. "Aye, I can." Would she tell me? I had heard from my doctor's nurse at home about an evil neighbor of her old mum's, in Ennis, who would answer a question that way and leave it at that. It amused the nurse's teenage daughter; it wouldn't amuse me right now. But the woman was not of that type. "Aye, I can indeed," she went on, her urgency all disappeared. "Could you ever be telling me, is it the Griffiths you're wanting?" It was. "Well, just take this left turning right here, and go on up the hill. You'll come to some gates, large gates, on the left, and that's it."

It was 7:35 when I cranked up the window, so hurriedly I doubt my guide heard me thank her. I roared up the hill, found the gates, and eased on through—thank goodness, for they opened onto a steep driveway that seemed to descend straight down for miles. Had I gone through them at my high-road pace, I'd have shot down the hill like a runaway sled and landed smack in the dining room, unless the brakes were of Herculean strength. That didn't seem likely. In Ireland, cars are kept in shape much as horses are; they're given their feed and water, a bit of exercise, and left alone unless they begin to act up.

At the bottom of the hill, an immense pink house of three stories with wings to either side rose up like a national monument from acres of graveled yard.

I skidded to a stop near another car. I assumed I had parked correctly, and I crunched over the stones to the door. Mrs. Griffith greeted me. "Come in. Walter will be right down, then we've just time for a drink before Mary will have dinner on." Usually, the Irish are fairly unconcerned about time. Mrs. Griffith had been, unaccountably I thought, quite nervous on the phone about my lateness of half an hour—and this in a land where a thank-you note can be written two years after the kindness and not raise an eyebrow. Her concern, however, had not been for herself, but for her cook, who wanted to get home to her own family and had, in any case, been working overtime.

The room we entered was the drawing room, which, she said, she had recently had redone. It was long, tall, light, and airy and furnished all in pale blue and pink. It set off Mrs. Griffith's blond beauty enormously well. Mr. Griffith mixed drinks, and we sat down to talk. "What can we do to help you with your book?" he asked.

As far as I was concerned, inviting me to dinner was enough. Ireland, despite many accidental and deliberate burnings over the years, is still littered with gracious homes like this one. Many, like Russborough House in Blessington, are open to the public, and they afford something of a look at how people once lived in them. But this was a chance to see how people live in them today.

One of the things I noticed first about the house was its warmth, not just the kind generated by its people, but the actual air temperature. "I have learned to like heat, spending half the year as we do in the United States," Mrs. Griffith said. "So we do keep the thermostat up. Luckily, we have a very good heating unit, and, though it's expensive, it's not impossible."

The Griffiths had bought the house fairly recently. Built in 1824, in classical high-Georgian style, it was lived in from 1970 until the early 1980s by American novelist Richard Condon. "He was the one who did much of the modernizing," said Mrs. Griffith. "In fact, there is even a place for an indoor swimming pool, though one has never been installed," she said as she took me on a tour of the lowest floor, containing the marvelously efficient heating system as well as a fitted wine cellar and a huge family area with a kitchen.

Upstairs, on the main floor, is the drawing room, an immense library, bathrooms, the main kitchen, and a morning room. There is more space as well—garages, a separate apartment, and so on. The library, however, was especially attractive, with deep mahogany shelving on all the walls. "It used to be white," Mrs. Griffith said. "I had it painted in faux mahogany." It was an excellent job and had fooled me at first glance, though I was still on the trail of faux finishes, as an adjunct to my major search. I had been commissioned to produce an article on them, and they were a large part of the elegance of Georgian art and architecture.

On the top two floors are bedrooms and more bedrooms. The Griffiths had bought the house furnished, but Mrs. Griffith had moved bits around, subtracted bits here, added bits there, until it had lost the incongruously modern feel it had had when it belonged to the Condons. "These bedrooms come in quite handy. Just about every weekend when we're here, my brother's children come to stay," she added. "I had hoped you were going to use one of them. I was so surprised to hear you were calling from a hotel. I had just assumed you would stay the night with us."

Therein lay the first—and undoubtedly largest—disappointment of my trip. I am a "house nut," having restored a few of my own on a less grand scale. And besides, the Griffiths were fun.

Rossenarra House had indeed a fascinating history. Situated on twelve acres, with a sixty-mile view of Kilkenny and Tipperary, it was designed by James Hoban, who also designed the White House in Washington, D.C. At Rossenarra, the racehorse Red Rum, three-time Grand National winner, was bred. Sir John Lavery, one of Ireland's most famous artists, lived there; it was his wife, Lady Lavery, whose portrait appeared on the Irish pound note until recently, when it was replaced by a portrait of an Irish lady sea rover (the famous seventeenth-century pirate Grace O'Maille).

The offering brochure the Condons had made to market the property states: "It is to be sold either furnished, or unfurnished. Robert Haughton [house agent] suggested a number of alternative uses for Rossenarra House: for very low-density upmarket housing on part of the lands; a hotel/restaurant; an executive headquarters for a multinational company; a sales conference centre."

Haughton also came up with this ingenious proposal: "The property would suit a successful rock group, with the in-house garage converted to a private professional recording studio, and the tennis-croquet court turned into a helicopter pad. Similar properties in England are put to this use."

God Save the Queen, and all that, I thought. But thank goodness Rossenarra was spared this last, particularly obnoxious, abuse. Americans have been deeply involved in Ireland, for both good and ill, for years. Walter Griffith is undoubtedly involved for good; it is one of the niceties of modern life that a substantial income from gentlemanly pursuits can save a noble house from ruin. It is equally nice that it is again lived in by an Irishwoman, Christina Griffith. Filled with family and friends and entertainments, as well as the more mundane pursuits of a modern couple's life, Rossenarra House has gotten another lease on the future. Its abundantly pink exterior—a color of the spirit in more than one culture—seems perfectly suited to it. There *are* faeries in Ireland, and I'm certain the music of the spheres was spared a serious disruption when they kept Rossenarra House from a loud, untimely death.

I stayed with the Griffiths until all hours, drinking more than one Irish coffee. And I sincerely wished I'd gotten my invitation straight.

Like Dublin itself, roads in Ireland are a mixture of graceful curves and sudden straight lines. And you can't so much drive as sail them, on a tarmac ocean. For a time, you'll find that you must tack against the wind, curving outward from your destination. You must perhaps run straight into the wind for a time. All the while, you must scan the sea and sky and look for harbingers of land—birds and insects. You might pass a porpoise leaping in the sea. Or a ghost ship. Or another vessel. You might be boarded; or you might board someone else. You may stay "at sea" for a long time, with no destination in sight. In fact, letting the winds of the Celtic landscape decide your next move seems often the right thing to do, as I did on my way south from Kilkenny.

I drove east from Cashel, partly to find a small crystal factory I had been told about, partly to see the countryside. I found the factory of the expansively named Kilkenny Crystal, a small, modern building about the size of a small suburban house. It was down a typical narrow lane between two rock walls in the Tinnamore section of Callan. The factory sat next to a neat, brick-colored suburban house where the proprietor, Patrick Clancy, lived. I drove through the gate and knocked on the door and rang the bell of the dark factory building. I was afraid it was closed. But, in true Irish fashion, in a minute or two a woman walked out of the house and greeted me. I apologized for disturbing her, and she assured me her husband was busy but would be over to give me a tour shortly. I explained that I was an American writer, and she kindly let me into the building to have a look around.

As promised, her husband arrived in a few minutes. He explained that Kilkenny Crystal was one of the oldest "new" crystal firms in Ireland. It was founded in 1969 by Clancy and a German immigrant, Hans Gross, who developed many new crystal designs. Unfortunately, Gross died in the mid-1970s, and the factory languished. But Clancy and his son, Richard, had a large stock of crystal "blanks," as the uncut crystal is called, and in a few months found Martin Duggan, who had just left Waterford Crystal after spending nine and a half years as an apprentice and cutter at the world's largest crystal factory. Why Duggan left is a purely Irish reason: he was bored with cutting the same patterns day after day. Moreover, as a farmer's son, Duggan liked to help do the work at his father's farm. Now, he can cut crystal for Clancy as needed, and farm as well.

Richard Clancy engraves and polishes the crystal Duggan cuts, and a local woman (Clancy referred to her as a "girl") marks the crystal for cutting and checks on quality. Kilkenny Crystal specializes in family coats of arms, and sells largely to local Irish businesses, some larger businesses, and the occasional tourist. Locally, it sells to "children of parents who first bought from us five or ten years ago," Clancy says. Obviously, Kilkenny is not going to challenge Waterford, but Duggan does make some unique and interesting designs, especially Avonree, a flowing pattern named after the local river of the same name.

Then I drove south, toward Thomastown. "What were all those rags I saw tied to bushes?" I later asked an acquaintance in County Limerick.

"Oh, you've passed a holy well," he answered. "They may be rags, or they may be bits of people's clothing. They hang them on bushes near a well to obtain the blessings."

The "haberdashery bushes" I saw were on the road from Kilkenny to Thomastown. I later learned even more amazing things. That particular well was dedicated to Saint Fiachre. Fiachre was a holy man from Ullard, County Kilkenny, who chose to spend his time in the isolation of a foreign country—France—in preference to the solitude of a monastery. He has become, over the years, the patron saint of French taxi drivers. Why? Because the first cabs in Paris congregated around the Hotel St. Fiachre. All this makes as much sense as obtaining blessings by hanging cloth on trees near natural springs. But such is Ireland, and so, apparently, is France.

When I reached the outskirts of Thomastown, I stopped for a man standing in the middle of the road and wearing a cap and long black balmacaan. He resembled greatly one of Dublin's "parkers."

"What's going on?" I asked him.

"The Thomastown Horse Show," he answered. "Entry is two pounds. Parking that way."

"What time does it get started?" It sounded like a lark, despite the blustery day—again.

"Well, they're started now," he said. "But sure, the best jumping won't be until later on, you know, after they get the novices out of the way and all."

I decided to find some lunch and return. He guided me around and back out the gate, and I headed down the road to Inistioge. I had no idea if food awaited me there, but I had a feeling an adventure did.

I had heard of the place from Tom Waters, back in Dublin. It is his hometown, his birthplace, and his mother still owned the family home there. Waters is a tall lanky fellow, with a wild mane of slightly graying hair, piercing blue eyes, and the stony bold features of Peter O'Toole. He had had a good education, in quite the English tradition, I had been certain from his speech. But he had a lot of the fey about him. It may have been due to being raised in Inistioge (pronounced "in-ish-teeg").

Inistioge is nestled between mountains on the River Nore. It is a fishermen's haven, filled with water from earth and sky. The Waters house—marvelous surname, in the circumstances—was surrounded by a moat, I knew, and I thought it shouldn't be difficult to find. I drove through the little town and out across the river and up a hill, and I knew I had gone too far. Back down. From the bridge, I took a few photos of fishermen. Where is the house with the moat? Would it be a big moat? What, exactly, was a moat these days? I stopped and asked.

Next to the river there was a car park, and across the street from it a Georgian building called The School House Café. I was hungry, but, knowing food was available, I decided to continue looking for the moat.

I had no idea how many souls Inistioge contained; there were probably no more than twenty houses in the town itself. But among these were a grocer, a petrol dealer, a tackle shop, a pottery, and two beauty salons, all shops with living quarters behind.

I stepped into the local MACE store—a sort of small rural supermarket found all across Ireland—and asked the owner if she knew of a house with a moat and a family named Waters.

"Aye, I do, surely. It's right around the corner from here."

I didn't see any corners, but I took her word for it and went looking for one. Eventually, I did see that the main street seemed to slip around and turn up the hill, or at least part of it did. The other part went round the square, where I'd already been, and on down to the river. I eased the tiny car up a street even tinier. There, with a stream running around three sides of it, was a house with green trim. It had a garden full of flowers and a short palm tree or two. Palms thrive in Ireland because of the proximity of the warm Gulf Stream air, despite the overlying, almost arctic, weather patterns. In that very stream, Tom Waters had had his experience with the supernatural.

"I guess Ireland is full of stories about supernatural occurrences," Waters had told me one night over dinner. "But I've got one that really happened.

"My father decided to cut down a stand of trees quite a few years ago, as it obstructed his view of the river. One of the neighbors came along and told him he'd not be wanting to do that; the last person who had cut down those trees had had terrible things happen to him. [It seemed the stream was a pagan holy-water well, and the trees had been planted in a pre-Christian holy bower, or so the local legend and superstition went.]

"My father was not superstitious, so he kept on cutting. It would be hard to make the connection, but the fact is, my father, who had not been ill, died soon after that."

Like most Irish, the Waters family held the wake at their home. When all the mourners had gone on the night after the burial, Mrs. Waters missed her silver tea service. "She didn't think that one of the mourners—all friends and family and neighbors—could have taken it. But we thought maybe a stranger could have come in through the crush and taken it." At any rate, Waters said, the case was not long in the solving.

"The next morning, my sister went to let the dog out, and there, not tossed or broken or thrown at all, was the tea service sitting in the moat, as if it had been all set out there for a party."

The Waters house was charming and it was for sale. Tom lived in Dublin with his wife and child, and had a job with the IDA; he had no need of it. Mrs. Waters wanted to move closer to civilization, too. As a house nut, I would have loved to own it. But Inistioge is far from much I care about—and very, very strange.

For one thing, it was the home of the Tighes, who in turn were the progenitors of Eleanor Butler and Sarah Ponsonby. These two ladies, one writer said, "exemplified the Romantic and the Gothic by running away together to live in a Welsh cottage." They were, aside from their eccentricities, tastemakers in the eighteenth century.

Then there is the Georgian house on the east side of the town square, with this very unusual inscription in a marble block above the door:

Make to yourselves friends with the manner of unrighteousness, that when ye fail [fall? it was quite weathered] they may receive you into everlasting tribulation.

Chilling thought, and an interesting perversion of the Golden Rule.

Finally, cold and hungry and wanting to return to the horse show, I went into the School House Café. It was the hangout for a number of preteens, all devouring oatmeal cookies and "minerals," or sodas. There was an Anglo-Irish family, all togged out in loafers and Fair Isle sweaters and London Fogs, going, I presumed, to the horse show, too.

It was warm in the shop, until the elderly woman and the black-and-white dog came in and left the door open. No one but me noticed. In any case, the cold was nothing to what I experienced later in the café's open air "loo." Reached by going out the back door and across a garden, the toilet boasted a corrugated clear fiberglass roof, that could be looked down upon (and through?) from the upper floors of the café building. It also had, high up in a wall, a permanently open window in the form of a man-made hole; this was the disinfectant system, I presumed. There was cold running water, and a community hand towel with blue flowers on it. But there was no toilet paper. And I knew that, as with drinking from an Anglican communion cup, no one ever caught anything from an Irish toilet. I hoped.

Fortified, I drove back to the horse show. The crowd had grown in the last hour and a half, no one seeming to mind the rain and chilly gusts. Stopping to pull on an extra pair of socks and a scarf, I headed for the far side of the field, where the novice horse-jumping was still in progress. Next to it, a ring had been set up for seniors' practice. As I walked, there was a huge roan horse carrying a rider in a tweed hacking jacket. Golden-brown ringlets stuck out from under the rider's hat; I thought for a moment it might be Eddie Macken, Ireland's great steeplechase rider. But no, it couldn't be, not in a tiny competition like this, which sported, besides the horse-jumping and the "professional equipment" stands and chips wagons, a family pets competition. I could hardly wait. I had read, and reread, watched, and watched again, the great English animal/people stories by James Herriot, *All Creatures Great and Small*. In one episode, Herriot, as a young vet, was honored with judging the family pets competition at just such a local outing in England's Yorkshire Dales. Here, too, were country people. Would I get a view of anything as uproarious as Herriot awarding prizes to the founder's own son, which was rewarded with booing and a pelting with ripe fruit?

I couldn't take my eyes off the man in the tweed hacking jacket. It really looked like Eddie Macken.

Generally, I am allergic to horses. A few years ago, I had a box on the rail at an historic race track. I enjoyed going: the races were fine, the brandy was better, and, as often as I could, I brought along good company. But I did itch. The horse dander mixed with the dry dust flew up my skirts, until I finally took to wearing slacks. But even then, I was in agonies, depending on the stillness of the day, with watering eyes and sneezing. But I love the beasts all the same. I haven't been on one in years and would be quite frightened of a canter now. In front of me, a group of slightly built thirteen-year-old girls and boys were taking enormous mounts over some exceedingly difficult jumps. Although this was just a country show, the riders were all smartly dressed, most in velvet, but a few, like the adult Eddie Macken clone, in hacking jackets. Without exception, though, the horses' hoofs gleamed, and the animals were well combed, and the saddles and tack were in prime condition. It shouldn't have surprised me; Ireland has had a love affair with the horse, going back hundreds of years. Today, Irish bloodstock makes up a good percentage of the stuff in the veins of the world's winningest beasts, in both flat racing and steeplechase.

Moreover, racing of either sort is so civilized in Ireland. Flat racing, like that I saw at Leopardstown, offers plush accommodations for beasts, riders, and spectators alike. Steeplechase doesn't. The horses and riders and grooms must provide for themselves, with trailers and equipment of their own choosing. Some have campers, so they can bring along their own food and have access to running water and indoor plumbing of a sort. Otherwise, they are left to contend, like the spectators, with snack wagons and port-a-potties. Still, the bracing aspect of the sport—fresh winds blowing over upland fields—offers a charm all its own.

Although I am ordinarily the silk cushions and bonbons type, my delight in the Thomastown race was complete. (*Could* it be Eddie Macken?) I had eaten well. I could have used some stouter shoes, but then, I hadn't been expecting to tromp muddy fields that day. I had been cooped up in an automobile for much of two days, and I was feeling almost as frisky as the horses.

After I'd watched the novices for an hour or so—Irish time was in effect—I decided they'd not be done soon, so I meandered over to the small ring where the owners of the family pets were gathering. It was a very informal affair. I never quite figured out who the judge was; I never learned who won. But, to be sure, it was worthy of Herriot. One tall, preppy young woman held a squirming cock-a-poo with a bandanna around its neck. There was a boxer straining at his lead. There was a cage containing, I assumed, a cat or a rabbit; I couldn't see it, and it made no sound. There was a marvelous huge St. Bernard, looking mellow, as they always do. Recently washed and combed, he was the perfect picture of a fictional dog, held on a bright red lead by a young boy obviously hoping his pal would win.

And suddenly, the Bernard flopped down in the mud and conducted a methodical search of his ear with his hind leg, swiftly moving from searching to rooting out whatever was biting him, and splattering mud and grass all over himself and his owner in the process. "You can't do that," the boy wailed. "Scratching's not allowed."

"Stand him up, then," his mother instructed from the sidelines. Obviously, not possible.

"Sure, he's more comfortable sitting down" came from a kibitzer, a red-faced countryman with a devilishly sly grin on his face.

I doubt if the boy and the St. Bernard won. I had to leave. The rain was coming harder, and I still had a long way to drive to Waterford.

And I never found out whether the dashing rider was Eddie Macken.

I traveled back through Inistioge, but quickly. New Ross was the only large city I would pass before arriving in Waterford, and I thought it might be worth a look. On the River Barrow, at the head of Waterford Harbor, New Ross looks like a rural San Francisco, its steep streets heading down to the bay. Its houses, gabled and seemingly pinned to the sides of the hills, are medieval-looking. It was a stronghold against Cromwell and saw major battles in the Wolfe Tone Rebellion of 1798. It is one of the few places remembered for the brutality of the Irish partisans rather than of the English forces. At the massacre of Scullabogue, hundreds of British prisoners were burned alive after the Republicans had fled the field.

Waterford, which is quickly reached and quickly left, is chiefly known today for its crystal. The sprawling factory lies at the south side of the town, housed in nondescript, almost Quonset-like buildings. One can tour it, but today much of the cutting is machine cutting, and there is not very much to say about it.

The city itself is a waterfront town; it boasts the derricks and dockside paraphernalia of any waterfront city. But it also offers dockside dining and a cruising restaurant.

On August 23, 1169, Waterford was invaded by a Welsh Norseman called Strongbow (real name: Richard FitzGilbert de Clare, Earl of Pembroke) along with two hundred knights and a thousand other troops. In a single day, the combined Norse and Irish within the city walls had been defeated.

The day had gotten grayer and grayer, and, I must admit, I was getting weary, defeated by the wet and cold despite the day's many pleasures.

5. CORK

I dine with one of the great cooks of Europe. I learn about industry in the port city, then linger in some ruins—and some former ruins.

There's something very Parisian about Cork. It may have to do with the way the streets open out toward the quays, and the wide and blinding quality of slanted sunlight that streams into the broad boulevards. The rather spindly trees, recently planted in front of imposing gray blocks of buildings, are reminiscent, perhaps, of certain traffic circles in Paris. There, too, the saplings are only a few years old, and have stood the crush of people waiting for buses, sprinting for taxis, having a chat. Or maybe the Parisian feeling comes from the multitudes of fashionably dressed young women and men streaming from the stone fastnesses of banks and solicitors' offices, ignoring the few retail shops in favor of a fast break to home.

These five-o'clock hordes seemed not so downtrodden as the hordes familiar to me from New York's subways. Indeed, they had expressions on their faces that, like those of the Parisians, told me their real day was just beginning. And so it was; but in a far different sense than the late afternoons and evenings of the cosmopolitan Parisians.

There are no sidewalk cafés in Ireland, save a humble few in Dublin. Nightlife as the Parisians, or even New Yorkers, know it is fairly scarce in Ireland. No, these were young married people mainly, going home to their families. Those who were single would not be stepping out until much later, well after 8 P.M., after eating dinner with their families. Most single people in Ireland live at home, with Mum, Da, and siblings.

Cork seems like Paris, with its river slicing it, like a plum pudding, into two succulent, steaming portions. Cork's Sean

O'Faolain, in his book *An Irish Journey*, understands Cork's magic situation thus:

> You soon find out that the city is not merely built on a marsh but on islands in the marsh, and that the streets are, often, covered canals or rivers. Patrick Street is winding merely because the river under it winds—one winter the river burst the wood-paving and we saw it underneath; and if you will lean over the parapet near Patrick's Bridge you will [or used to] see it emerge there into the Lee. . . . Drawbridge Street indicates that water was near.

Cork is now more than eight hundred years old, but water no longer pops up into the streets; the streets are no longer paved with wood, in any case. I was there during Cork's anniversary year, and the city, along with the national government and local cultural groups, had planned all sorts of festivities. Cork was drawing crowds of American tourists. Understandably, because there was a lot of immigration from Cork, because it, and neighboring and still crumbling Cobh (Morton remarked on this, too), were major ports, especially for cargoes of human life. Passage to America was relatively cheap—cheaper, certainly, than feeding a fourteen-year-old until she got married, cheaper than housing a young man who could find no work. And work is still hard to find in Cork.

Today the progeny of the Cork immigrants are returning to celebrate. But what? I wondered. I pondered. Most of them were celebrating their own good fortune in having been born in the prosperous United States, though they wouldn't put it that way. I think the Irish would, and do, though. It has been said that the Irish with energy and imagination left. The unwanted also left, of course, among them prisoners of the English government of the last century. From whatever cause, the Irish know that the American Irish are not cut of the same cloth that forms the social fabric of the mother country. Moreover, so much of the Irish economy has depended for years, as it still does, on Irish-American tourism that certain resentments have, naturally, developed. The bulk of tourists are, as well, what my father always called "sloppy, sentimental" Irish. These are the ones, I have observed, who think a Kerry slide must be an Irishman falling down, rather than a piece of music. All these American Irish seem to know is "Danny Boy" and brown bread.

But that's the bright side. On the dark side, many of these people (or ones like them, not born on the old sod, but having a connection) provide aid to the bombers in the Six Counties. Indeed, one of these Irish-Americans, who runs a travel agency in the United States, told an official of the government of the Republic of Ireland that she would continue to support rebellion in Northern Ireland—bombings, maimings and other outrages—until the last Protestant had died. Naturally, she had never herself been in danger. She had not, for that matter, taken the pulse of the country she was "helping," sheltered as she was on a tourist bus with others like herself and living safely in America.

Irish-Americans, generally, believe that Ireland is quaint, an idyllic landscape of happy, fresh-faced maidens and handsome lads. "When people leave, they take with them the culture as it is at that moment," I had been told by Miriam Logan in Dublin. She herself had a relative who had left, before the Troubles got started again in 1969. "When I talk to this person, who lives in another European country, I find she is militant about rejoining North and South. Nor does she care whether there is much bloodshed about it. Of course, she has the luxury of being far away from any danger. And she has not been home enough to know of the change in attitude." There is no blood feud between North and South any longer, Logan thinks, and I agree. Rather, it is only a handful of perennial malcontents and hired provocateurs who cause the problems. Not, mind you, that the situation will ever be perfect. Even so, while many Americans think that it is taking life and limb in hand to travel even to the Republic of Ireland, never mind Ulster, it is not so. The civil strife is well-contained. It is perpetrated, as our civil strife here, mainly in the areas neither tourists nor any thoughtful person would walk blindly into.

Ireland is no longer a pastoral society, but it still is a garden spot. Cork, in particular, shows the diversity of modern Irish life. For one thing, Cork is a music haven, with far more going for it than "My Wild Irish Rose." Nomad composer Sean O Riada (1931–1971) was born in Cork, educated at Cork, and founded the Ceoltoiri Chualann, a traditional music group that fostered, among other great things, the Chieftains. O Riada turned his back on the European music he had learned at school and composed, with his Ceoltoiri, two settings of the Mass in Irish in traditional music idioms.

Cork boasts concerts frequently at Connolly Hall and the Opera

House. Cork School of Music offers regular evening concerts from October to June on Wednesdays and Fridays. Every spring, there's the Cork Choral Festival, and there are band concerts as well during July and August evenings. There's also an annual country-music festival. In Ireland? Indeed. Much of what has become American country music began in Ireland. The tune of "The Connemara Cradle Song" has become, in the States, "On Top of Old Smokey." The Chieftains have even recorded an album, in Ireland, called *Cotton-Eyed Joe.* Why? Because, on their tour of Texas a few years back, they took refreshment at a country-and-western club. On hearing the band there play "Cotton-Eyed Joe," Paddy Maloney instantly recognized the melody as an ancient Irish one, which the group also plays on the album. Even American mountain clog dancing is Irish in essence; watch some step-dancers sometime, and you'll see why. And the cadences our mountain folk speak, often thought to be English Elizabethan, are just as likely to be the lilting leftovers of Irish accents. Or even the more musical, and also Gaelic, Welsh.

Maybe that's why Mrs. Shan O'Keeffe, wife of the Returned Yank managing director of Sifco Turbines, Ltd., found the Cork version of talking to kids so amusing. "I don't find things too different here," she said, commenting on the family's relatively recent arrival from America for her husband's job. "But there is one thing Shan teases me about all the time. It's when I'm taking the kids somewhere in the car and I say 'Get in.' The proper local terminology is 'In you go' and, of course, 'Out you go,' when you're unloading. It's a small thing, but I think it's representative of the way things are done here. 'Get in' sounds too abrupt to them. 'In you go' is more polite," she added. And more musical.

Mrs. O'Keeffe, a teacher in the United States, is a go-ahead woman in Ireland, helping to set up conferences as an adjunct to her husband's work, but enjoying the gentle side of Irish life as well. The O'Keeffe children, born and raised in the United States, were finding horse-riding lessons almost as interesting as American TV (though they do miss Saturday-morning cartoons) and other high-tech pursuits. "And they do seem to have more sniffles here," she added. "I think it's the weather. You just can't dress them right; one day in February it may be seventy-five, the next, thirty-two. And you can have exactly the same fluctuation in May. It's impossible to make them keep their coats buttoned. But then again, you may not want to."

Mrs. O'Keeffe isn't regarded much as a foreigner or tourist, because her husband is native Irish. "And my children have adapted so quickly to the local patterns of speech and behavior that they are not singled out in school. In fact, one day a substitute teacher told the returning teacher that she only had one American in the class, not two. 'Oh, yes,' said the class teacher. 'The O'Keeffe boy is American, too.' "

Mrs. O'Keeffe seems glad of this. Perhaps, like me, she agrees with Morton. "There are certain things in all historic cities which tourists and no other people do. They are generally of a nature to confirm local inhabitants in a belief that all tourists are half-witted. In Cork you are supposed to kiss the Blarney Stone and hear the Bells of Shandon."

I did neither. I regard myself as a traveler, not a tourist. The Blarney Stone was out. As for the Bells of Shandon, perhaps they rang while I was there: I was very busy visiting factories and cooks and so on, and didn't especially notice. Unlike Morton, I did not ask for a special playing.

The truth of Ireland is in what its natives do and speak. But that's more than just the "What will you be drinking now?" from the barman in the hotel pub. Ireland's prize-winning Cork-born author, James N. Healy, finds a way to combine the truth of the matter with the tourism of it.

Writes Healy, in *Cara*, the in-flight magazine of Aer Lingus Irish Airlines, "Shandon Steeple [is] Cork's best-known landmark—the Statue of Father Matthew, Apostle of Temperance. He stands there with his right hand held out in a gesture which the wags interpret as saying 'I was drinkin' since I was that high.' It is one of the few in a city curiously short of monuments: perhaps that is why it is generally known as 'the Statcha,' in Cork vernacular, and the city's most celebrated meeting place.

"Cork has recently spread out to meet what were formerly the separated suburbs of Blackrock, Douglas and Wilton. New dormitory towns have been established and one hopes that the green belt between them and the city will remain, as otherwise the intimate character which has always been such an integral part of Cork will be eroded.

"This lovely city in its valley on the Lee is generally regarded as a prosperous place, with a renowned independence of spirit, but the recession of recent times has hit it perhaps the hardest of all

Irish cities. But then it always needs the promise of a good fight, or a suggestion that his is not as good as the next, to goad a 'Rebel Corkman' to his best endeavours, and one likes to think that, in this tradition, he will have the courage and the pride to fight his way out of the complicated problems of modern times."

"The Corkman" is, at the very least, beginning this uphill battle. Unemployment in this city of 140,000 people has been running, in recent years, at 25 percent. There are rows and rows of Council Houses; luckily, they have been built in an Irish adaptation of international style that's not half bad. And they have been placed in outlying neighborhoods, rather than plunked into the middle of historic districts. This is only sensible; the new factories are on the far side of the "green belt," so that the new housing is, in fact, close to the potential employment.

Helping to alleviate the 25 percent unemployment rate are numerous IDA schemes to attract foreign businesses to Cork and to spur indigenous Irish business. During my trip, I visited three relatively new and sophisticated plants built by American-based firms, all of which are located in new industrial parks. Driving through downtown Cork to reach these modern paragons of industry, however, provides ample evidence of Cork's plight—everywhere empty, rundown factories from as early as the nineteenth century line the narrow side streets of the city.

Cork gained its first prosperity in the nineteenth century—and even earlier—as a major port city for shipping the whiskey from its distilleries, and local beer, as well as for shipping raw grain and other agricultural products from the rich Irish countryside, including fertilizer, a by-product from all those cows. Cork was also the home of the world-famous Butter Market, located beneath Shandon Steeple. The Butter Exchange, as it was called, was one of the world's largest food-distribution centers during the mid-1800s. It shipped salted butter in wooden boxes, and salted beef and pork in barrels, all over the world, first in windjammers and later in clipper ships and steamships. The exchange underneath the steeple died during the 1920s and the building became a textile factory.

Before 1867, the five largest independent Irish whiskey distilleries were all in Cork. In that year, they amalgamated and became the present-day Cork Distilleries. In 1917, Ford Motor established a tractor factory for the European market, bringing thousands of jobs, but this was changed over to automobile assembly during the 1950s, reducing the number of jobs by the hundreds. Finally, a few years ago, Ford and Dunlop's, which had made tires in old Ford facilities, both shut down for good.

Today, Cork is the home of many of the European facilities of large pharmaceutical and health-care manufacturing firms. And an increasing number of electronics and high-technology firms are locating in Cork, spurred not only by the additional incentives offered by the IDA. Shan O'Keeffe, the Sifco managing director, told me his firm located in Cork because Cork has an excellent airport facility with speedy and cooperative customs facilities. Sifco Turbine repairs and rebuilds jet engine parts for major airlines, such as Lufthansa, Air France, Turkish Airlines, and SAS in Scandinavia; O'Keeffe must get the rebuilt engine parts to them as quickly as possible. Aer Lingus, the Irish national airline, operates scheduled service from Cork to most major European capitals.

Cork has, of course, been an important seaport for eight hundred years, so that its world-class deep harbor is its most taken-for-granted asset. But Cork has gained another one, also essential to Sifco's choice of Cork: natural gas. During the mid-1970s, Marathon Oil and other oil companies found a substantial supply of natural gas in the Celtic Sea not far from Cork. In the early 1980s, Cork gained Ireland's first natural-gas pipeline. Sifco's processes require large amounts of natural gas burning at very high temperatures, and the local gas company offered Sifco a very favorable long-term contract at very low prices. (Since then, natural gas has been found in, and is now pumped from, an area near Dublin.)

Equally important to Sifco and other American firms locating in Cork is the large supply of well-educated and skilled people. Another U.S. firm, Liebert, employs more than two hundred people to make air-conditioning equipment for computers for the European market. During my visit, Liebert's Irish managing director, Ray Geaney, another Returned Yank who used to work for General Electric in the States, pointed out his window across the road to the Regional Technical Institute. "With the institute next door, we always have a good supply of competent people," he said, adding that he also makes good use of the local AnCO training school for his semiskilled employees.

AnCO is the Irish government agency responsible for training semiskilled modern industrial labor. In facilities all over the country, AnCO gives basic training in industrial processes, then further trains to suit a company starting up. From these well-trained employees, the company can pick those that best fit its needs, giving industry access to a "college" of excellent, highly motivated employees for all industrial crafts. In a country where tourism, agriculture, and the domestic arts (needlework, lace making, and so on) have been the staples of the national product, "male" industrial employment is a great need for the Irish, and they get from this arrangement as much as they give, in most cases.

But Sifco, Liebert, Ridgid Tool, Cado Computer, and numerous other U.S. firms in the Cork area all seem to succeed not only because of what Ireland gives to them, but also because of a particular combination of resources or characteristics they share with Ireland. For example, Sifco makes unique use of the Irish propensity for the "lateral thinking" I talked about before. Says O'Keeffe, "Our work requires a very high degree of skilled labor. We didn't expect to find people with the skills we needed, but we did expect to find—and did find in abundance—people skilled in metal-working trades. Although there are five separate jobs involved and a range of skilled work, each skilled employee does all of them. And our people enjoy moving around, doing different jobs and being responsible for the quality and results they produce. This situation is unique in Ireland, unique in an organized [unionized] shop in Ireland, and unique within Sifco's organization."

Without really knowing it, Sifco brought to Ireland a philosophy that states that quality cannot be inspected into a product. Quality must be built into a product. "To help improve quality and the proficiency of each person, our operators move around. They know the results and effects of their work versus that of others and their impact on the other phases of the total product. And they like it. They do not get bored doing the same thing over and over, because they do not do the same thing over and over," O'Keeffe notes.

With his comments, O'Keeffe perfectly expresses the essence of the Irish lateral thinking: their minds easily and quickly move from one subject to another. They love challenge and competition, and they hate to be bored and do the same thing repeatedly.

While Americans often pay lip service to the importance of people in industry, for the Irish the service must become action. Liebert, says Ray Geaney, brought with it a very strong commitment to its people. "Liebert believes the purpose of business is to create and retain customers. Doing that effectively is what gives you a profit. And as an outsider coming into the organization, the customer and employee orientation here was very noticeable.

"When Liebert first introduced this orientation to Ireland, the Irish were naturally very skeptical," he adds. They'd heard lip service from unsuccessful companies. "But once we got over their resistance, they became hooked on the Liebert culture. Liebert is also very team-oriented and does not suffer prima donnas either."

Geaney compares Liebert's approach to Ireland to that of Saint Patrick. "If you know the Celtic Cross [an early Christian cross with a cross placed over a circle], you know that Saint Patrick is said to have imposed his culture—the new Christian cross—onto the existing pagan culture which worshipped the sun, the circle symbol. Liebert is trying to get the best of both cultures, the Irish and the Liebert."

Liebert's approach blends well with several Irish traits: a strong concern for the family—Liebert often invites employees' families to the plant; a strong commitment to job security; a strong orientation to teamwork—the Irish are fanatics about team sports—football (European soccer), hurling, field hockey, and so forth.

Despite these and many other successes, the hundreds of jobs created by the new industries cannot replace the thousands lost by the decline of heavy industry. It is unfortunate, but in Cork it is clear that the Irish government has had no choice but to carry out a kind of industrial triage in which older workers without marketable skills are put out to pasture so the government can attract modern, high-technology industry to employ the increasingly younger and well-educated population.

Perhaps Cork's greatest hope for its industrial future comes from two very different directions—chips and curds. No, not potato chips, but semiconductor, integrated chips. And yes, curds, as in "curds and whey." In cheese and computer chips, Cork is leading Ireland toward the future.

The National Microelectronics Research Centre, located appropriately in a restored old distillery building on the banks of the River Lee, is the first pure microchip research facility in the country. The Centre hopes to emulate, on a small scale, AT & T's and Bell Laboratories' highly respected commitment to both basic research and commercially profitable applied semiconductor engineering. Says Dr. Gerry Wrixton, from his office in the old building, "We have three roles: educational, industrial, and developmental. We are working in the specific area of designing and fabricating integrated circuits. The emphasis in the electronics industry today is to integrate more and more customer-designed circuits into conventional products. And one of our goals is to help Irish and European electronics firms design and make these integrated circuits for their customers."

The Centre is a joint venture of the Irish government, the IDA, University College—Cork, and private industry.

How do computer chips relate to cheese? Not directly, but they are a component in the Irish move to a place in world markets, whether the design of a new chip, or a "designer" cheese. Every day, in a dairy in Imokilly just outside Cork City, fourteen *tons* of an Italian hard cheese called Regato and a large quantity of a Greek cheese, Kefalotyri, are made—not for consumption in Ireland, where the taste for cheese remains sharp cheddars and English Stiltons, but for Italy and Greece.

Why would Italians and Greeks want their cheeses developed and made in Ireland? Because of the enormous quantities of high-quality and high-butterfat milk taken from the legendary Irish dairy herds. Imokilly Cooperative, a subsidiary of Mitchelstown Creameries, successfully exports the cheese to Italy and Greece as well as to markets in the United States, Canada, and Australia.

This unusual occurrence took place because of a fire that destroyed the old, rundown Imokilly dairy. Rebuilding the dairy in the late 1970s forced general manager Tim O'Connell to think about new cheeses for new markets, especially since the enormous surpluses in European milk lakes and butter mountains threatened the Irish dairy industry.

O'Connell combined the dairy knowledge only the son of a working farmer could have with the spirit of a true entrepreneur to forge this new path for the Irish cheese industry. The cheeses Imokilly produces also show how good the results of joint private and government cooperation can be. The cheeses were developed with the help of the dairy and food science faculty at University College—Cork, the National Board for Science and Technology, Bord Bainne (the Irish Dairy Board), and the cooperative itself.

But O'Connell says he has just begun. Imokilly has just introduced two new cheeses for the Italian market—a hard Parmesan and a soft Mozzarella type called Pasta Filata.

These two enterprises illustrate how Ireland can substitute

brains for brawn and use its indigenous advantages to expand its industrial base and compete successfully in unimagined ways around the world. At the same time, chips and cheese can help rejuvenate a city that has gone through the worst the industrial age can offer.

I am not given to visiting cathedrals and churches for their own sake; it seems to me they are best seen with a service going on, and there are only so many Sundays in a year, far less in a journey. Still, I wanted to see St. Finbarre's Cathedral for a couple of reasons. Only 115 years old, it is a young church for Ireland. But it bears artifacts from an earlier time, particularly from the Georgian era, which I particularly love. A brass memorial hangs there, a memorial to Elizabeth Aldworth, the only woman Freemason. Hidden behind a library curtain at Donerail House, she heard, when still a girl, the secret proceedings of her father and his fellow Masons in council. There was no choice but to make her a member.

St. Finbarre's is Church of Ireland and still offers both sung Eucharists and Evensong. Unfortunately, I was not in Cork on a Sunday.

Drisheen is a kind of sausage made mainly from sheep's blood and milk and I refuse utterly to eat it. Nevertheless, it is such regional specialties that have gotten the Cork area recognized throughout Ireland for gourmet cooking. Or it could have been Myrtle Allen.

Mrs. Allen lives and works, most of the time, in a huge late-Georgian house on a working farm hard by the coast in Shanagarry, south of Cork. She and her husband, Ivan, bought the house a few decades back to raise a family in; they have done that, and have turned it—the Ballymaloe House—into a hotel and restaurant the likes of which is not exportable. Nonetheless, the Irish have tried. Mrs. Allen also has set up, and oversees, La Ferme Irlandaise, an Irish restaurant in Paris that is all the rage. "My son-in-law, John Whelan, is the official manager. Both of us, however, pop out there every couple of months to see that it's doing well. The staff is entirely Irish, and two of the chefs were trained here at Ballymaloe House," Mrs. Allen says. "It's a nice experience for them. Some of the staff are offspring of local farmers who might not get the experience otherwise."

Mrs. Allen suggests that the popularity of the Irish restaurant in France is because of the astonishing differences in the food styles. "Our food is first cousin of English, Scottish, and Welsh cooking," she says. "Much as Chinese and Japanese are cousins."

Mrs. Allen is a "comfortable" woman, but more businesslike than motherly, as the last half of that sobriquet usually goes. Ivan Allen is a tall, tweedy man with a shock of white hair and a manner rather bookish; he was, in fact, going off to play bridge the day we met, but not before he had superintended the wine for the luncheon we shared—surrounded by about a hundred small children and their parents.

"I must apologize for this," said Mrs. Allen when we were seated in the dining room. "I had forgotten that it's Communion Weekend. It's traditional that the families take the children out for lunch after they've had their first Communion, and, well, here they are. Many local ones, anyway."

The food was set out buffet-style, and the children seemed to have endless appetites. There were roasts and potatoes and turnips and liver and breads. "There was a time when our food was even more influenced by English food—but that was being influenced by French food, through the big hotels. I don't think that was really right for us. A country's food has got to be based on what has historically been available. That form of cooking was not natural to us. For instance, we might make a peach melba—but we understand a gooseberry fool much better," Mrs. Allen explained. A "fool" is little more than pureed local fruit and cream—which Ireland has in abundance.

Mrs. Allen has taken Irish food to other places besides France. New York's Bloomingdale's, the year it had an Irish promotion, asked her to give cooking classes and demonstrations of Irish food. "Here, I cook fish in a little cream with a bay leaf and a little onion, and it's delicious. There, where I had the cooking schedule for ten days, I had a hard time with the fish. Or maybe the cream." In any case, it wasn't turning out as it did at home. And no wonder. Irish cream is like pale molten gold, nothing at all like our overprocessed, drizzly, white-as-a-sheet stuff. And no doubt the fish were fresher and, coming from Ireland's colder water, tastier at home.

"The materials you work with are part of your living conditions, part of the land of the country you live in," says Mrs. Allen. "Here, we use salted butter. I understand that it is regarded in a bad light now in America.

"Translating cooking from one country to another seldom, if ever, works perfectly or, at least, authentically. The ingredients are just different."

Mrs. Allen is a "walnut-sized hunk of butter" cook, like my grandmother. "I get recipes because people come and tell them to me," she says. And, of course, she invents her own new ones, or adapts and improves on the Irish traditions.

But she does lean heavily on the native food. Stuffed leg of lamb is traditional. So is horseradish sauce, currant jelly, mint sauce, and bread sauce. "Dressed crab is a specialty of this district," she adds. "But I add chutney, which improves it."

All potted meats are good old-fashioned English-Irish cooking, she says. "Turkey Baked in Butter and Watercress is New Irish Cooking—using local ingredients and making a new Irish food out of it."

After our meal, I waited for Mrs. Allen's staff to bring me some photos I had asked for. The day was black as night and again, for May, the lashings of rain were extraordinary. I thought it was a great Irish day, however. I wished that I didn't have to drive on, and could have taken a book from the Allens' large library (all available to guests) and cozied up by the drawing-room fire. I'd have ordered some tea and biscuits and spent a wondrous, dozy day, until Mrs. Allen's staff again filled me with all sorts of earthly delights—skipping the drisheen, of course.

6. Kerry

I find disappointment in a tourist attraction. I find solitude among the ghosts of the monks, adventure twice recalled on a wild coast, and hope and despair in the heartland of Ireland.

Almost everyone who visits Ireland for the first time wants to trace the Ring of Kerry. From Cork to Tralee, this southern route boasts a multitude of lakes, vistas, peaks, panoramas, castles, and waterfalls. But it is an area equally popular with the Irish, I discovered, or, at least, the angling Irish. For Kerry boasts some of the best sea trout and salmon fishing in the world.

Waterville is, specifically, the town they all flock to. Ellen Lynch Heggarty, whom I had met in Dublin for tea, fishes there with her husband.

The Waterville System, as it is known, is unique, offering early fishing for sea trout, from mid-April until October 12. The fish are reputed to be larger than elsewhere, despite the longer period open for taking them. Included in this angling haven are the Waterville River, a very short one, and the "long" River Comeragh (five miles total), plus Lough Currane. There are three smaller lakes as well—Derriana, Namona, and Cloonalkin—and a number even smaller than that; in this area, any large pond with fish seems to be rated a lake.

By far the most interesting part of Lough Currane was, to me, Church Island. Boating over, I could scarcely wait to see the sixth-century ruins, believed to be the oratory of Saint Finan, the small chapel used for private devotions. Later ruins nearby are from the twelfth century. These show the Carolingian influence brought by the Vikings in their Hiberno-Romanesque stylings. They are more fanciful, certainly, than the earlier church, but they are less interesting. The crude blocks of the oratory seem to speak more truthfully.

But I was most charmed by the flowers. Like the Burren, a region of rocky uplift I was to visit later, Kerry possesses rarities like the giant butterworth, seldom found elsewhere in Ireland but abundant here. The Kelly lily, just into bloom when I arrived, grows here—and nowhere else in Ireland or Great Britain. And everywhere there was fuschia, with its stunning deep-red and purple teardrop blooms. I had been amazed the first time I saw it. I couldn't believe something so vibrant in color, so delicate in branch and stem, could cover walls and barn sides and cottage fences in such profusion in such a cold country. It looks so tropical in its abundance, like the lush beauties of a South Sea island. Often growing wild against the gray-golden thatch of a derelict cottage, it could be mistaken for a bush of hibiscus growing against a reed hut—except for the cold blue-gray of the background sky and the bundled-up farmers cutting hay nearby.

I hadn't known, before I went, that Ireland, gray-green half-frozen Ireland, had so many tropical delights. The palm trees. The monkey puzzle trees, so named because it is impossible for monkeys to climb their spiky boughs. The orchids of the Burren, yet to come. Even the cabbie who fetched me at New York's Kennedy Airport after my trip knew about it. "They've got palm trees, don't they? I'd really like to see that!" he said. He was from Puerto Rico. Maybe that's why he knew about palm trees in Ireland. Being Spanish, maybe he knew about the Armada, too. The Armada is credited for much in Ireland. And maybe he shared the Irish dedication to "mañana."

Mañana—or rather, a leisurely way of passing through this life—is perhaps more evident in Kerry than in other areas of Ireland. Except, that is, when you're staying in a modern hotel on a main street in a rural town. I came to know this the hard way, by being awakened by animals grunting below my window. So, I realized, had Morton. Since further sleep was impossible, I decided to read his impressions of the men who travel the country roads on market days.

I had not stopped very many men trudging the country roads, though I surely saw them, mainly in Wellington boots, carrying a stick and herding a bunch of cows—just as Morton saw them fifty years ago—down the road, sometimes to a market day, sometimes just from field to barn. They always had a dog with them and almost always a young lad—their son—dressed much as the father, learning the trade, even if he was expected to go to university first before returning to the family business.

The people I did speak with—in stores, before the fire in a lounge bar, on the docks of a dozen little seaport villages—all displayed a homespun erudition. Just as Morton found amazing the common Irishman's skill with language—and the logic behind it and the information to fill it out—so did I. I have never heard ugly-sounding, vulgar speech in Ireland, no matter if the speaker's fingernails were crusted with dung, streaked with petrol grease, or trimmed and polished like a show horse's hoofs.

As for the rest of it, it was not at five in the morning I was awakened, as Morton had been, but eight. Farmers in Ireland do not seem to rise early anymore. I was told the logic of it was that the cows don't care what time they're milked. Their comfort depends rather on being milked twice a day, to be sure, but it is the interval between that counts, not the hour at which the milkings occur. Indeed, the market days never begin much before ten in the morning now, especially in winter when Ireland has precious little sunlight, starting late and ending early. Because of its closeness to the Arctic Circle, which Americans never think of, it has very nearly midnight sun in the summer, with sunset sometimes as late as 10 P.M., sunup by three-thirty.

Despite its fame, the Ring of Kerry, a road only 112 miles long, seemed highly overrated to me. Killarney is not a pretty town, and is far too ready to cater to the least of the tourists who come by. Waterville is mistily spectacular, I will agree. But for the beauties of the south, I prefer Dingle.

It is said Saint Brendan sailed to America from Dingle; perhaps that's the connection. Indeed, when explorer/writer Tim Severin re-created that voyage in the 1970s, he used a Dingle launching place, and a Dingle-built curragh, a boat of wood and cowhide. Dingle does jut far out into the Atlantic, almost daring a crossing. Wild and remote, Dingle, for sheer beauty, wins over Kerry in my ledger.

I entered the spectacular Dingle Peninsula from Tralee, itself a regional market town most famous for the annual Rose of Tralee Festival and the national folk theater, the Siamsa. At the Siamsa, the customs and traditions of the countryside—thatching, weaving, butter-churning, storytelling, and so forth—are reenacted in music, song, and dance.

Ascending the Dingle Peninsula (for it is very steep) took me up and around the sides of a very substantial and famous range of hills, the Slieve Mish Mountains. Irish legend says the last battle between the land's original inhabitants—the dark, small Firbolgs—and the invading Celts was fought in these hills. Legend also says that the hills are the home of the leprechauns. This latter legend must have developed because of the Firbolgs whom they greatly resemble. Like real people, leprechauns are not always nice. They've malice aforethought, these ones. They'll trick and deceive you as often as help you. And no one yet has found their golden treasure.

When the Celts finally did conquer, the surviving Firbolgs retreated to the mountains, much as the Celt-Viking-Norman Irish did from the invading English in Wicklow. In the mountain fastnesses, both groups maintained their identities and customs for decades, slowly absorbing and being absorbed by the new population—but never being totally subsumed.

I did not meet any leprechauns, but I did see several small, dark Irishmen. I followed the scenic coast road to the end of the peninsula to Smerwick and Dun 'n Or, or Del Oro. This, too, is one of the few areas of the Gaeltacht, the Irish-speaking region, and the signposts and day-to-day language were Gaelic. Gaelic shares its roots with the Teutonic languages of northern Europe, not the Romance languages of southern Europe. Yet, unlike German, Gaelic is a soft, melodious language with little clicks and "tu" sounds. It is very musical and appealing to the ear when spoken softly.

Along the Dingle coast are many stretches of white sand beaches, but I was not eager to sample the cold North Atlantic waters. At the end of my quest for Dun 'n Or (literally translated "Fort of Gold") I found much more than a golden coastline. I found Sybil Head, an enormous mountain that seems to reach to the heavens and then plunge straight into the sea. And the sea, apparently angered at this affront, pounds the base of the mountain with twenty- or thirty-foot-high, vicious, gray-green waves. As I stood there in awe of this scene, a deep black cloud, pushing galelike winds ahead of it, seemed to rise out of the North Atlantic like a Celtic bull god. It charged into the coast pouring heavy rains all around.

I rushed into the Hotel Dun 'n Or to get away from this howling mad beast and commented on it. The bartender looked up and said, "Oh well, a bit of wet out today." Nods and smiles and that characteristic drawing in of breath that means "That's life," "Tomorrow will be different," "Tomorrow will be the same," "A shame, isn't it?" or any other prosaic afterthought the listener wants to attribute to it. Typical, his statement and the weather.

At Ballyferriter, during the same lashing rainstorm, I visited a well-preserved oratory—a stone, cantilevered and watertight cell. The oratory is shaped like a boat; in fact, the only boat-shaped oratories in Ireland are found in Kerry, leading to the popular surmise that Saint Brendan or his followers built them in boat shapes because they were seafaring monks. More realistic is the idea that they were built five or six hundred years later and were patterned after wooden oratories that had been built hundreds of years earlier. In any case, the small cell was watertight, as it has been for hundreds of years, despite the lashing rain outside. Although the oratory itself has only tiny slits for windows, the view from its small door is lovely. It looks down across wide fields and across Smerwick Harbor.

I could imagine the serenity a penitent monk might have felt as he gazed at this scene for months or years. But his life would also have been a demanding one. The weather there, as I found out, can be bad even for Ireland.

I drove back along the southern coast of the Dingle Peninsula because I hoped to see the Blasket Islands, a renowned group of islands off the coast, which had aroused my curiosity. In Dublin, I had read in a newspaper that a wealthy private owner wanted to sell his two-thirds of Great Blasket Island to a real-estate developer who wanted to build a luxury resort. The other residents were opposed to this sale because they did not want their rural lifestyle disrupted. However, into this largely local dispute stepped a very prominent Irish political leader. He supported the voices of protest—for what I thought were curious reasons. First, he was in opposition to the government in power, so he was likely to disagree with anything it favored and agree with anything that could embarrass it. But—and I thought this suspect in a member of the party that supposedly favored the "little man"—he *owned* one of the neighboring islands. Clearly, although the politician did not say anything about his personal interest, he had a direct financial interest in the manner in which the land on a neighboring island was disposed. It seemed to me a case of "He who lives in glass houses . . ." But such is the personal nature of Irish politics. No one I mentioned it to seemed to think it a conflict of interest. "Oh, well . . ." followed by that sharp intake of breath that means "That's life" or "Tomorrow will be different . . ." Ad infinitum. A most troublous people.

All of this demonstrated, yet again, that the Irish will behave exactly opposite the way you might reasonably expect. Of course, there are exceptions to this.

Leaving the beautiful Dingle Peninsula behind, I abandoned Morton's path again to cut through the heart of Kerry and Limerick to visit Doneraile Court, a large Georgian house being restored by the Irish Georgian Society.

Doneraile Court is an imposing three-story house overlooking a broad, green demesne that sweeps down a hill to a pool and small river and then sweeps up a steep hill. Doneraile Court was purchased by the Irish government in 1967, and the demesne, or grounds, was transformed into a lovely national park. The house itself, however, despite its textbook Georgian architecture and fittings, was left to fall apart, as is the Irish government's unfortunate habit. After nine years of vandalism and futile protests to keep the house up, the government finally sold the house to the Irish Georgian Society.

Since that time, the Society has been restoring Doneraile Court—but slowly, because of a lack of funds. The founder of the S. S. Kress stores a few years ago gave the Society a substantial sum of money to fix the roof. Today, says the Honourable Desmond Guinness, the Society employs one carpenter who works on the house as he can. But, more interesting for Americans, the Society also invites young Americans—high school and college students over the age of sixteen—to spend a few weeks during the summer to help work on Doneraile. Many have taken advantage of this chance to learn about Georgian architecture and gain some carpentry skills while mucking out the worst damage to the house.

I hope Doneraile Court might become a symbol of a more harmonious future for the divisions in Irish society. The park and grounds are green and lovely, and many people in the area use them for afternoon strolls, walking their dogs, or a weekend outing. But restoring the house and using it as a showpiece of the best of Anglo-Irish architecture and culture seems to me just as appropriate. Not to do so would seem to be cutting off one's nose to spite one's face, a pity when the whole appearance could be so beautiful.

The great gray weathered wall of Doneraile put me in mind of the contrast between the suspicion in which the Irish hold their great houses and the pleasure with which we regard ours. I considered the awe in which we hold our own Mount Vernon, Jefferson's Monticello, and many similar homes of great national leaders, and I again considered the Irish attitude toward the great homes of their leaders. The Irish respect more the small cottages where some of their leaders lived. And, to be sure, some of the Republic's greatest heroes were of modest birth and means (though as many, or more, did spring from a higher station in life).

I wonder if their rejection of the great of means in favor of the humble of birth doesn't belie an infantile and self-defeating rejection of their contributions to world history and culture. I know of no other nation of its size and population (smaller than the state of Maine, less than half as populous as New York City) that has given more in people, brains, talent, and energy to world affairs, and on which more crucial historical events have been played out. Yet the Irish seem to be handicapped with tunnel vision or an inferiority complex that prevents them from taking pride in their ethnic group (or all of their ethnic groups, if you will), their culture, and their matchless history.

By the end of my visit to Doneraile Court, I was filled with both hope and despair. But I yawned in the suddenly bright sunshine. "Oh, well . . ." and I sharply drew in my breath. I was learning.

7. Shannon

I visit castles and factories and make five new friends, not all of them human. I search for the Celts. I meet two entrepreneurs and discover Irish nouvelle cuisine.

Most people arriving in Ireland disembark at Shannon Airport. Once upon a time, before truly long-range jets, almost every transatlantic flight stopped there for refueling. I have met the nephew of the first Irish woman to make the "pond crossing" solo, but I can't recall his name, or hers. But she did it from Shannon, which was, at the time, little more than a hard-packed field and a Quonset hut.

The Quonset huts are still there, used as storage facilities. The terminal building is new and modern, and there's a very satisfactory hotel on the airport grounds now. There is also, within the confines of the airport encampment, a very large free-trade zone. Within its boundaries, foreign companies can assemble, without paying import duties, any number of goods for reexport—also basically without tariff—to the European market. Needless to say, dozens of forward-looking companies have taken advantage of this.

To serve them and their employees, a totally new town was created. Built primarily by Shannon Development Corporation, a semistate agency that's also involved with "Shannonside" tourism, Shannon New Town offers little of the charm of the rest of Ireland, but it does offer a collection of modern amenities rare outside Dublin, all collected into a shopping center. There's a large supermarket, a hairdresser, a bank, a post office. And there's also, naturally, a newsagent selling daily papers, books, stationery, and candy bars. Though close to the airport, I doubt many tourists visit it, because it is not touristy—it's life. The newsagent, like his confreres nationwide, knows his clients, speaks with them, takes endless pains helping them. Nor is he oblivious to the newcomers—Shannon gets lots of those—and makes special efforts with them. The same holds true of the chemist's shop, which carries not only the usual prescription and patent medicines, but baby formula, cosmetics, and a few fancy gifts. What it doesn't carry, which most rural and small-town chemists do, is animal medicines, from "black draught" to antibiotics.

It appeared to me that living in Shannon New Town is little different from living in any of hundreds of American suburbs. The shopping mall is the center of what little community life there is, and the focus of most of the families' lives is a spouse's job at the airport or in the industrial estate. A modern invention, Shannon New Town has little character, unlike other Irish villages. But the achievements at Shannon Industrial Estate in creating hundreds of new jobs is very impressive. These jobs are urgently, if not desperately, needed in Ireland.

Shannon Development, founded in 1960, has created several concepts about industrial development that are standard practice in most countries of the world today. It created the first of the duty-free shops and free-trade zones at international airports; the Shannon Industrial Estate sprawls just outside the fence next to the runways at the airport. Shannon New Town, built from the ground up long before Maryland's Columbia, is now home to more than five thousand people who live in what is euphemistically called "mixed-use" housing: single-family homes, semi-detached homes, apartments, town houses, and so forth.

At the beginning of my first trip to Ireland, I landed at Shannon Airport. And I was somewhat disappointed. With the modern airport terminal, I felt at first that I had landed in an American city in which all of the crazy drivers were merely driving on the wrong side of the road. Leaving the airport, I drove along a modern, four-lane highway, called a "dual carriageway," and could see only very modern buildings: on one side, modern factories, and on the other, modern apartments and town houses. My first experience of historic Ireland came as a shock about six miles east of the airport. I was driving along, looking for a sign of the Ireland I had heard about, feeling more let down each moment. Then, around a sweeping curve in the road, commanding the heights near the river and with a fine view of the Shannon River estuary, was an enormous castle. That, I felt, was Ireland. But I was wrong. It was a "tour castle," open for eight hours a day as a museum.

Since then, I have come to appreciate how the Irish blend the ancient customs and traditions and the modern necessities of industrial development and housing.

Shannonside—that area extending from Loop and Kerry Heads at the mouth of the Shannon River inland to Limerick—is as rife with history as the rest of the country, maybe more so. The area is littered with still-intact castles. It boasts Ireland's most mighty river and its incredibly abundant estuary. It offers a fair share of sandy ocean beaches, while encompassing in its splaying reach the steep, sheer Cliffs of Moher. It boasts what is reputed to be Ireland's prettiest town, Adare, and some of its most decrepit. It has Ireland's most modern-looking town, Shannon, and the most medieval-looking, Ennis, which, of course, are within a few miles of each other. It has its share of early Christian sites, such as Dysart O'Dea, as well as a healthy concentration of pre-Christian monuments and artifacts, including a number of Irish Elk antlers in collections, with others still in the bogs waiting to be discovered and hung on the wall of some great house or castle. For all this, Shannonside doesn't get much press, except for the touristy articles about Bunratty Castle banquets. To my mind, these are among the lesser treats, or even less than that.

Bunratty Castle is, however, that first castle I saw early on my first trip. It is a tourist attraction, surrounded by a folk park and village. The castle banquets, the folk park, and the rest of the tourist shtick are other creations of Shannon Development that have since been copied all over the world. Although I don't care much for these tourist attractions myself, they have created plenty of jobs and brought in needed dollars. And they are well done.

More interesting to me, and something that the touristy veneer cannot bury, is the fascinating history and still-imposing presence of Bunratty Castle. It is worth a tour and a consideration of its place—and the place of the great lords—in Irish history. It is hard by the Shannon at the foot of a very steep hill, on a site originally thought to have been fortified by the Vikings, who were only too well aware that commanding the river and the height would be of great strategic use.

Around the year 1250, Robert De Muscegros, a Norman, built a castle there. Upon his death, Thomas de Clare, having been given title to the land by England's Edward I, built a stone castle and imported English soldiers to defend it. Soon a town grew up around it.

Subsequently, it was destroyed half a dozen times: by the native Irish in 1305 or earlier; after the de Clares were defeated at the Battle of Dysart in 1318; by the O'Briens and Macnamaras in 1332, again by other raiders in 1353; and so on.

In 1450, the present castle was begun, to be completed in 1467. It was owned by the O'Briens for centuries, and was defended once by Admiral Sir William Penn, father of William Penn, founder of Pennsylvania. (Possibly that's why, when I got to the banquet, there were so many honeymoon couples there from the Keystone State.) In any case, Penn surrendered it, and it languished through a succession of owners for a couple hundred years.

In 1954, the castle was bought by Lord Gort, and has been very well restored indeed. Recent years have seen the addition of a folk park next to it. Consisting of a typical Irish village of yesterday, but equally of today—at least on the outside—I found the park too Disneyland-ish for my taste. After all, any small village in Ireland looks substantially like it. Signs over the butcher's, or "victualler's," are still painted on boards and hand-lettered. Shop interiors are still small and for the most part less well-lighted than Americans expect. There are still families—many of them—using turf stoves to cook with and baking bread the traditional way, kneading it on a four-legged kitchen table and setting it in a crockery bowl to rise near the smoldering turf.

Having been stuffed with creamed and fried and baked Irish specialties for several days, all through Cork and Dingle, I was in great need of the sort of low-fat, low-protein international food I feed myself at home. In Limerick, I found an Italian restaurant. A plate of fettucine à la pesto and a half bottle of red wine—and nothing else—sounded fine.

On the road to Limerick, a modern but also a very historic city, are three structures, seemingly built in a straight line, that illustrate what modern Ireland is all about. Just beside the road is a ruined castle tower, about seventy-five feet tall, standing like a proud chieftain surveying his field of battle. This represents Ireland's proud past.

A few hundred yards behind the castle tower, or "keep," on a low ridge, is a modern motel. It welcomes the tourist trade that makes up 40 percent of Ireland's gross national product. It is a figure of Ireland's recent history, with its economic dependence on service industries.

But behind the motel sits a symbol of Ireland's hope for a prosperous future. Twin radar towers, their missile-shaped bases sitting stoically on the hill like futuristic castles, spin their antennae through the skies. Advanced technology is Ireland's future. Limerick is trying to blend the three. As a result, it has growing pains.

Traffic on the main roads during evening rush hours can be as slow as that in any major American city, and I was frustrated. But I was having a homesickness attack, and was determined to find the Italian bistro. I had booked ahead and didn't want to miss my table. I had gotten the feeling, from the hotel receptionist who recommended it, that it was pretty popular among the "Guppies." Indeed, its hostess was in the best tradition of a modern Irish preppy—a longish, smooth hairstyle, tortoiseshell glasses, fashionable but not trendy clothes, and upper-class accent.

The restaurant was a quaint little place, in the best Italian-export tradition, couched in a cellar space, set with red-and-white-checked tablecloths, hung with plastic grapes and raffia-covered wine bottles, and maitre d'ed by a Yugoslav immigrant. And it was quite full of Guppies. Two of them were discussing the best of international cuisine and a friend of theirs who cooked it. Halfway through my meal, eaten silently and alone (though I was eavesdropping), a table for six filled nearby. My ears flapped. Did I discern one of those piercing midwestern twangs? I did indeed, and it was issuing forth from a member of what some Irish friends had called "the Polyester Platoon." These are younger, in general, than members of "the Blue-Rinse Brigade." Often, they are a bit wealthier, but not so greatly that they have been forced or persuaded to learn manners. And they are completely self-centered and obnoxious. This representative of the Platoon was a heavyset woman with a loud voice.

We Americans tour more than most of the rest of the world. Nor are most other countries wealthy enough that even their most average citizens can afford to go abroad, at least not in the numbers Americans have been able to. With the dollar strong, as it has been throughout the 1980s, Americans, it seems, are everywhere, and in such numbers that it is not so easy to get lost and absorbed among the natives wherever we visit.

We therefore stick out. Often, we overwhelm the resources of the country we visit. We carry attitudes and attributes we were brought up, for good or ill, to admire: boldness, brashness, curiosity, good cheer, an ability to be demanding and to speak up, friendliness. Our major failing is that we forget that there is a reason for the saying "When in Rome, do as the Romans do." We think, naively, that the "Romans" should do as we wish they would. And there the trouble begins. The best travelers I have met, from whatever country, soft-pedal their natural proclivities after assessing which of them will or will not be acceptable to the natives. Americans, generally, do not. We no longer walk softly and carry a big stick. We tromp. Who needs the stick?

Many of us forget that it is not written that a traveler must be supremely comfortable, much less at home, while traveling. In fact, the occasional discomfort, the disjointedness, the calculating and balancing and juggling to maintain one's self, absorb the "otherness" of the strange land, and enjoy it all—that is what travel is all about.

Still, there are occasions when familiarity is a blessing. I had experienced a need of familiar comforts right before I left Dublin. That's why I sought out the Italian restaurant. But the fat woman? Was she homesick, too? Is that why she had an uncontrollable need to regale, loudly, her Irish host and hostess with tales of her business savvy at home, the first step, sentence, and sniffle of her grandchild, the earning power of her slightly embarrassed husband? Or was she just plain obnoxious? I could see her Irish hostess visibly shrink into the corner of the booth formed by the table and the grape-hung lattice. I could see the veil descend across the Irish husband's eyes as their foreign companion rattled on. It is a veil I have seen often when the Irish are in the presence of something they find insulting or at odds with their own view of polite behavior. They are not given to speaking up, directly, in such circumstances. The wise-guy rejoinder seems to be, rather, a product only of the Brooklyn Irish—a James Cagney character—rather than of the Celts themselves.

I had heard about ugly Americans from the Irish, too. A newsagent in Galway later asked me to write about how foolish Americans look when they invade Ireland at St. Patrick's Day, wearing green all over and waving flags and generally sporting about most sentimentally and noisily. Miriam Logan, at Malahide, had put her finger on the syndrome—the idealization of the land lost, and the lack of realization that the motherland has not been trapped in a time warp and thus is not the way you left it. The Honourable Desmond Guinness agreed with that assessment of the phenomenon, but he was much more charitable, a characteristic of the better-off Irish people I mentioned it to. He found the behavior touching, and thought it flattering that anyone would find so much unabated joy in so simple a thing as a saint's feast day and the parades and parties that go with it. Amazed and fascinated that they undoubtedly put themselves in debt to "cross the pond" and celebrate with their rootstock, it's probable he well knows the economic impact all of it has. In some years in the past, Ireland was desperate for the tourist dollar.

The American lady in the Italian restaurant never shut her mouth. I finished my dinner, satisfied with my pasta and feeling more like myself than I had in weeks. I was ready to tackle the exotic once again.

I was staying in a lovely suite at FitzPatrick's Shannon Shamrock Hotel, a shameless copy of upper-crust American corporate-style hotels, and a successful one. It is not a way to get to know how the Irish travel (few except international businessmen and -women use it) or how they live (its cuisine is more international than Irish). And yet its owner, Paddy FitzPatrick, is one of the great Irish characters and great Irish oddities of his own generation and a couple of generations since.

On this trip, I renewed my acquaintance with him, which had begun about eight years before. "Mr. FitzPatrick, isn't it?" I asked, seeing a large fellow, late-middle-aged and wearing an impeccably tailored blue suit, in the hotel's lobby.

"Indeed, yes. And aren't you the writer we've got staying with us now?" I hadn't expected him to know. But then, there had been some confusion about the booking, which his manager had quickly made right. I reminded him of my earlier visit; in fact, I had stayed there several times passing through. But my first stay—and this one—were undoubtedly the most noteworthy.

That first time, I was writing specifically about Shannonside for an American magazine. Mr. FitzPatrick, whose hotel was not only putting me up but was to be featured in the magazine, invited me for drinks at his chalet and for dinner afterward.

In Ireland, women are still expected to drink only sherry. But I loathe the stuff. Still, it is part of the atmosphere, so I usually just drink it in, so to speak. But there are those homesick times when the only thing that will do is an American mixed drink—like one night in a well-regarded restaurant in Nenagh. I was with a mixed group of Irish and Americans, all of whom I had met in the United States. We had to wait some time for a table, and so were having drinks in the lounge bar. "I'll have a bourbon manhattan," I told the "girl." The others eyed me strangely.

Shortly, the girl returned. "I'm afraid the bartender doesn't know how to make that. Could you ever be telling me how it's done, then? Sure, once he's got the recipe, it won't be a moment."

I rattled off the recipe. But soon she was back again. "I'm sorry, but the bartender says he has no bourbon. Would it be all right, he says, if he uses whiskey instead?"

I agreed to this, though I knew Irish whiskey is not like our blended variety, but is closer to Scotch.

"I'm sorry to bother you again," said the girl. "But the bartender says he has no sweet vermouth. Would you be minding if he made it with white vermouth instead?"

By that time, my drink was a laughingstock. But I agreed, and christened the concoction a "staten island." (After the old joke. Henrik Hudson, sailing into Manhattan, exclaimed, " 'Sdat an island?") I did not order a second.

In any case, Mr. FitzPatrick, from his well-stocked bar, produced the real thing. At dinner, we consumed a couple of bottles of fine red wine to go with it, and with the food, of course. And topped it off with Irish coffee, elegantly made at table by the hotel's world-class maitre d'.

Mr. FitzPatrick is a world-class kidder as well, having twitted the wife of New York's former governor in public. So public, in fact (at Eamon Doran's East Side Irish watering hole in Manhattan), that the incident made the *Daily News.* I mentioned it. I had enjoyed reading it immensely.

Mrs. Hugh Carey had appeared in the restaurant wearing a turban. "You'll excuse my saying so, ma'am," FitzPatrick said. "But your hair must be a frightful mess under that thing."

"You know, the lady was very gracious about that," he said. "She and her husband are both fine people, and I like them both a lot." One shouldn't wonder. Like Hugh Carey, and like Evangeline Carey's family, Paddy FitzPatrick is a self-made man. Sometimes, I found, his countrymen resent it.

Bright and brash, FitzPatrick married a famous model early in his career. There are those who've told me snidely that her presence did him no harm. Indeed not. And why should it? She has decorated his hotels for him. Together they have produced a family of sons and a daughter highly qualified and highly worthy to carry on the family business. The only one I have met is the daughter—Eithne Junior, as she is known. Also lovely, she had recently "married the Abbey Tavern," as her father puts it. (The Abbey Tavern, in Howth near Dublin, is renowned for its Irish music. In fact, it exports numbers of its singers to the United States around St. Patrick's Day. I saw some just this year.) She had also become pregnant, and by now she has had the child she was carrying when she refused to leave the business. "There's an overseas hoteliers' conference she was supposed to go to," Mr. FitzPatrick told me during our brief encounter. "Neither her husband nor I want her to go, but she's adamant. She wants to stay in the business until the last possible minute, and she plans to come back as soon as possible." A go-ahead woman, looks like to me. And definitely a Guppie.

"If there's anything you need, let me know," Mr. FitzPatrick invited.

There wasn't. FitzPatrick's staff is always very attentive and responsive. He has a wonderful laundry service; all my clothes were clean for the first time in weeks. And my room was full of all sorts of amenities: a fruit basket, miniature bottles of Bailey's Irish cream liqueur, a pants press (which I managed to use on a tweed skirt), color TV, radio, alarm clock, balcony, and a very useful little information booklet guests are invited to "take away with you."

In the booklet, I was amused to read this notice:

> **Police Notice to Tourist/Business Travellers**
>
> **Attention!**
>
> Should you encounter any problem during your visit to this country do not hesitate to enlist the help of An Garda Siochana.
>
> We would remind you that you are probably carrying considerably more property with you than usual. We recommend that, as far as possible, property should not be left unattended or exposed in your vehicle—it is safer in the boot.

It is doubly safe at FitzPatrick's, where the suites offer room safes. In any case, the doors at FitzPatrick's actually lock. In most of the country, except Dublin, hotel-room doors do not lock. I don't travel with priceless jewels, and my cameras are generally pretty close by me, "in the boot." All the same, if being able to leave room doors unlocked in public hotels means that Ireland is a moral country, fine. It is very pleasant not to have to look upon your other numbers as thieves. And I've never, knock wood, missed anything, whether at Shannon or elsewhere, locked door or not. About which other so-called underdeveloped nation can similar be said? None, I think.

Also in the booklet was an advertisement:

CASTLE MATRIX

Rathkeale, Co. Limerick

Built in 1440 by the 7th Earl of Desmond, the renowned Norman-Irish poet. It was here in 1580 that Spenser and Raleigh began their lifelong friendship. Authentic furnishings, *objets d'art* and historic documents.

28 km (18 miles) south-west of Limerick on main Killarney road, Castle Matrix is headquarters of the Irish International Arts Centre and the Heraldry Society of Ireland.

Castle and grounds open 15 May to 15 September. Saturday to Tuesday 1300–1700 hrs.

I had never heard of this castle before. I had heard of all the other local and open ones, of course—Dunguaire, Knappogue, Bunratty. But Castle Matrix? Dromoland, now a hotel and basically a modern structure, is on the site of a castle. And there are dozens of privately owned castles, not open to the public, and hundreds of ruins in Limerick and Clare.

I decided to visit. Thank goodness. I discovered some of my favorite Ireland there.

I don't think I had paid any attention to the opening hours. I was well within the season, however. I found the castle without too much trouble, although it is not as well signposted as the "big ones." It lies at the end of a narrow lane, across some of the ever-present cattle grates, protected by a rusting iron gate. The car park contained one other vehicle, so I walked up to the front door and knocked—loud, but not long. Shortly, a young woman with long dark hair, carrying a redheaded baby, opened the door. I'm not sure how I accomplished the task of introduction, but I was drawn inside. The other visitors were just leaving, and I was directed to wait, as Sean would be with me directly. The woman's accent was distinctly British. Sean's was quite American. The baby gurgled internationally.

Soon we were sitting in the keep, at long board tables used by researchers. Sean O'Driscoll is the president of the Heraldry Society, for one thing, and keeps records and documents galore. He is also an artist, having studied for a time at one of my own old haunts, New York's Art Students' League—although he did it somewhat before me. He was a colonel in the U.S. military, involved in developing military jets and many esoteric defense systems I don't understand. He was with NATO's parliament for fifteen years; and has known some of the most fascinating international cultural figures, including Eion O'Mahony, often called "The Last Bard."

Elizabeth O'Driscoll brought tea and biscuits, and left to settle Kieran, the baby, down for his nap. Sean O'Driscoll discoursed on one of his many favorite subjects.

Having just said good-bye to a group that had come for a heraldry lesson, we began with that subject. And, too, O'Driscoll had been lately, he said, reading a book I also admire, *Drawing on the Right Side of the Brain,* by Betty Edwards. But it was not only the artist in him that drew him to it, it was the student of heraldry as well. The book's premise is that art ability lies in the noncognitive right hemisphere of the human brain. You've got to "leap" into it to produce worthy art. Not everyone can do so with equal agility.

"You know, Jung believed that certain symbols were inherent in the right side of the brain," O'Driscoll said. Children, he noted, instantaneously made up symbols for things. Primitive people do it. Schizophrenics do it. There is a genetic memory for symbols. If the symbols are subverted, Jung believed, neurosis resulted. "In heraldry, this shows up in the symbols used by sets of people. The Celts, for example, use the boar a lot; it is believed to be one of their preconscious symbols. Three of our members are right now researching pre-Celtic symbols," O'Driscoll added.

The name of the castle itself is a language symbol of the earliest, most fundamental kind. "The original for it was Castle Matres. 'Matres' means the 'mother of all gods.' And the castle is built on the site of a Celtic sanctuary."

Suddenly, O'Driscoll offered a tour of the building. He wanted to get to the battlements so that I could see the beauty—and the symbolism—in its setting.

"Look at how these are constructed," he said, pointing at the battlements. "They are built so that a man can stand behind them and shoot arrows, or whatever, and probably won't be hit with return fire. The crenellations protect his head. The angle at which the stones are cut prevents a shot bouncing off them reaching a man flattened against them." Ingenious. And who said modern war technology was superior?

Looking out over the plain, I could see clusters of farm buildings, roads, new housing, and stands of trees. And I could see a stream. "It's called the River Deel here," he said. "The name relates to the number three.

"In France, the Celts always built their sacred altars near the tributary of a sacred river. We are on a tributary of the Shannon, which we know was a sacred river to the Celts. Moreover, the mother god was always in three parts, hence Matres—mothers. She symbolized babies, wheat, and fruit. In Greece, she was the Three Sisters. Even in Shakespeare, the female trinity arises again in the three witches. In Irish folk tradition, there are three mother gods, all Bridgid. The Catholic Church changed them to one—Saint Bridget. There's a holy book from 1487 in which Saint Bridget is called the mother of the gods; only later was it changed to God. After that, she was changed to the foster mother of Jesus. In still later books, she has disappeared."

Now I understood why I had never heard of Castle Matrix. Too heretical. It didn't fit with the common wisdom about the slightly stupid, abundantly backward, totally pagan Celts and pre-Celts. "The sacred stone, or altar, was always thought to be an umbilical connected to the mother goddess," O'Driscoll said. I had learned about the omphalos in my college theater courses, the stone in the center of an ancient Greek theater that was said to be connected to the mother goddess. A revelation: the Celts had it, too.

On a clear day, the battlements offer a thirty-mile vista, taking in part of Counties Clare, Kerry, Tipperary, and Limerick. In the castle grounds, shrunken now to little more than a few acres, there are nonetheless twenty to twenty-five species of trees, one of which is represented by a magnificent stand of yew trees. "Those trees are undoubtedly progeny of the ones that stood here when it was a pre-Christian sacred grove. They stand in a line from the sacred rocks. In Celtic mythology, they are the most sacred of all trees, and their berries are the most poisonous."

"Aren't you afraid your sheep will eat them?" I asked. I *thought* they were sheep I had seen on the way in. But strange ones.

O'Driscoll laughed. "Not those sheep. They're smarter than that. They're Jacob's sheep, the kind that was found in biblical times and is, in fact, featured in the Bible. Notice that some have three or four horns. But unlike modern sheep, they don't fight. In fact, they are bigger than commercial sheep, their wool is finer and thicker, and they are infinitely smarter. These are sheep as close to nature as possible; it's only man's interference that makes creatures eat poisonous things."

O'Driscoll hopped down from the battlements and ran to a set on the other side. "Can you see those circles?" he asked.

Not well, I told him.

"I'll show you the aerial photos inside. There were at least three, but as many as five, stone circles near this castle. One farmer has made a garden of one. These things were sited based on the Celts' mythology; later, most of the Christian churches were placed on the earlier holy sites." Just as Geaney had said of the cross overlying the Celtic circle, probably due to Saint Patrick's genius, resulting in the magnificent High Crosses, among other things, I mused.

"From everything I can find out, it appears that Castle Matrix—that is, its original Celtic sanctuary—was believed to be the source of the sacred river. And the sacred river was the source of all power."

Pre-Celtic to pre-Christian to Christian—to now. O'Driscoll was a fount of much information. Somewhere in our talks of mythology and religion, he mentioned the Holy Grail. "Most people think of the Grail as a cup of blood the knights were seeking. That is not the case. What they were seeking was a member of the bloodline of Christ." And there is such a person, such a family. O'Driscoll knows them. He recommended to me a book, *Holy Blood and Holy Grail*, by Henry Lincoln, Richard Ley, and Michel Bergerac. I fully intend to read it, lest I run into European nobility and know not who they are. For the bloodline does run through the worthies of that continent.

"You know, of course, that everyone on earth today is related to everyone who ever lived on earth?" O'Driscoll asked. I had never thought of that. I am not a one-worlder, as I said. But what he said is, mathematically and logically—and very likely spiritually—true. It just happens we don't all like each other. Like any family. Nor have we all the same talents.

As we clambered back down the winding stairways, O'Driscoll stopped frequently to explain the interior. Each level contained a most amazing piece of furniture, or was connected with a most amazing world event, or both. So why had I never heard of Castle Matrix?

There was something about a cabinet in one room—how it magically ended up in O'Driscoll's possession and later was found to have been created for the castle in the first place. Or the Raleigh statue, which had also taken a circuitous route back by way, if I recall, of Williamsburg, Virginia. My head was already swimming from the conversation. I had seldom met anyone so full of so much knowledge of so much.

When we got back to the main floor, Elizabeth was back, and so was Kieran, bumping into the furniture in his toddler's scooter. The afternoon was fine, though the inside of the castle was cool and dark. Elizabeth suggested we all have some cake at a nearby café. But alas, when she called, she found it was closed until later in the season. In the old days, it is rumored, a restaurant owner would go out and kill a cock if need be to feed a hungry traveler. No longer does hospitality extend that far. I was sort of disappointed.

Instead, we said our good-byes, lingeringly, while the sheep and the dog and the horse—a two-year-old female named Honey—sniffed us all about. Honey, who roamed free like all the other O'Driscoll creatures, investigated what she liked. Often, Elizabeth said, she ate it. Specifically, Honey was attracted both to my husband and to his brass blazer buttons. The horse was doing two things. She was toddling, so to speak, like Kieran, who also liked to taste things. But unlike Kieran, she was becoming sexually mature, and found my husband a worthy object with an almost correct dose of pheromones. With any luck, she'll find a real stallion some day.

Spurred by my conversation with O'Driscoll, I drove the seven miles from Rathkeale to Askeaton, the site of the FitzGeralds' ancestral castle. Askeaton today is a small Irish village, far from the tourist trail, but on the way to Foynes, a major industrial site. Askeaton sits on two hills and is split down the middle by a small river. I drove through the center of the village, following the snakelike path of the road, and crossed the bridge. Like every other bridge in Ireland, it is not straight. On the left were the ruins of the FitzGeralds' most fabulous castle. Nothing remains today but a corner and a partial wall. Or so I thought. Parking nearby to walk the site, I noticed, but a quarter of a mile downriver, the ruins of an enormous abbey, perhaps even a cathedral. And following the river was a large, solid wall. I followed the wall with my eyes to another wall split off from it, and another from it, and so forth all over the area.

I gradually realized I was looking at the outlines of what had been Askeaton Castle, a castle-town-fortress-religious center that was much larger and much more prosperous than the small modern village. The complete disappearance and destruction of the Anglo-Irish nobility is too bad. I knew these nobles were aggressive, often violent, and despotic men and women. But I realized, looking at Askeaton castle, that Ireland must have lost a lot of its sense of place, its sense of national purpose, and its spirit of enterprise when Elizabeth destroyed the Irish lords. It certainly lost much prosperity and leadership.

Today, unlike the governments of Scotland, Great Britain, France, Germany, and many other places, the Irish government is letting the castles fall into ruins. The Irish seem to attach their hatred of English domination to all of the castles and great houses, and many want to tear them all down. While the Irish government has made national monuments of many of the ruins, it refuses to provide any money to restore or take care of them. I believe that Ireland is making a mistake by thinking only about where it is going, instead of where it has been. Despite their wishes, the English influence is dominant—the Irish legal, educational, and governmental systems are based on it. And its current prosperity is based in part on the fact that it is an English-speaking nation. It would seem better to reclaim the castles and great houses as their own, tweaking the noses of their former "oppressors" by making showplaces of the art and architecture and using the turbulent history itself as a source of strength.

Moreover, these were Irish lords. Some may dispute my belief that the FitzGeralds were Irish. They were, it is true, Norman invaders. But the FitzGeralds and dozens of other Normans became "more Irish than the Irish" and fought against English domination for generations. The irony is this: Around Shannonside, the Irish government has paid to help restore three castles of the Earls of Thomond, who were among the staunchest supporters of the English crown. These include Bunratty, Knappogue, and Dunguaire castles. The ruins of the FitzGeralds and other pro-Irish lords have been let go. Only O'Driscoll, the Knight of Glin, and a few other private owners have saved any of the FitzGerald castles.

On the road back to Limerick is still another FitzGerald castle ruin, near a tiny parish called Kildimo. It, too, lies in ruins, but it sits on a rock promontory jutting out of the landscape like a prizefighter's iron jaw. It commands a panoramic view of the Shannon River, and although I had to drive down a dirt road and trek across a field to get to it, it was worth the ride and the walk. I could almost see and hear the noise of the dozens of workmen as they hauled and lifted and fit the stones of the castle; the clatter of horses' hoofs and wagons and carriages; and the bustle of the villagers when the FitzGeralds ruled the land.

I'd had about enough "foreign-ness" for one day, I decided. So, I turned on the telly in my room. Lo and behold, there was a BBC documentary about silk-making in China. Following that, I was treated to a locally produced newsmagazine feature about two sets of Guppies who had given up the good life to live in the wilds of the Burren, with scarcely an income among them. One was making hand-dyed wools, the other something more industrial, bronze forging as I recall. Different, and yet so much the same.

I had seen, on American TV, a program about a group of people in England who had tried to live as prehistoric people of the British Isles had lived. They wore clothes of skins from animals they slaughtered themselves, they raised sheep, and they spun wool with crude implements. What they didn't grow, they didn't eat. And, for a year or more, there was no commerce with the modern world—until the camera crews arrived, of course.

The couples on the RTE (Radio Telefis Eirann, or Irish Radio and Television) did not go anywhere near as far back as that; they didn't really leave the current century. But they could have gone as far back as 600 B.C. if they had wanted to really find their roots. Ireland, and particularly the Shannon area, boasts a wealth of information about the early Celts in Ireland.

These people, brave and warlike, spread out from central Eu

rope and, from 450 to 250 B.C., were the most powerful group in Europe. Because Ireland was never brought under the aegis of the legions of the Roman Empire, Celtic life existed there undisturbed until the Vikings began to raid. So, not only are there abundant excavations to be found, the customs had longer to imprint on the bloodstock of the natives and the intermarrying invaders.

Most of Ireland's Celts lived on isolated farmsteads, the house surrounded by earthen ramparts and the farm itself spreading out in a circle beyond it. The farmsteads were called forts; now, because of their shape, they are called ring forts. Throughout the countryside, despite thousands of years of subsequent cultivation and various uses by other people, the ring forts are still easy to view in aerial photos like O'Driscoll's. In 1970, a replica of a ring fort was created at Cragganouwen, County Clare, and it is a marvelous historic attraction. This re-creation also boasts, however, another form of Celtic habitation—a crannog. These I find more intriguing than the ring forts, and their remains, too, are clearly visible all over the country, even from the window of a car.

Each crannog, archaeologists think, was the home of a single family rather than a group of families. These people, too, were farmers. But, as they lived near lakes, they constructed artificial islands not too far from shore. The islands were, of course, circular. The circle—recall Saint Patrick and the High Crosses—was sacred to the Celts, symbolizing their all-important sun god.

Although the crannogs were generally reached by boat, some, including the replica at Cragganouwen, could be reached by strategically placed rocks just beneath the surface of the water. The inhabitants, from practice, could easily escape on these rocks from their lakeshore farms to their home. Enemies, not knowing where the stones were, would have had a harder time of it.

In Adare, not far from Cragganouwen and on the way to Askeaton and Rathkeale, there is a new temple to gastronomy, a half-timbered house where nouvelle Irish cuisine is getting a send-off. The restaurant was only three weeks old when I visited. But its young owner, Daniel Mullane, was planning great things. I sampled among the first of these, and so far his great plans had provided equally great results.

Adare itself is reputed to be the most beautiful of Irish small towns. It is quaint and clean. But except for another huge ruin of a FitzGerald castle outside town, it isn't, to my mind, Irish. In fact, with numbers of half-timbered houses around, built by the English, it looks like an English village. That's OK, of course, the English having been much a part of all of Ireland for so long. My only question is this: Why do the Irish find it acceptable to glorify a collection of very humble English houses, and find it loathsome to so much as restore an Anglo-Irish castle or great house? Such contrariness is hard for a foreigner, even a sympathetic one, to fathom.

Mullane's restaurant, the Mustard Seed, is in a very well-preserved half-timbered house. Inside, he has created a drinks room with several tables around a cozy fire, and two dining rooms. "I wanted to redo an old house," Mullane confided. "But I couldn't afford to do it unless I put my house on show." That didn't appeal. But putting it on show as a restaurant did. Mullane was trained in Europe by the best chefs. And he also has an eye for promotion. Knowing that he is located in a tourist area, but wanting to cater to locals with refined palates as well, he produces two menus every night. The main menu is very heavily endowed with marriages of European nouvelle cuisine and the abundant and terrific Irish raw materials, from cream to scallops. The "Taste of Our Country" menu, which is a bit less dear (that is to say, lower-priced) offers more traditional dishes, although these, too, are cooked up in a lighter style than those of the original "farmhouse" hands that created them.

A sampling from the main menu:

Stir-fried scallops and spring onions with bean sprouts
Melon and crab with lemon mayonnaise
Mosaic of layered spring vegetables bound with chicken in a fresh tomato sauce
Lentil and tomato soup
Escalopes of Fresh Salmon with light lemon sauce
Pan-fried Loin of Veal with lime and watercress sauce
Almond tulip and strawberries
White chocolate mousse in berry sauce

The "Taste of Our Country" menu offered:

Sauteéd ox tongue with a marmalade of onion
Hot buttered mushroom filled with crab
Nettle and leek soup
Pan-fried pork fillets with Bulmer's Cider sauce
Nuggets of chicken breast pan-fried with tarragon

Pancakes with Irish Mist
Bailey's Ice Cream

I had time to peruse the menus while Mullane tended to other guests. I had dropped in the afternoon before, seeing him taking out the trash, to ask if I might speak with him and test his restaurant and cooking theories. The Shannon Development people who put me onto him had suggested he would be a worthy addition if I wanted to do anything about new Irish restaurants and the entrepreneurs they, like the IDA, wish to encourage. Shannon Development, along with the IDA, has been very professional in its dealings with me, pulling no punches beyond the merest hint of public relations, so I decided this might be on the money, too.

"We have such abundance in Ireland," Mullane said. "We have the best blackberries, rose hips, crab apples, and wild mushrooms. Even the nettles. I can just go out to any car park and pick them when I need them. This evening, before you arrived, I went out and picked watercress." None of these delicacies is cultivated; like the country's huge babies, they just grow.

"There are herbs native to this area, too, which I use," Mullane added. "Honesty, tansy, dandelion, even bay leaves. I got some bay from a car park in Limerick this week."

Mullane, though qualified, is not his own cook, preferring to plan menus with his chef. He runs the front of the house instead. The chef, Tim Gibbons, is even younger than Mullane, by the look of him. But he, too, is a risk taker, although he learned his trade closer to home. "When I began to plan opening this place, I also began scouting a cook," Mullane says. "I wanted someone with skill, but I wanted imagination. And I had to have someone willing to cast his lot with mine."

Gibbons was locally trained at the Galway City Hotel School. He was working in a large hotel in Limerick when Mullane discovered him.

"Dan walked in and said he was opening a small, high-quality place, and asked would I like to join it as chef," Gibbons says. "He offered me the opportunity to develop menus with him. But he warned me that it wouldn't be a secure type of position, with the need to start up and build up our fortunes. But I took it. All I've ever wanted to do was cook professionally, and I wanted to get away from being one of a number of cooks in a big hotel kitchen."

For a chef, Gibbons is highly voluble. He's also, like everyone in Ireland, highly literate. His menus show it. Knowing I was coming, and that I wanted to collect some recipes, he had written out two of his favorites—and the customers' favorites—for me before I arrived. I ordered both of them, but since there aren't very many soup nettles in the United States, I offer this one, as he offered it to me:

Bailey's Ice Cream

5 egg yolks
150 grams, or 5¼ ounces (½ cup plus 1 tbs., plus 1 tsp.) Castor sugar
½ vanilla pod
1 litre (1 quart plus a splash) milk
½ litre (½ quart plus a splash) cream
1 glass (8 ounces or to taste) Bailey's Irish Cream
60 grams (approximately ¼ cup) pralines

1. Cream the egg yolks and sugar to the "ribbon" stage. Transfer to a double boiler and cook until light and creamy.
2. Bring the milk and vanilla to the boil. Add half to the egg yolk and sugar, whisking all the time. Then add the other half. Over a double boiler stir with a wooden spoon and continue to cook until it coats the back of the spoon.
3. Remove and allow to cool.
4. Prepare the praline by cooking equal quantities of sugar and hazelnuts to the caramel stage. Turn out on an oiled marble slab. Allow to cool. Crush finely.
5. Semi-whip the cream.
6. Transfer the Creme Anglaise to a rotary-type freezer. When on the point of freezing, add the cream and flavouring.
7. Freeze for at least 4 hours at −18 degrees Centigrade. (25°F.)
8. Serve with a suitable biscuit, i.e., Lemon Shortbread.

Indeed, the Mustard Seed is, as it says, "an Irish restaurant in the new style." That Gibbons signed his recipe is proof enough for me that Mullane's place is one of the forerunners of improvement in the much-maligned (although I think unnecessarily) food of Ireland.

* * *

Thus fortified, I was able, the following morning, to complete my tour of Shannonside with a visit to an industrial estate in Limerick.

This estate was on the east side of Limerick. I was staying at FitzPatrick's on the west side; once again, I joined the Irish not in a pub crawl, but in a crawl through the snarling traffic. Again I marveled at the hundreds of school-aged children in their parochial-school skirts and jackets of many hues. The Irish certainly have an abundance of human resources on which to build their future.

The Raheen industrial estate is a mixture of the advanced high-tech industries—American floppy-disk maker Verbatim has a large, new factory there—and more mechanically oriented industries. On the other side of Limerick is the National Institute of Higher Education (NIHE), the heart of the Irish government's push to develop a generation of technically educated and oriented students. The NIHE, founded in 1972 in what had been a beautiful Georgian manor house, has burst into a full-fledged modern campus of brown, modern, functional, heartless buildings. But not gutless. There is no doubt that NIHE's seven hundred plus graduates each year are highly trained and skilled in electrical and mechanical engineering, the applied sciences, and even government and public policy. And the cooperation between NIHE and area industries, including Wang (it, too, has a sparkling new, modern factory across the road from NIHE) in providing job opportunities is very laudable. I visited the NIHE and discussed its booming future as an educational institution later the same day. But at Raheen, where I began my morning, I encountered a dissenting view of Irish industrialization.

Almost everywhere I went, the Irish road toward industrialization appeared to be paved with silicon chips and well-educated engineers. But I knew from Ireland's very high unemployment rate and from reading about the various disputes in the contentious Irish newspapers (by American, if not by English, standards) that road has been and will continue to be a difficult and painful one. During my encounter in Limerick with an industrial manager, I found some of the reasons why.

This manager's firm had apparently been made various promises and had been persuaded to move into a facility in Nenagh, although the firm wanted a building in the Raheen estate. Soon after the deal was struck, the manager found out that the factory in Nenagh had flooded during a large storm. In fact, it had been flooded at least twice. When the company asked the IDA to change the location, it was turned down because of some inexplicably strong desire in Dublin for them to stay at that site. Only after the factory flooded a third time, and the company threatened to move its planned operation to another European country, did the IDA agree to let the company have what it wanted in the first place—the factory its operation now occupies in Raheen.

The same manager—not, by the way, Irish or Irish-American—also said he had stopped participating in the local chamber of commerce after he overheard several local Irish businessmen sharply criticizing the foreign industries that were located in Limerick. He said, "These people had been very friendly to my face, but after they had had a few drinks, they began to make sarcastic remarks, suggesting they did not like the presence of so many foreign companies in their town."

Now, this manager has joined with other foreign, non-Irish managers in the area to form their own association.

This unfortunate situation, I believe, is of a piece with the treatment of the castles of the Irish lords and the Irish attitude toward the "haves." Even many of those Irish who today are the haves—bank presidents, industrial executives, government officials, etc.—seem to be what are known as the "begrudgers." The begrudgers, very prevalent among Irish workers, resent and envy people who do well or, at least, better than they themselves do. They want to tear down the castles, burn the great manor houses, and bankrupt the wealthy or tax them into poverty. This attitude, I believe, comes from their believing that Ireland is still an oppressed land, though it certainly is so no longer.

It may also come from a feeling of powerlessness, but, more than that, I believe begrudging comes from those who simply wish to blame others for their troubles and who refuse to take the action they can to help themselves. Of course, for many Irish people, plagued by unemployment or too old or poorly educated to be retrained in the new technologies, the future holds little promise. But the Irish government has done an incredible job of providing food, shelter, and support for the unemployed and the underprivileged. Ireland is too fertile and the government too generous and mindful of the harsh past to allow real hunger or deprivation to occur ever again. But among some of the Irish, reminiscences of the autocratic past linger long. Unfortunately, these attitudes are mortgaging the future.

Ireland is said to be divided between the Republic and Northern Ireland. I disagree. Ireland today is divided between what I call the "doers"—the energetic, enterprising, busy people working to forge Ireland's place in the world—and the "don'ters"—the resentful, begrudging, envious, complaining people who want to penalize others for their talents, efforts, and success and keep Ireland a backwater, pitied and preyed upon by stronger nations.

Fortunately, during my travels, I found far more doers than don'ters, though the latter make a lot of noise and a bit of trouble. The spirit of progress and enterprise seems to be on the ascendancy in Irish business, government, and industry. Maybe the long-awaited Celtic Rising will happen after all.

Market day during a rainy spring. Ennistymon, County Clare. (Bryce Webster)

The Great Hall at Bunratty Castle, where noblemen gathered and dined. (Shannon Development, Ireland)

The Botanic Gardens, located in the working-class Glasnevin section of Dublin. (Paddy Tutty, Bord Failte)

A lake in Killarney, part of the beautiful Ring of Kerry. (Brian Lynch, Bord Failte)

A Rent-an-Irish Cottage vacation in the Shannon Region of Ireland provides varied opportunities for families interested in outdoor sports, including an outing with one of the famous Irish hunts. (Shannon Development, Ireland)

Typical round tower, like dozens of others that pop up in the Irish countryside. (Bryce Webster)

Connemara Lake fishermen get an early start for spring "rough" fishing, or "coarse angling," as it is known. (Bryce Webster)

A view of Waterford City. (Bord Failte)

Street scene, Dublin. (Pat O'Dea, Bord Failte)

Plant manager McCarthy checks assembly at Ireland's Cross pens factory. (Bryce Webster)

The main street in Blessington, County Wicklow, and the hotel where tea is still traditionally served. (Paddy Tutty, Bord Failte)

The Hyster assembly plant, Galway. This facility of a U.S. company makes heavy-duty lifting equipment for EEC countries. (Bryce Webster)

Irish "lounge" scene. Women frequent lounges, but never pubs. (Arthur Guinness Son & Co. [Dublin] Ltd.)

The Lady Patricia—*one of two Guinness-owned vessels that ply between Britain and Ireland—loading at her berth in the Port of Dublin. The world's first beer tanker (with a capacity of 206,000 gallons), she was originally designed to carry transportable tanks and was converted at a cost of £500,000.*

Stout is pumped on board from road tankers, which connect with short insulations and link up with the ship's automatic loading system. (Guinness Ireland Limited)

One of Ireland's technological institutes, the main corpus of the National Institute of Higher Education, a mix of old and new buildings—but very new ideas. (NIHE, Ireland)

Doolin, a seaport-fishing port-artist's colony on the wave-battered coast of County Clare. (Bryce Webster)

Ideal family entertainment is just literally "around the corner" at most of the Rent-an-Irish Cottage centres in the Shannon Region of Ireland. Traditional Irish music, song, and dance sessions are held at the local "Teach an Cheoil" centres in the villages and, here, the visitor can get a unique insight into Irish culture while mingling and chatting with many of the local people. (Shannon Development, Ireland)

The ancient skill of "squaring" the world-famous Liscannor Stone with hammers is kept alive today at the spectacular Cliffs of Moher, forty miles from Shannon Airport in the west of Ireland, where a small private firm extracts the 350-million-year-old quartz sandstone lying under the Atlantic coastline surface for use in home and export markets. The two main varieties quarried—the smooth-faced Lough stone and the fossil-patterned Moher flagstone—are used for various purposes in domestic and commercial life in places as far apart as Germany and the United States. (Shannon Development, Ireland)

Bunratty Folk Park, a reconstructed typical Irish village, County Clare. (Shannon Development, Ireland)

8. Lisdoonvarna

Lisdoonvarna is an amalgam of the old and the new in Ireland, offering both an old-fashioned spa and the very modern concept of the singles bar, Irish-style. Nearby there are the Cliffs of Moher, Lahinch and its magnificent golf course, and the Aillwee Caves.

The name Lisdoonvarna has always attracted me. On many visits to Ireland before I actually visited the place, I had dreams about it, about fairy-tale cottages and young women in peasant skirts strolling gaily along, waiting for young men in leather knee-breeches to come home from work looking for them. In fact, the town of Lisdoonvarna has little indeed to do with leprechauns or any other fairy-tale creatures. It is indeed old, in part, but it has some modern "charms" such as the big new music hall attached to a fairly modern hotel, where thousands of Irish lasses do appear each September, hunting husbands.

Most of the year, however, Lisdoonvarna is simply a sleepy, slightly inland village, which boasts Ireland's only developed hot springs and a spa to go with them.

The afternoon of my arrival, I dropped my bags in the hotel, had a bath and a nap, and went looking for dinner. I found it and later followed my ears into the lounge bar. There was music playing. It was only mediocre, and really quite loud. Sitting behind the next round table, apparently waiting for her companion, was a very pleasant-faced dark-haired woman in a blue sweater, or, as they would say, jersey or jumper. She spoke to me.

"Is it from Dublin you're visiting Lisdoonvarna, then?" she asked. It was not the first time I was to be taken as a Dubliner in Ireland, nor the last.

"No, we are from New York. We've come to take the waters at the spa."

She was surprised at that; I was later to learn why. We chatted about this and that until her husband, and mine, returned to our tables with the drinks. And then we all chatted some more. It turned out that the couple was from Donnybrook, a suburb of Dublin, and they had two friends with them who joined the party in a short time. But the small dark woman and her most astonishingly tall husband were far more lively and interesting, and, in fact, the other couple shoved off shortly for their guesthouse and their bed.

The Tall Man and his Short Wife, as we have always since referred to them, were on a four-day trip. The man, it seemed, was an amateur explorer, and, as they had no children, they often stole away for a long weekend to see more of their country, staying in guesthouses or bed and breakfasts to make it all affordable. They were middle-aged and seemed to be firmly middle-class, verging on upper-middle. And the fact that they had no children was certainly unique. In fact, it made me think they might be Protestants: Donnybrook had been a very British enclave, and it would have been nature's choice alone for a couple of their age not to have children if they were Catholic. But I didn't ask.

We parted from them at closing time, which is 11:30 P.M. in Ireland. They said they were staying about three more days and perhaps we would see each other again. I wanted to ask them for their address, but was reticent. Because I react in foreign countries much as the natives do (I call it the chameleon act, taking "When in Rome" a step further), I tend, more and more, to believe the couple must have been Anglo-Irish, who are more reserved than the rest of the Irish, if not so unfriendly and offputting as I have often found the English.

The next morning we drove down to the spa. It is nestled in a natural amphitheater formation, with a swift and boisterous stream dancing through it. Alongside the water there are elephant-ear plants with leaves as broad as a wrestler's back. There are water lily–like plants growing in eddies at the stream's edge, anchored by roots that, if made of hemp, would have served to hauser an Atlantic freighter to the Galway docks.

From the car park, you must enter the older spa building to make appointments for baths, saunas, massages, facials, beauty-salon services from cuts to manicures, and, amazingly, the tanning machine. If you cannot be taken right away, there's a brand-new building across a wooden footbridge where coffee, tea, biscuits, and even some heartier fare is served while you wait. You can also get a newspaper to while away the time, and you can shop for souvenirs as well.

My husband decided to treat himself to an extra massage one morning, but I wasn't in the mood for being stroked and pounded, so I went to the coffee shop (tea shop, I suppose) and ordered a "white coffee" and a local paper.

For at least two hours, I sat happily in the sun that was streaming through the Scandinavian-style plate-glass and teak-trimmed windows. And I'm sure I had more "white coffee," which is merely the highly descriptive Irish way of saying coffee with cream.

The spa itself is a museum piece, a rambling late-Victorian building that had, at some time in the past, been partitioned into men's and women's bath areas, and had, sometime more recently, acquired some rather jarring modern amenities, such as plywood partitions and modern office furniture at the reception area, and the like.

The baths themselves take place in a dormlike area, with small cubicles off a long hallway. In each cubicle is a chair, a cot, and a small closet. Behind each two cubicles is a shared tub room. So high and deep are the tubs that wooden steps are provided for getting in, and a rope pull hangs over them for getting out. The matron fills the tub with the sulphurated water of the natural springs, made boiling hot on the premises, and calls you when it's about chest deep. Once she has helped you in, she points out the hot-sulphur tap and cold-water tap and invites you to stay as long as you like—even if you are scheduled for a massage afterward. The waters may rush from the ground, but they respect Irish time when they're above it.

I found the bath itself relaxing and the panorama of clouds, seen out the windows set high in the wall, entertaining. When I got out, I lay dripping-wet on the wool blanket on the cot, as instructed, and pulled a second one up around me. I was afraid at first it would be a scratchy and clammy and uncomfortable experience. But I found that I had never in my life been so pleasantly and cozily warm, and I soon dozed off, waking only when the matron called me to the masseuse, the unmarried girl I mentioned earlier to whom childlessness by choice was a new concept.

After this first visit, I knew why the Tall Man's Short Wife was amazed that two young Americans were going to the spa. When most Americans think of health spas, they think of gleaming white walls, masseuses named, and looking like, Brunhilda (or Jack La

Lanne), maybe a terse lecture on the evils of smoking and drinking—altogether a chastening experience from the ranks of the physical elite. At Lisdoonvarna the matron was just that, at least when I was there—a matronly woman whose upper-arm strength came more from beating "barm brack," Irish traditional bread, than kneading the flesh. The masseuse was a lithe but by no means either muscular or bony (bonny, more like) young woman. And far from being white and tiled, the facility itself is painted in every conceivable Victorian shade. The floors are wood or lino or may even have a bit of Navan carpet in spots. In fact, the tea shop looks like a spa, and the spa like a tea shop.

On the third day of our stay, we decided to make a day trip to the Aillwee Caves. Formed by an underground river, the caves date back to 2,000,000 B.C. After the river vacated the space, bear and other wild animals moved in. But even they were long gone when the caves were rediscovered by a hunter in this century. The government has taken over the caves, and there is now a very fully stocked, and not at all tacky, souvenir and snack shop at the entrance.

The cave itself is not as spectacular as those Americans are used to—Luray, Howe, and others—lacking brilliantly colored stalactites. But the descent is steep enough, though fully handrailed and well-guided, to intimidate many. And when the guide puts out the lights, so that the tour can experience true total darkness, many hearts are fainter than their owners think, mine included.

Back at the surface, I, and most of the other women on the trip, sought out the ladies' room. While I waited in line inside the door, someone lightly touched my shoulder, and I jumped at least a good meter off the ground. Who could be wanting me in a strange land? Surely not my husband, in "the ladies' " (as the Irish shorten it), and I didn't know anyone else. I thought. But it was the Short Wife of the Tall Man. They had just entered the shop, and she saw me. We all, together, had a little chat after that. And once again, I was too reticent to ask for names and addresses—as were they. I have an idea that I could go to Donnybrook, their residence the only thing I know about them, and describe them to local shopkeepers (or maybe the librarian, as I assume the Tall Man to be an avid reader) and locate them. I yet might.

The Aillwee Caves are at the edge of an area called the Burren. A vast expanse, sitting on the County Clare coast south of Galway

Bay, it is an area of striking contrasts. The landscape itself appears to be made of lumps and mounds and walls and forts of dun-colored rock. But between the boulders, which lie close together like quarry tiles in a modern house, grow alpine flowers of great delicacy and beauty. In May, however, the barren landscape sports gentian, geraniums, and even wild orchids growing along with the alpine growth.

The same misty day, after a drenching night, that we visited the caves, we went for a ride through the Burren, beginning in Kilfenora. We met a young woman, standing bigger than life along the road, a hitchhiker, we presumed. When we stopped to pick her up, a young man got in with her, with their packs, no mean feat in the continental version of a Ford Escort we had rented. They were Americans, of course.

The boy had been in Ireland for only a week or so, and was on his way to England, France, and, apparently, a summer-long discovery of Europe. The girl, however, was a seasoned Ireland hand, having spent three months already backpacking and camping in Ireland.

For myself, I cannot think of a more inhospitable climate in which to live out of doors. The ground never truly gets warm, the sun never truly shines meltingly hot, it may rain buckets for an hour and be misty for a week thereafter—except for the thirty-minute intervals of sun in a cloudless sky that might lull one into thinking the weather had broken. The best one can hope for is a series of "soft days," days on which a superfine mist hangs in the air, the breezes are balmy, and the sun shimmers beguilingly behind it all. The weather patterns in Ireland are, no doubt, why the bulls are shaggy even in July, and there's no shedding problem with the dogs.

But this girl claimed to love it, and indeed she did have the rainwashed complexion one is supposed to get from green-and-white-striped soap. Her blond braids glistened. She smelled fresh as the morning dew, and I can't remember seeing anyone else on quite the same natural high.

All this is not to say I mind being, temporarily, outdoors in Ireland. In fact, for civilized fresh air, it truly cannot be beaten.

Kilfenora sported the Burren Display Centre, where we had a snack and found a multitude of fairly classy souvenirs. The town also contains several High Crosses. One of them, Saint Doorty's Cross, lay in two large fragments in the churchyard until 1950.

Created in the twelfth century, the cross shows the Carolingian influence imported by the Vikings. The scene on the front shows Christ as abbot of the world, directing his earthly disciples to destroy evil, which is in the figure of a ferocious bird. On the back of the cross is an emblem of Christ crucified, surrounded by birds. Much of the work is cracked, and the deep relief in which the cross was originally worked is worn shallow. But the intricate Celtic decoration is still visible.

Not far from this spiritual site is an even older site in which more earthly wars were waged—Caher Ballykinvarga. This double-walled stone fort has been tentatively dated to the Middle Iron Age, the few centuries surrounding the birth of Christ. Scholars believe it was the home of a small band of bellicose men. The castle itself—more like a raised earthworks fort, really—was surrounded by a *chevaux de frise*, the ancient equivalent of antitank traps. The *chevaux* consists of sharp boulders, half buried around the fort at close intervals, making it impossible for more than one person to walk through at a time. And it wouldn't be anything you'd want to attempt in the dark, even now.

Similar fortifications are found elsewhere in Ireland, though I didn't see any of them. I am told that the most widespread use of the *chevaux de frise* is to be found in central Spain and in Portugal. Although most scholars thus believe there had been trade between the two ancient locales, others think each made the discovery independently. I vote for commerce: even today, there is a band of Celtic-speaking people in northern Portugal, and they are seafarers like the Irish.

Throughout the Burren are structures commonly called "wedge tombs." Any number of them are visible in fields of rocks, the wedges themselves being huge flat rocks set up lean-to fashion, often in the middle of a wide expanse. Berneens Wedge Tomb, which was in my guidebook, caught my eye. "To visit the wedge tomb at Berneens," it says, "stop just before the first house on your right after Cahermore." Typical Irish directions.

I stopped, and agreed with the guidebook author that the tomb was marvelously situated, with a wide panorama of hills, run up and down with the rock walls peculiar to the Burren. These walls, rather than using rectangular rocks piled intricately atop each other New England–fashion, use flat slabs standing face to face rather than edge to edge. They lean, against gravity, uphill and downdale. They resemble gray dominoes placed on end, just slightly tilted but not enough to fall.

These wedges are assumed to have been built about 2,000 B.C., and they are assumed to have been used for burial and covered over with earth. But surely more people had died than there were stones. How could a society living in close barter with capricious nature have afforded the luxury of such constructions for every member that died? Indeed, Ireland would be nothing but a monumental graveyard. Of course, it could have been just the leaders who were treated to such impressive interments. Or it could be that the wedges were something else completely. I favor the theory that they were not covered with earth but were used pretty much as is for any number of purposes. For instance, they might have been communal worship areas. Or they might have been staging areas for battles. Or they might simply have been erected as shelter for people out patroling or tending sheep or cattle.

I like to let my imagination run away with me in Ireland. It has frustrated me, both during and after my journey, that the Irish themselves apply very little of their immense creative powers to finding out the truth of the ancient sites. The nation is overgrown with fantastic historic realities and possibilities. And yet, due mainly to the influence of the Roman Catholic Church, very little imagination is used concerning the distant past. Invariably, anything not instantly understood (or worse, perhaps, understood and rejected) is attributed to paganism. And anything pagan is attributed to burial—never religion, though the ancients had one, and never technology, though they had a technology of their own as well.

In the Burren, going from one site to another involves trips of as little as eight-tenths of a mile. It is impossible to cover all the sites you could, or even all the ones you want to, unless you've endless time. And there are sites for every interest, from the pagan monuments to settings and artifacts of the early Church, to the habitations of the more substantial citizens of antique times. This last is my favorite. A joyful voyeur into the lives of long-dead humans (though I equally like to discover how people live now), my favorite ruin in the Burren is Leamaneh Castle. Not fitted up and tourable, as so many castles in Ireland are, it is indeed not in the classic mode of a castle at all. To be sure, it is made of stone, with thick walls that have allowed it to stand since it was built in

1480. But it is not a classic castle, because it has only one section that could be properly defended, rising to great heights with only tiny slits for windows. The rest of the castle, built as a fortified house in the seventeenth century, boasts unusually large, attractive windows.

Another unusual feature of the house and castle are the stairways. In most castles, they spiral to the left. In O'Brien castles, like this one, they spiral to the right. Why? Because the tribe was mainly left-handed, and constructing stairways to favor their needs put their mainly right-handed opponents at a disadvantage.

There are small things in the Burren, too, to get excited about. Ludlow, one of Cromwell's generals, noticed them: "Of which it is said," he is credited with writing, "that it is a country where there is not water enough to drown a man, wood enough to hang one, nor earth enough to bury him, which last is so scarce that the inhabitants steal it from each other, and yet their cattle are very fat, for the grass growing in tufts of earth of two or three foot square that lie between the rocks which are of limestone, is very sweet and nourishing."

Indeed, the earth nourishes an abundance of plants not found elsewhere in Ireland. There are spring gentian, maidenhair fern, helianth, and orchids. Growing side by side with the alpine flora, the orchids range from the so-called Irish orchid (which is really a Mediterranean species) to spotted orchids, early purple orchids, scented orchids, and more. Nero Wolfe would have had a field day.

On the day after my Burren trip, I journeyed to the seaside village of Lahinch, by way of Doolin.

About two years earlier, during the annual rock-music festival held in nearby Lisdoonvarna, three American young men drowned while attempting to swim at Doolin. It occurred to me then, and has occurred to me since, that they must have been influenced by drugs, or insanity. Doolin is the port from which sails the Aran Islands boat to Innishere—when it can. I've stood on the Doolin docks, mesmerized by the brute power of the ocean fighting to cross the tiny land mass that stands between it and England. The ocean was apparently quite riled up about the impediment after its five-thousand-mile roll across the seabed's mountains and valleys, pushed by winds and sliced through by the intrusive warmer waters of the Gulf Stream that curve around Ireland's western coast. There was nothing that morning to suggest to me that any human could claim victory over it. It was then that my teenage readings of Synge's sea-drama classic, *Deirdre of the Sorrows,* made most sense to me. It was then that I knew why Irish seamen traditionally don't learn to swim and prolong the inevitable—and why the Aran-knit sweaters had a distinctive pattern knitted by only one family, as markers to claim the dead should they ever be tossed back from the sea.

Despite its exalted position among tourists everywhere as a port to the Aran Islands, Doolin is, like many Irish coastal towns, a one-horse affair, having only one main street, but two bars. One of them, the one beyond the bridge I have been told, offers exceptionally fine traditional Irish music. But I visited in the daytime and found, serendipitously, a tiny shop instead.

I wasn't sure, at first, that it was a shop. There was a black-and-white dog lying by the half-open "Dutch" door. There was a small handpainted sign next to the window, however, so I looked in. Right on Doolin's main street, in the center of town almost, it was nonetheless an ageless, ancient, Irish three-room cottage. The main room, which I found myself standing in, was the shop itself. From a room to the side, through a flowered curtain, a young man with dark, almost black hair, appeared. He wasn't dressed for commerce, and, through the course of our conversation, I discovered that he was an unemployed fisherman, native Irish, but that his wife was an artist who had been born and raised in New York City. I didn't meet her, as she was busy with the baby. But I bought an atmospheric watercolor of a scene that must have been near Doolin.

I wondered how there could be any unemployed Irish fishermen, since every restaurant menu was abundantly filled out with fish dishes, especially the ubiquitous plaice, a type of flounder.

"You know, they're just lazy," said my informant, a restaurateur in Galway. We had been discussing local seafood, as he runs a seafood restaurant, and I mentioned the unemployed fisherman in Doolin. "If they have any other means of support, they won't go out until the wolf is at the door, and sometimes not then. It seems to me your fisherman may be one of those."

For a while, this made sense. But then I recalled the crashing of the waves, pounding the cement docks at Doolin to powder, no doubt, and I found it hard to think of wanting to stay at home as lazy. Maybe the young man's ancestors were all fishermen and he felt bound to be one, too, without having inherited the love of the sea and the life that would make it possible. Maybe his wife had some income of her own, beyond the art (or maybe she sold enough at 20 punt each, the equivalent of $21 at the time), to keep them comfortable in the tiny cottage, baby and all, and didn't want the father of her child risking his neck when the sea was mean.

Or maybe he *was* lazy.

Finally, we got to Lahinch. One of my first stops was at the car park near the strand. I wanted to see the ocean again, and Lahinch was a summer resort town, not a port. Indeed, the sea was still crashing up the beach, but it didn't seem nearly so vexed as at Doolin. It was as if it had gotten its tantrum over with in the confining rock-filled and rock-bordered estuary that sits at Doolin's feet. Now, it could afford to be a bit more gentle, teasing the few children on the beach to leave their sandcastles and the watchful eyes of their mothers and play with it. But none of them did. There are days you can swim at Lahinch, and days you can't.

One thing you can always do in Lahinch, however, is eat well. The Aberdeen Arms Hotel, which is not right on the strand but rather tucked up on the town's high street beyond the MACE store, has a well-earned reputation for its fine dining room. The menu features nary a trace of plaice—well, maybe it does, but there are so many other delightful things to choose from. There is a maitre d', unusual in Ireland at a small hotel, and he runs the room in the best Irish tradition. Regular patrons are treated no differently than guests, but more so. To explain: Ireland embodies, to me, the pinnacle of politesse. While the British have more form in their manners, the French more style, the Italians more largesse, the Japanese more ritual, the Americans none at all (I have now covered the major tourist groups), the Irish have made an art of blending good sense and civility.

What the maitre d' does is this: When regulars arrive, with or without reservations, they are assured that the hotel is delighted to have them there to dine *again*. They are shown immediately to a table, if there is one, or invited to have a drink or coffee in the lounge bar. If they choose coffee, it will likely come from the dining room, and will be free. A waiter will be sent to tell them when a table is ready.

If a new patron—either a new hotel guest or walk-in—appears, with or without a reservation, the preceding courtesies are followed precisely, except for the use of the word *again*.

Another thing one can do in Lahinch is play golf. Perched on a hillock above the sea, the Lahinch Golf Club boasts a championship course and a club full of dedicated members, many of whom live, or at least summer, in the substantial modern houses that ring the course. Windswept and spray-drenched, the houses near the course are among the best in modern Irish home design, using the thick masonry walls of the traditional cottage, but formed with steeply sloping roofs, balconies and interior galleries, and tall, narrow double-paned windows to let in the light and keep out the gales.

Nongolfers can shop at Sue's, a knits and woolens store backing up to the beach. One can also buy Lahinch Golf Club sweaters there, enabling one to add to a preppy wardrobe without actually participating in the sport. In any case, shopping at Sue's can be a sport in itself. The day I was there, both my husband and I chose golf club sweaters, and he got a tweed jacket as well. My brother was soon getting married, so we bought a mohair throw for him and, while we were at it, one for ourselves. Aside from that, we bought a number of smaller woolen goods as gifts for family and friends. When we went to pay, with a charge card, the proprietor asked if we had cash. Of course, this happens in the States as well, because of the profit loss when the credit-card company charges up to 6 percent or more to the merchant. We didn't have that much cash, and said so. But the owner then offered to take a personal check. We didn't have one of those either, only some company checks. He was, indeed, perfectly happy to take one—though it did not have our names on it, and would, in any case, take up to a month to clear, what with flying back and forth across the Atlantic.

This behavior, unheard of from a merchant in the United States, is typical of the Irish attitude. He didn't think we would be dishonest, and figured he would get paid for the goods. But this is not blind faith; having depended so much on tourism for so long, the Irish have come to expect certain things from certain groups. There were some European travelers, the proprietor told me, of whom he would be suspicious even with cash, and from whom he would be very reluctant to take a traveler's check, so often did this group forge them. But with Americans, he had had few problems. Indeed, he found Americans to be quite pleasant to deal with all in all, and they seldom wasted their own or his time without intending, at least, to buy. The southern Europeans, on the other hand . . .

In all my trips back and forth between Lahinch and Lisdoonvarna, I had tried, in vain, to stop at the Cliffs of Moher. Many days, I could tell at a glance that it would be too misty or cloudy or rainy to see a thing. Other days, I set off from bright sun in Lisdoonvarna, only to find Moher socked in. One day, indeed, I spied picnickers along the road, their sleeves rolled up, enjoying a feast on the verge. They were not three miles from the cliffs. Nonetheless, when I got there, huge billows of theatening—and, soon, delivering—clouds rolled in off the Atlantic.

So, I have never seen the Cliffs of Moher, nor the sights one can see from them. I am told the gray risings of the Aran Islands are part of the view. On an especially clear day, the Twelve Bens of Connemara, miles and miles away across Galway Bay, glimmer and shimmer into view. Closer, peregrine falcons rest on the almost sheer cliffs, along with more common birds such as puffins, razorbills, and a variety of squawking gulls.

I'm sure it is worth a visit. Knowing Ireland is like peeling an onion, and I'm sure I will return to peel the next layer soon, when the winds and gods are willing, and I will see the horizon from the cliffs.

9. galway

Galway, the gateway to Connemara and a good jumping-off place for some points in County Clare as well. I visit some factories, some shops and restaurants, and take a harrowing ride along the Coast Road.

One of the sentimental favorite Irish-American tunes is named "Galway Bay." It makes immigrants go teary-eyed in Stateside Irish pubs. Americans who've never even seen the auld sod adopt a faraway look, the one of a person imagining heaven.

But if heaven it is in their minds, I hope their heaven includes a Key West, a Greenwich Village, a San Francisco Telegraph Hill. For Galway has the character of these. It has also, however, the character of Dayton, Ohio. And of Coney Island. And Stamford, Connecticut. . . .

Galway is, to my mind, the quintessential Irish city, a conglomeration of perfectly meshed opposites and analogues. A new city; an old city. A cosmopolitan outpost in the west of Ireland; a provincial seat. A factory town; a seacoast resort. A city of sea-shanty back streets on crumbling quays; a hometown with a healthy population of squeaky-clean prep-school kids and their golf-playing mums.

My first two visits to Galway had left me, to say the least, unimpressed. But it grew on me. And the more I learned of Ireland, the more I learned that my first two visits to Galway had revealed essential features of the land and its people that I later came to appreciate.

The first visit was for the purpose of visiting industrial estates, vast sweeps of land dotted with low-rise factories making everything from rubber bands to fine china and crystal. I arrived in a heat wave and checked in at a modern hotel, the Corrib Great Southern, on the outskirts of the city proper but close to the factories. It had been booked for me by one of the Irish government agencies I was working with at the time. It was a stunning lesson in letting—nay, encouraging—the Irish to be Irish, and adapting myself instead.

The modern hotel had a swimming pool, a very large dining room, lots of guest rooms, and central heating. It had mingy little windows of the kind you'll find in many a Holiday Inn in America, things that open only a wedge. It had gleaming tile bathrooms, U.S.-style, and no mold had begun to grow in the cracks as yet. It had a harried manager. And it had a house full of touring Evangelists. But worst of all, it was the middle, truly, of a heat wave—over 80° F outside and no way at all to shut off the heat in my room, nor any room to move me to.

I spent the first sleepless night I'd ever had in Ireland. In the morning, I went to church to pray, literally, about what to do. The revelation? Change hotels; tell the government guys about it later. So I drove out to Salthill, a section of the city that rises on the side of a hill above Galway Bay. At the top, I knew, there was a fine hotel in the European tradition, and I hoped they'd have a room for me. I asked in the lobby, but the manageress, who would know such things, was not about. Still, said the clerk, "Have a seat, and the girl will bring you your tea while I see can I find her."

It was about 11:30 A.M. The lobby was lovely and cool and had prints of flowers on the wall. The tea was good, too, and I had hopes—and a whole Sunday to spend before my industrial work took me back to serious business.

In good time—which is to say, just when my tea was almost done and, as an impatient American, I was about to "inquire"—the manageress appeared. She had already looked up their bookings for me and said that they could put me up that night, but not the next, but I could come back the one after that. She said she didn't think I'd want to do all that moving around (and she was right) and that she'd call down the hill to a hotel that often took their overflow, "To see did they have a suitable accommodation." Would I like some more tea while she did this?

The little hotel had room indeed, and she had booked me in for the three days. I could take my bags down right away, she said, and though the room wasn't ready, they'd look after them and put them up when it was. I could go off and continue my holiday.

Now here was, again, the Irish character in action. The manageress didn't have to put herself out; she didn't have to send me away where I'd be happier and do herself out of the two days' room rent. And in the States, I'm sure she wouldn't have. Nor did the little hotel, the Rockbarton Park, have to be so nice about handling my baggage.

I ate dinner at the large hotel that night and thanked the manageress for her help. I stayed happily at the Rockbarton Park, where I have stayed happily half a dozen times since. I stayed once, a few years ago, at the European hotel on the hill, but it had changed. It had been bought by a conglomerate; the wonderful manageress and the welcoming feeling all were gone. I moved out, after one day, back down to the family-owned Rockbarton Park.

The Irish are a family people; Americans are corporate. While the Irish government acknowledges that it must become a more industrial society to compete in world markets—and it must do that to survive—the character of the nation is, thankfully, not changing along with it, at least as far as I can see. The culture is not changing as rapidly as the country is successfully putting on line first-class production in electronics, pharmaceuticals, apparel, and information. But this, too, is not surprising. Ireland is a nation of well-mixed contrasts, and has been so for hundreds of years. For example, it is an island nation, but has none of the political upheaval associated with other island nations, like Taiwan, Cuba, Jamaica, and Cyprus. In fact, it has a long history of political stability, whether under British rule or its own.

Even the rift is stable. Within the governments of the Republic of Ireland and Ulster, there is great stability, and no hint of bloody coups, or even bloodless coups. Both are, and have always been, staunch adherents of due process, thus providing the political background needed for the economic growth desired. The occasional bloodshed is, to them, no more than the race riots were to us: significant to those involved, and even to the population as a whole, but not enough to blow a whole people out of the water.

So, while the Irish are successfully founding new factories, and recycling old ones, they have not gone button-down all the way. The best hotels are the old style, either family-owned or, if company-owned, run as if by family. The telltale signs are many. Such a hotel will generally not be constructed along international style lines: it may be a very old building, or a very odd building, or, like the Rockbarton Park Hotel, a simple suburban family home that grew into a twelve-room hostelry, complete with dining room and lounge bar. Very likely, not all of its guest rooms, even today, will sport their own baths. The decor may range from European upper crust—fine old furniture and heavy draperies—to hodgepodge—a leather chair here, a grouping of Danish modern, a "snug" near the fireplace, venetian blinds, and sheer curtains. Prices may range from near bed and breakfast for a small family hotel, as little as 6 punt per night, to the top rate for the country, 50 punt and more, in an historic hotel or one with an especially fine menu and chef (a punt equaled approximately one American dollar in value in 1985; this fluctuates monthly and yearly).

Seeing the day going, and knowing I had to tour factories the next day, I decided to make the best of the local attractions and the beach. The Rockbarton Park was merely three short blocks from the beach, which stretches in a gentle curve for at least two miles, my hotel almost at its center. The heat wave had not abated, and the sand was filled with picnicking families, the children splashing happily in the water. None of the adults swam, and later I found out why.

It was August, holiday month in Ireland as on most of the continent, and the small shops at the town end of the beach were doing a land-office business in plastic pails and shovels. They sold one pail that, when filled with sand and overturned, produced a molded castle, complete with parapets. I couldn't resist, and I bought one to bring back for my small nephew. I also bought a chocolate bar, which was to come in handy later on. There was saltwater taffy for sale. There were game rooms, with both mechanical and electronic games, and the ubiquitous teenagers hanging over them, shoving in their twenty-punt coins for another shot at getting the highest score. There were huge signs advertising the night's entertainment at a dozen pubs along the strip, many with dancing. There were elderly ladies, still in "jerseys," toddling up the porches of beachfront hotels and guesthouses named St. Agnes, Stella Mare, and Farrell House, to meet their friends for tea. There were nuns strolling two by two, dogs frolicking with small boys or large girls, small girls wheedling their "Da's" for pinwheels, large boys pleading with girls for a kiss. There were elderly couples striding shoulder to shoulder in sturdy shoes, young couples pushing huge red-cheeked babies in prams, brazen unmarried couples walking arm in arm and taking an occasional bold peck at each other's cheek, and smiling shyly when they'd done it, knowing most of the passersby would be clucking their tongues at it.

At the city end of the promenade, I went into a small hotel for tea. When I came out again, the sun was down. A gathering of clouds had entered the harbor and was rolling fast by us. I was getting chilled and hotfooted it back to the hotel for a sweater. But reveling in the almost breathless freshness of the sea air, I went back out to walk the other end of the promenade, away from town. At the end of it, there was a huge cement pier from which adults were diving. One was sitting on a sort of bleachers built into it, drying himself.

"Is the water cold?" I asked.

"It is pretty cold," he answered in a Canadian accent. "But not too much worse than the lakes at home. It's just when you get out in this wind, it's enough to steal your breath away. But I had to do it. For one thing, I haven't had a bath in a couple of days, and just getting wet feels pretty good."

The young man was on a camping tour of Ireland, having come once before for a standard hotel tour with his parents. "To tell you the truth, I don't mind this. Everyone has been so friendly. I've had people share meals with me, and I have been offered that lovely field across the road to camp in as long as I'm in Galway. The man who owns it said I can even come up to the house to shower whenever I like, but I don't like to take advantage of his kindness like that." The camper's last name was O'Dea. "We pronounce it 'O'Day' at home, but here I've become 'O'Dee,' " he laughed. It brought to mind other vagaries of the Irish tongue, for it surely is not English.

A friend of mine had years before gone to Ireland. Jack Mahon his name is, a good Irish name in the States, but pronounced quite Germanically, like Mann. In the airport, he had been paged: "A telephone call for Dr. John Ma-hon, please," he had heard several times before connecting Ma-hon with himself.

I would shortly discover that our American Gallagers and Gallaghers (pronounced 'Galla-ger' here all the same) are Gallahers in Ireland. I had a great uncle, long dead, named Mr. Dunahy; it was he to whom Jackie Gleason's Joe the Bartender character said good night all those years. Gleason had played with my uncles (my father was much younger) in his salad days in Brooklyn and knew Mr. Dunahy quite well. Why should this name have passed into English with the *H* intact instead of the *G*? After all, in Ireland the name is Dunaghy. Why had it not come into America as Dunagy? Probably because it sounds so awful. I can't even conceive of Gleason saying "Good night, Mr. Dunagy." It's too harsh, too un-Irish.

The next morning, the weather was back to beautiful, a fact not wasted on me as I bundled into the car for a trip to the industrial estate at the edge of town. I didn't fancy being cooped up in factories all day. But, as it turned out, that wasn't to be the case, exactly.

The pace of Irish business life is much more akin to that of our own in the 1920s, or even before, than it is to U.S. business conduct today, despite the fact that Ireland has made tremendous leaps into postindustrial enterprise. It's just that they do it their way. Indeed, they entirely skipped the "smoking factories" phase of industrialization.

In going from the agrarian era to the space age, Ireland has had a share of errors. For instance, an early entrant into the Irish industrial sweepstakes was a Dutch high-tech corporation. The Dutch managers of the Irish facility decided to run round the clock, with clearly delineated breaks, clock-punching, inviolable schedules—in other words, Dutch orderliness. They wanted, in short, to turn the easygoing Irish into the highly organized Dutch. It didn't work. Despite providing some of the highest wages in the area, and the best working conditions, no one stayed very long, and the turnover rate alone was enough to finish the Dutch. In time, no Irish would even apply to work there, so different was it from the Irish idea of how to put in a day's work.

No one in the Industrial Development Authority wanted to talk much about this failure. And I don't believe it's because they are particularly upset over it, in and of itself. I rather think this is the natural civility rising again, preventing them from casting aspersions, even on people who clearly are in the wrong.

Nonetheless, there are numerous prosperous foreign companies operating in Galway's industrial estate. Digital Equipment Corporation (DEC) has made minicomputers and peripherals in an enormous factory there since the mid-1970s. Northern Telecom, a Canadian manufacturer, has also had a firm there for many years. Wilson Sporting Goods makes tennis racquets; Thermo King makes refrigeration units for large trucks; Farah Manufacturing has three plants that make casual clothes for men and boys; Beckman Instruments makes very specialized titanium and aluminum alloys.

All this is partly due to the special interest shown in Galway and points west by the IDA. The west of Ireland has been, for centuries, an ignored and abandoned area. It was where the native Irish were driven by the Puritans in the 1640s and by the Protestants after 1690. But the progress being made in the west, and especially in Galway, has been astounding. Modern attractive suburbs circle the older and historic downtown, and the population, which has long been eclectic because of Galway's port and fishing industry, is very sophisticated.

After visiting several factories in the estate, I escaped into the sunny winds for a wild drive to Ballinasloe, to the A. T. Cross pen factory there. Run by a Returned Yank, Peter McCarthy, it had adapted to a surprising array of unusual problems. One of them was, indeed, almost unmentionable.

There had been, it seemed, a problem with the electroplating of the gold pens, the plant manager told me. For a whole month, they'd have near-perfect production runs, and then, one day, the electroplating would go wrong. They'd have to do batch after batch of expensive pens over again and again, or even scrap them. Finally, they discovered that the problem was with the electroplating-machine operator, a premenopausal woman. It seemed, and they later found scientific research to support the hunch, that the electrical impulses from her body (the machinery was very delicate and very much hand-operated) would upset the electrical field of the electroplating machinery. In the United States, I can imagine the young woman in question bringing a discrimination suit. Switching her to a different task during her premenopausal days seemed logical and effective—the Irish solution. Accommodation was made in the interest of getting the job done. Does this sound stereotypically Irish? Hardly. But the image of the Irish as laggard workers is, one must recall, one conjured up by the British, who traditionally desired the Irish as servants and nothing more. The facts, today, belie that the Irish are lazy, or ever were.

While they are unique in their ways, today's Irish are a far cry from the "shanty" Irish of song and fable, or even the alternately sycophantic or obstreperous multitudes Morton says he found in

1930. In fact, the industrial Irish are capable of many small acts of genius, as the country is filled with other sorts of small workable miracles.

One example is in a factory that makes electronic components. Because the parts are fragile and need to be shipped and received in perfect condition, the factory uses mountains of extruded foam-chip packing material. One of the factory's major problems has been efficiently getting the static-filled stuff into the boxes without having it also stick to the tables and fly away in any breeze from a door opening or person walking past.

There is not in Ireland, at least to my knowledge, a machine to do this. Still, the plant manager wanted more efficiency and less waste and asked for suggestions. The winner? A huge sack, suspended from the ceiling and made of readily available blue denim, with a nozzle and valve. The "girls" had made the sack (the size of a suburban bathroom), and the men had hung it from the ceiling in such a way that it can be let down for them to fill it with foam chips and haul it up again. The packers simply place the boxes under the nozzle, cock the valve until the box is filled, and move on.

The Irish character is full of adaptation, as I have said before. But there are certain underlying facets that seem never to change. My experience with a rented car proves it.

While I was generally spared driving in Ireland by my husband when we traveled together, after he returned home and my mother joined me, I had to do the driving. I picked up a larger rental car and settled behind the wheel, with her next to me, fresh off a harrowing flight. The flight movie had been about airplane crashes; was showing it part and parcel of Irish humor? And the plane, she said, had hit some severe turbulence—followed by two hours of circling the fogged-in airport.

I put the key in the ignition, and nothing happened. A man was getting out of the car next to me, probably picking up a visitor himself, and I asked him for help. "These things can be tricky," he said, reaching in and giving the key lock a little twist. "I'm afther forgetting how to start the t'ings meself sometimes," he added. "Aye, it's a wonder how these mechanical objects have a mind of their own, and them taking up your driveway most of the time, a useless hunk of metal and all."

He had cleverly made my stupidity the car's fault. Elaborately he did it, and on purpose, not wanting me to lose face and feel a dolt in a foreign land. In this respect, the Irish are practically Japanese. But I think, in the end, they go further. While a Japanese man wouldn't have wanted me to lose face, and he in turn would have lost face if I had, the Japanese seem to know it's all a game of sorts, though a serious one. The Irish, influenced by centuries of legends and tales, are able, quite normally, to make a leap into a world of disbelief—in this case, a world in which an ignorant tourist is an honored guest. And if it is less than mentally inhabiting the Irish magical world, then—at the very least—he was a master at practicing the nonjudgmental ideals of modern psychotherapy. For we both left the encounter feeling good about ourselves.

My musings on the Irish character got another workout later on in Galway. On the day of my industrial tour, I was taken to dinner at a rousing restaurant called Paddy Burke's by a local bank manager. He lived in Salthill, in a lovely house, and had three daughters, all studying to be doctors. His house was filled with fine old furniture, he drove a Mercedes, and his wife played golf and shopped frequently in the better stores. Nonetheless, they subscribed to the archaic Irish idea that they were no better off than anyone else.

The drink at Paddy's was ample, as was the food, but, expectedly, the place was not posh. I've been back since and found it a sort of open-collar place that attracts the Irish version of the Yuppie, as well as tourists. The leap to disbelief that worked so well at the car-rental agency, it seems to me, cuts both ways.

Historically, Ireland has been a poor country, at least since the British invasion eight hundred years ago. There's little way around that. It has always had, however, an abundance of natural resources. It is true, not to put too fine a point on it, that the British regarded Ireland as their supply depot. They used its lush forests first for their hunts, taking boatloads of upper-crust English across the water for sport and the pleasure of killing foxes. As Dublin's expatriate genius, Oscar Wilde, put it, they were "the unspeakable in full pursuit of the uneatable." (Amazingly enough, the Galway Blazers Hunt still rides, although now the unspeakable ones are Ireland's own.)

Later, the British cut down Ireland's forests to fuel its own industrial revolution. In 1932, ten years after Irish Independence, the British government imposed a tariff of 40 percent on Irish exports to Britain in retaliation for Ireland's confiscating some still-British lands. This tariff was not repealed until 1938, when, it could be argued, England was in no position to be warring with its nearest neighbor on any account.

The laws enacted in Ireland by the British were intended, always, to keep the nation poor. Regulations that would be today considered unfair trading practices had been carried out by the British against the Irish for hundreds of years.

Silversmithing had been, until late-Georgian times, a proscribed profession for an Irish Catholic; one of my most prized finds is thus an early-Georgian ladle made by Irish hands and, for obvious reasons, not hallmarked. It is utterly lovely in shape and feeling, with a shell bowl and chased handle. But the work itself is crude, that of someone learning the trade that would, along with crystal and lace, later put Irish workmanship into the world's best homes.

The country itself, however, rid of the yoke it had borne since before the Danish invasions, and then the British, is unbelievably rich in natural agricultural abundance. It is warmed by the Gulf Stream, and thus things grow year round. Though it rarely gets really warm, neither does it get below freezing very often. Plants love it. Cows love it. And so do babies, who are born enormous and stay that way as long as they drink the rich, unhomogenized cows' milk and eat the healthful oat porridge that has been a staple of the Irish diet and Irish agriculture since a pre-Celtic people introduced the grain to the island.

However, the Irish had to unite to get their country back, and unite they did. Despite that, they are still a fractious people. The saying goes that if you put two Irishmen together, they won't agree on the time of day. And this may be so. But the time of day is not important. What does matter is that Ireland is eternal. That's why the Troubles that resulted in independence, in 1922, and the troubles with the partition today, while serious, are not fatal.

Why are the Irish more Catholic than the Pope? Not long after the pagan Celts had adopted Christianity, Norman and British invaders began trying to prevent the new religion from growing, preferring allegiance to the invaders' government than to God, or any god. The British, of course, were brutal in their assault on Ireland's Catholicism; they prohibited Catholics from performing many trades and all the professions, and from owning their own land—in short, from living. Indeed, the British are morally responsible for the potato famine's ravages, which killed or caused to emigrate seven million of the country's population of nine million in the 1840s. The British occupation of Ireland, lasting eight hundred years, united the Irish in their Irishness and in their Catholicism. Indeed, it has made them fiercer crossbearers for it, I think, than the free-spirited Irish would ever have become otherwise. Their infinite capacity for melding disparate factors has made them, today, completely religious, but not obnoxiously pious, strong in their own faith, but not strident in proselytizing it. In fact, I can't recall having met a single "Jesus freak" in the whole country.

But the Irish are united, at last, in belief in themselves. Part of the social fabric that upholds this belief is that even the well-to-do regard themselves as average Irish men and women. As they were once lumped all together as "Catholics," they now are all Irish, the difference being that they accept the current label because they awarded it to themselves.

This idea was hard for me to accept. But I was, unwisely, trying to see why the Irish weren't more like us, instead of seeing them as they are. If the bank manager wants to deny his status and his superior lifestyle, so be it. Not a single one of the cottagers I have met is unhappy with his own lifestyle, although there are "begrudgers" around, those who think the "swells" ought to be done away with. Usually, however, these people are themselves misfits in the Irish life fabric and often become criminals or members of the IRA, which are, I've been told, often one and the same.

"Bobby Sands? He was just a t'ug," said a local restaurant owner as we idled for an hour after an excellent meal, on which we had complimented him. "Dey are all t'ugs, if you ask me. Just look at Sands now. He joined the IRA and became a national hero mainly because he couldn't do an honest day's work. He had an arrest record for petty crimes as long as your arm. Becoming a 'revolutionary hero' was a step up for him." I got the gist of his statement, but it was a while before I figured out "t'ugs" meant "thugs." (There's no soft *T* sound in Gaelic. In spite of eight hundred years of the English, it's a rare Irish man or woman to whom this sound comes naturally. In the 1800s, it also was transmuted into Brooklynese: "Da corner of Terty-terd Street," and so on.)

Ireland's great playwright, Sean O'Casey, pointed out this very thing shortly after Independence. In 1926, Dublin's great Abbey Theatre—which has trained so many fine actors, including Milo O'Shea and Geraldine Fitzgerald, for starters—produced *The Plough and the Stars.* In this work, O'Casey suggested that the slum-dwellers of North Dublin were not saints. In fact, they were motivated in their part in the Troubles as much by drink, malice, cowardice, and indolence as by God and dear old Ireland. The reaction to this play—and remember, the playgoers were the Irish "swells," not the slum-dwellers—was outrage.

Galway has the usual entertainments cities anywhere provide. One evening, I decided to try out the movies there, to my delight. They even still show a travelogue before the main feature.

Galway is an old city. During the late twelfth century and early thirteenth, the Normans replaced the Viking hordes as invaders of Ireland. In 1235, they finally crossed the Shannon River and drove northward. All they left to the Gaelic Irish were parts of counties Leitrim and Roscommon. In the Gaelic kingdom of Connaught, they held sway, and built two formidable walled cities, Athenry and Galway. Today, Galway stands as the more important, and impressive, of the two.

But Galway is a city like other cities, in many respects. Like Dayton, it has industry. Like Stamford, it has a suburban life of lunching ladies planning charity fairs and men in pinstripes who go to the office to make money for the lunching ladies and charity fairs.

Galway has, however, eccentrics of every stripe, as well. That's because it has been a seaport for hundreds of years. Christopher Columbus is known to have hired several Irish sailors from Galway before he sailed to find the New World. On any given day, you can find ships from all over Europe in Galway Harbour. And from the swarthy aspect of some of the Galway "Irish," it is clear many Greek, Italian, and Spanish sailors decided to stay after their ships docked.

Although I've seen gypsy children begging or, these days, selling flowers, in Dublin, I've seen more in Galway. On the roads leading to and from the city there are officially overlooked encampments of "travelers," as the caravanserai are called locally. Some are Romany gypsies with dark hair, flashing eyes, and fine horses; others are cut from the usual fabric of Irish cloth, but gone wrong somewhere in the warp or weft. They take easygoing to its zenith; their belief in magic is not only legendary but an operating factor in their daily lives. Even the Irish love of the horse is exaggerated in them. They may own two pans and one pair of shoes and a TV; but they will have horses tethered near their motorized caravans.

I've even had lunch in a shortly thereafter-departed health-food restaurant staffed by a group of Rastafarians who were, indeed, the only black faces I've seen in the whole country, save one busboy at the Shannon Airport Hotel. Near the Spanish Arches that signal the start of the wharf area, where oceangoing freighters are in good supply, there are people from every race. The chandleries and the Customs House all look quite Georgian, as they should. There are no restrictions around the docks, as we are used to. You can walk literally right up to any ship from anywhere, and, I imagine, you could walk off it as well.

As early as 1493, the complexion of Galway was likely to have been vaguely Mediterranean—and this long before the purported "black Irish" descendants of the wrecked Spanish Armada took up residence on Ireland's western coast. At that time, the chief tribe in Galway was the Lynch family. One of them who was mayor in 1493 is supposed to have hanged his son on the current site of St. Nicholas Church, which is near the docks. The son had stabbed a visiting Spaniard, and the father, having pronounced sentence, found no one else would step up to do the dirty deed. (Hence, our American word, "lynching.") At St. Nicholas, too, Christopher Columbus is reputed to have attended Mass.

These days, the dark-haired residents of Galway might well be Oriental. Like Bray, it has a Chinese restaurant, this one on a second floor near the department store Moon's. In it, my mother and I "adopted" a middle-aged Chinese man; he gave us good-luck tokens and a candy and called us Mommy Number One and Mommy Number Two. My mother gave him her address, but he has never shown up to claim his kinship or teach us Chinese cooking, as he promised. I think he got the impression, as the Irish did years ago, that the streets of New York are paved with gold, and he wanted some of it.

Galway is the gateway to Connemara, a region that still retains its wild character, wilder in its way than Wicklow because of its proximity to the sea and its dependence on the Gaelic language. And its poverty.

Connemara does, however, have a rich legacy of song—sea shanties, mainly, because so many of its sons went to sea and were lost there. It has hauntingly beautiful lullabies as well. And it has some tunes that crossed the Atlantic in a changed form. One night at a pub sing, I heard the starting notes to "On Top of Old Smokey," I thought. But it wasn't. It was the far older "Connemara Cradle Song," sung by mothers to babies long before the Smokey Mountains were breached by the first settler. And maybe that first settler was Irish.

At the far end of Connemara is Clifden, a storybook village with a church steeple rising right out of it as you drive down to it from the east. The vista has been used liberally on travel brochures. Unfortunately, Clifden doesn't live up to its looks. A simple market town, it now has small stores, small pubs, small houses—and the large church. It's a supply depot, these days, for youth hostelers who have climbed the nearby Twelve Bens, or are about to. But it isn't notable.

Far more notable is Maam Cross, which is, as its name implies, a crossroads. It's also the site of an annual pony sale. The sale occurs on Halloween, a bank and religious holiday in Ireland. Although I had seen lots of Connemara ponies in fields and on the roads, I wasn't aware of the sale until the end of my journey. Setting out from Galway after breakfast, I had decided to take my mother to Clifden, where she could look out across the sea to America, a substitute for Donegal, which she had missed. But we never got there. And we almost didn't get anywhere else.

We stopped in Oughterard, a lake fisherman's haven on the way, and I noticed, as we pulled away from a shop where my mother had bought some gifts—woolens and pottery—that the car I had hired was misbehaving. But I knew there wouldn't be a garage open, not one to fix a car anyway, even if gas pumps were open. And the problem didn't seem serious; the car was just a bit sluggish.

So we went on toward Clifden. Right after the road sign indicating it was two miles to Maam Cross, however, I saw a huge line of cars parked on both sides of the road. Suddenly there were cars ahead of me, and every now and then a car coming toward me, springing at us, really, as if belched from the throat of a snake.

By now there was also a line of cars behind me, a crush of people walking beside, and no possible way to turn around. I was in a serious traffic jam, the worst I'd ever seen in Ireland. But it amused me, anyway, so I kept on. The car, however, was giving me more trouble. In fact, I had to double-clutch the whole two miles to the center of town—and then things got worse still. I had figured out by then that there was a fair of some sort, even possibly that it was a pony sale, and the Irish are daft for horses, particularly these.

Connemara ponies are sturdy beasts for riding or farm work, and they are prized all over the country. Selling them is big business and great fun if you're in the know and in the mood.

At this point, my mother, unfamiliar with Ireland and never having gotten closer to a horse than a seat at the circus, was beginning to panic. She knew the car was not functioning properly. It didn't help any when an aged crone stuck her toothless face in my window and asked for "a half crown for the Blessed Mother." I gave her a pound note and she toddled off, her putty-colored clothes drooping in the fine mist that had gathered over the road.

Shortly, a policeman on foot came alongside us and motioned that we were to follow him through the crush of children and couples and beggars and ponies and "chips" sellers and beer wagons and, despite the raw day, ice-cream vendors. The double-clutching was becoming a serious problem, both for the car and my ankles. I had decided that, once through, I wouldn't risk the rest of the ride to Clifden or try to go back through Maam Cross, but go on ahead to Recess, where I knew a road over the hills would take us to the Coast Road. That we could follow around the bay back to Galway. It was longer, to be sure, and wilder, but surely shorter than another wade through a sea of humanity and beasts in a dying car.

When we'd gone a quarter mile or so through the throng, the "gard" left, to lead some cars a similar distance in the opposite direction. It appeared he meant to get us head to head.

At any rate, we were stuck again, this time right in front of the path used to take the untamed ponies from the vans in the field to the selling tent in front of the school building.

One high-spirited yearling, which had no doubt been conceived, born, and reared away from humans on one of the pony-filled islands off the coast, flashed his hoofs—mercifully unshod—above the "bonnet." Led across the street by a small lad, he reared up, whinnied, and did a fair imitation of Trigger holding a robber at bay. But the lad got him under control in time. Everything in Ireland, I had begun to think, happens just in time.

But that was not the end. A group of bulls was then let out to cross the road. Each one of them—and there must have been a dozen, all with dripping, flaring nostrils and a yellow eye—weighed more than my Ford Escort rental car. And they certainly had more power than the car did in its diminished condition. To say we were shaken is the literal truth. Besides that, I had to speak very sharply indeed to my mother to calm her.

But soon we were out of it, the bulls having been the worst of the ordeal. The gard had long since disappeared—probably for his tea at one of the stands—but whatever he did worked. No one crashed head to head, and we all, eventually, got through.

The Irish police, the Gardai (pronounced "gar-dee"), don't carry weapons. They no longer ride bicycles, as they did in 1952 when John Wayne's great west-of-Ireland movie, *The Quiet Man,* was made. But often they are, seemingly, just as quaint to us. But they do get the job done. I often think of them as New York cops because so many New York cops are or were Irish. I have seen New York's finest be very gentle with an elderly man who was knocked down by a bicycle messenger—and in the next second deal very harshly with the messenger. The Gardai are much like this, taking time when time is available, taking measures when they're needed. (In Ireland, there is a national police force, as in England, rather than the local police forces of the United States. The full name of Ireland's force is the Garda Siochana. It was founded after Independence in 1922, and was intended to be, and is, an example to the world of a successful unarmed police force.) But the most telling example of the mysterious ways of the Irish police is one I was a part of in Galway when I first arrived.

I was lost, and saw a policeman in the middle of a crush of traffic, so I pulled up next to him and asked him the way.

"Well, you know, I'm not just certain how to get out to Salthill. It seems to me you'll take a right turning off the High Street. Or no. I'm just not certain, do you know, and I think, maybe, will you just go around here and see can you find a petrol station with someone more familiar with Galway. I'm just now posted to Galway, you see. I'm from Portumna," the young gard told us. "Or wait, maybe I do know, now. Wait till I think a bit."

And this he did, with a five-corners blocked in every direction, and me the cause of it. But no one beeped. Eventually he decided he would possibly be telling us wrong, and that we'd better go to the petrol station indeed, and to please enjoy our visit, and forgive him for not being knowledgeable, but we knew, he supposed, how it was to find one's self the first day in a new place, unfamiliar, and he was a country boy and all that.

He was a slight man. He didn't remind me at all of the joke I'd heard about luring Kerry lads down out of the hills with a "lump of raw meat" to become gards. And after all, he was from Portumna, about nineteen miles away from Galway. His new job as a gard was probably the first experience of city life he had had—and he after having a crazy tourist to deal with right away and all.

Out of the throngs at last, we made for the Coast Road. The shortcut I knew of is normally a beautiful road, crossing high up over some minor "bens," or mountains, winding down past gates to neat farms. The road is often littered, it is true, with sheep. Ireland is mostly open range, and you drive such roads at your own peril; should you hit a sheep or other livestock, you will pay for it. The sheep seem to know this, and to know you know it, and have invented a game called "Scare the Tourist." They customarily lie at the side of the road on the verge, not in the tarmac, as it is less comfortable than the grass. But they may have a tiny hoof sticking into the road. Or a whole stupid lamb, ignorant of the rules, will lay itself smack in the middle of a curve. And, once in a long while, a curmudgeonly ram will lie in the road, daring you with his curled horns—and I think a curled lip as well—to hit him. So you stop. You beep. But you don't get out and move him; if you do, he will ram you. But it's fun. There is nothing like it in any other highly civilized place I know, though I'm sure the whole amusement is somewhat vexing to natives driving on their daily business.

I had been over the road before, but this time it contained an unfamiliar pothole. And I hit it. A hundred yards later, the car decided it didn't want to go any farther. We were by then only thirty miles or so from Galway, but we may as well have been in China. I hadn't passed a single car since leaving the pony sale. Everyone was there and would be until dark at least. But I saw a house with a car in front and coasted and coaxed my car into the driveway. I knocked on the door but got no answer. I settled down to await the return of the owner. It was at least eight miles to the nearest crossroads with hope of a phone; when the owner got home, on the other hand, perhaps he or she could call a taxi out from Galway, or drive us in. I'd send the car-rental company after the Ford in the morning.

But my mother, fearing highwaymen and brigands, leaped into the road at the sound of a car approaching from the Galway side. It was an old Corvair, but much bigger than the Escort. Two women and three children were in it. The driver got out, and together we looked at the Escort's engine. No hope. We didn't know one wire from another. She said there was a garage back about eight miles, at the crossroads, and she thought maybe the man would be back from the pony sale by now, so she'd drive us there.

We piled in with the kids, who looked at us with wide eyes. They wouldn't have seen very many Americans in those parts; in Ireland as a whole, scarcely anyone would have seen two women traveling without a man. And my mother's eyes were just as wide. Mine, on the other hand, were drooping with fatigue. The two women began to talk in Gaelic, to each other, and even I was uncomfortable. Not that they were rude: it is impossible, I am convinced, for the Irish to be impolite. It was just easier for them to think in Gaelic; English was their second tongue.

In any case, the man was not home, and, said his wife, not expected for hours. Another quick conference in Gaelic. And not a peep, not a complaint or a request, from the kids the whole time.

"Well, then," said the driver. "We'll just go on back to your car. I'm almost certain the man who lives there is something of a mechanic himself, and we'll see is he home yet. If not, then you'll come on home with us until we can sort things out. But don't worry. We'll not leave you stranded."

Back at the car, our savior said, "I can't imagine why this lady isn't home. It's not likely she'd be at the pony sale. I'll just knock again." And she did, and the lady answered. She'd been home the whole time, but in the back baking bread, and hadn't heard me. She said yes, her husband could likely help us out, but he and the two boys were still at the pony sale. But would we come in and have a cup of tea?

The two ladies drove off, and our new hostess wondered how they knew so much about her, as she didn't know them at all. But then, she was a Returned Yank, an Irishwoman who'd gone to live in Boston, but had come back when she saw her boys could be raised better in Ireland, with no danger of drugs and worse. Because they had been born in America, they were U.S. citizens, and could therefore make up their own minds, when they were grown, about where to live.

Her husband got home remarkably soon—or maybe the tea and conversation were so pleasant that, in Irish style, we didn't notice the time. He went out to the car and in a flash he was back. "It's OK now," he said. "Whoever serviced it last simply hadn't put the spark-plug connectors on tight, and each time you hit a bump, another one flew off. Finally, you got them all. But it'll be all right now."

To the sounds of the telly—the kids, like kids everywhere, had turned it on as soon as they came home—we were off back to Galway, a little later than I'd planned, and a little colder, but with a little more discovery under our belts. Nothing bad ever happens to anyone in Ireland.

The following evening, after a relatively quiet day of shopping in Moon's and at O'Maille's, which specializes in Irish woven and knitted goods, we decided to have a drink at the pub in the hotel.

The landlord's daughter was tending bar, and there was only one other patron, a young man in casual clothes. And he was, casually, quite drunk.

The landlord's daughter asked me how we'd enjoyed our shopping spree, and we made small talk from there. The man asked, "It's from New York you are, are you?" I said I was. "You've a great mayor there," he said. "Ed . . . what's his name now? It'll come to me. Koch. Yes, Ed Koch."

It turned out an interview with Mayor Koch had been picked up by one of the Irish television stations, and he'd been his usual, quick-witted, humorous, irreverent self. All qualities that are greatly appealing to the Irish.

"You know," said my tipsy companion. "I'm afther t'inking he must be Irish."

10 cavan

I visit Cavan, Ireland's lake country, and find cows, fish, dogs, babies, and a white horse. I disbelieve the common wisdom about Ireland's ancient past: I meet professors and vets and hoteliers and singers.

I had been told that County Cavan was a magical place; indeed, I had heard it was like heaven. But often, I discovered, such pronouncements have more to do with what is happening at a given moment in the life of the pronouncer than with the place itself. Still, when I first got to Cavan, I was prepared to believe. It is lush country, in the best Anglo-Irish tradition, with hedgerows, all neat and tidy, rolling hills with fields and white sheep or cows dotting them, and, very often, a blue sky. For Cavan lies one county inland from the Irish Sea and is not, as far as I have ever been able to discover, quite so thoroughly buffeted by the Atlantic weather patterns or storms off the Irish Sea as the rest of the nation. (Drogheda, which I visited from my base in Cavan, is right on the Irish Sea, however; looking out at the waves that kick up in that port, it is easy to see how the Irish Sea claimed so many lives in the calamitous Fastnet Race, the annual sailing race between Dun Laoghaire and England.)

That some "veddy English" charms should linger in Cavan is not surprising. For many years after England first took hold of Ireland, Cavan was the home of some vociferously dissenting Anglo-Irish nobility. Catholics, they were solicitous of the welfare of their native land; royalists, however, they believed Ireland could prosper under the crown. But in 1611, their belief was terminally dashed when Parliament enacted the most onerous acts eroding the rights of Irish Catholics. They left Ireland, did the Earls of Tyrone and Tyrconnell, in what was called the "Flight of the Earls." These earls later were known, in France, as the "Wild Geese."

After their departure, the crown saw a golden opportunity to colonize the area—including the lands the earls left behind—with English and Scots Protestants, and they took it. Over the years, however, the Catholics have returned to ascendance in Cavan. Indeed, on any given Sunday, the Church of Ireland across from my hotel in County Cavan might have only twenty-five attending. But the landscape itself seems to have acquired an irrevocable English tinge—another proof of Ireland as a land of living contrasts.

Cavan's tranquillity was a welcome relief, as was the hotel I stayed in, the Park Hotel, in Virginia, on Lough Ramor. I had an introduction to the owner, Mrs. Helen McDonnell, and was lucky to get two small rooms, one with bath, at short notice during Dublin's Annual Race Week. (Though Dublin is more than a one-hour drive from Virginia, the Park, consisting of an earl's hunting lodge and stables—the latter having been made into self-catering units—is a popular lodging for the week.) The rooms were both charming, decorated individually and personally by Mrs. McDonnell; the lady herself is more charming still.

I left my bags, once again to be taken up by the housekeeping staff when the rooms were ready, and went on a ramble. In the early 1970s, the town of Virginia won the prize in Ireland's Tidy Town contest, and it's easy to see why. So many years later, it is still brightly painted, its main street swept clean as a tin whistle, the park on Lough Ramor kept in fine condition for men, women, children, and dozens and dozens of ducks. And the shopping there, for a tiny town (and not a market town at that), is excellent, having to do, I think, with the attitude of the merchants. I have bought in it French yogurt to soothe a tender tummy, elegant Georgian-style wallpaper for my bedroom at home, and several hundred dollars' worth of silver plate in a Celtic pattern unavailable in any country but Ireland (though the company that makes it does export other wares) and fairly unavailable even in Ireland—because the people prefer the very British Georgian-looking king's pattern, consisting of threading and a shell motif.

The store where I purchased the silver plate caters mainly to the sportfishermen who flock to Lough Ramor. It does a big business, especially in the fine months of sunny May through holiday August, in tackle and lures. But they also carry other "hardware" goods, such as alarm clocks (in fact, it was to replace a broken one that I went into the shop in the first place), pots and pans, and silver plate.

I had admired the pattern in several restaurants and hotel dining rooms and, when I saw it in the little shop, decided to buy a service for eight.

"Would you be wanting the Irish service or the American?" the woman shopkeeper asked me. (Actually, she ran it with her husband; he sold the fishing goods, she the housewares.)

"What's the difference?" I asked.

"Well, in the Irish service, you'd be wanting a fish knife, completely separate from the meat knife, and you'd want a dessert fork. Americans usually don't get the fish knives, nor the dessert spoon, nor the table spoon, which we use as the dessert spoon."

I told her that I was probably neither fish nor fowl myself, and would therefore take the dessert (table) spoons, but not the fish knives. I ended up choosing salad forks (a double number, so I could make them do double duty, in a pinch, as dessert forks or dinner forks for larger crowds), dinner forks and knives, table spoons, soup spoons, and coffee spoons.

"I'm afraid we've not that much stock in the Celtic," she said. "But I'll be glad to order it. How long will you be here?"

When I got around to this, I was only staying one more day, then flying to France on business, and coming back for a couple of days eight days later.

"That's all right, then," she said. "I'll just call them, will I? and have them send it right out. So, 'twill be here for you when you return."

I agreed, and offered a deposit.

"Oh, that won't be needed. I'll just look for you, then, a week from Wednesday, is that it?"

A week from Wednesday I did not return. I had missed a flight and couldn't get back until twenty-four hours later. I kept imagining how an American shopkeeper would have reacted. First, of course, she would not have taken an order, and a several-hundred-dollar one, without a deposit to ensure my return. Second, even if she had, she'd have been cursing me roundly, probably both in and out of earshot, should I ever turn up.

But in Ireland? Not at all. When I finally entered the shop, two days after I was to have arrived, I apologized. "It's no matter," she said. "I knew you'd be back when you got around to it." Of course, maybe she did have some thoughts or words on the subject, but she certainly didn't show them to me.

It helps, when touring any country, to have a pleasant base of operations, rather than pack up and pick up your bags every day or two. I found the Park Hotel convenient for discovering a wide area of Ireland, bounded by County Monaghan and County Fermanagh, Ulster on the north, Drogheda on the east, Navan and the Hill of Tara on the south, and Lough Sheelin on the west.

Lots of other creatures have found it a very congenial watering hole as well. One of these was Henry.

Henry is a basset hound. One evening, as I was taking my dinner early in the elegant peach-and-gold Georgian dining room, the most sorrowful-looking animal I have ever seen ambled up to my table. Instantly a waitress ran to him, shooing him out, but in the most friendly of tones. As I had ordered a cold "starter," which hadn't arrived yet and would wait for me anyway, I followed the dog into the lounge off the lobby, where he had lain down right in the foot traffic to the main desk, but near enough to the roaring fireplace to get warm. Irish dogs are smart.

I sat down with him, petted him, and gave him a piece of buttered roll I had brought from the table. He seemed to like it, but was not overjoyed.

"He really likes chocolate, you see," a voice told me. I looked up to find it was Billy, the combination bellman and barkeep for the hotel. "He often comes to my house at night and beats the door with his tail until I wake up, let him in, and give him a piece of my chocolate. We both love it, you see."

Billy told me the dog's name was Henry, and that he belonged to the new local veterinarian, who lived on the Dublin road.

I didn't see Henry again for the two days before my trip to France. And he wasn't around the hotel when I returned, either. Finally, I talked my husband into looking for him, considering we knew where he lived—approximately—and all.

We drove out the Dublin Road after breakfast one morning, looking for a relatively new house; there weren't all that many, and it was probable the new vet had moved into a new house. When we found a likely candidate, a modern suburban house with the yard landscaping still in progress, a little station wagon in the driveway, and snowy net curtains at the windows, we decided to take a chance.

"Yes, this is where Henry lives," said the petite red-haired woman who answered the door. She said it as if it was every day a couple of Americans pulled into her driveway and inquired after her dog. And she invited us in for morning coffee.

We were led into the kitchen/family room, where her toddler son was playing with his cars and trucks on the floor. "Wait 'til I go see can I fetch Henry," Mrs. Aidan Whelan said. "Did you also want to see Midge?" We hadn't known about Midge, but since I for one have never met a dog I didn't like, I said sure.

I played with the baby, and my husband took his picture. Like all Irish babies, he was huge and healthy and smart. This characteristic of Irish babies may sound like a tall tale, but I believe it is true. I don't think Irish M.D.s have yet started to starve pregnant women and the resulting babies. And I do think the fact that the mothers are healthy and have never heard of Babe Paley's dictum "You can never be too rich or too thin" has much to do with it. Add to that the fact that they are fed on the incredibly rich Irish milk—particularly in the dairy counties—and that legends of giants such as Finn MacCool must have sprung from somewhere, and you have a prescription for big, healthy babies. By the time they are five, however, eating a diet more filled with the usual family fare seems to slow their growth down to a more normal rate.

When Mrs. Whelan returned, dogs in tow, she put on some coffee while we took probably a hundred photos of Henry. We asked, I suppose inevitably, if her husband's veterinary practice, since it was in a rural district, was anything like that of James Herriot in England's Yorkshire Dales, the exploits of which he has chronicled so well in his All Creatures books.

It was, she said. In fact, they'd just recently learned how very much like that it was. Naturally, her husband was desperately busy during the spring lambing season; he was likely to be called out any time of the day or night. And it was hard to get away even to Dublin for a day to shop or go to a movie. So, they had finally installed an answering machine so that they could, at least infrequently, get away for a day together.

"The first time we used it, we had a message on it that set us laughing half the night," she said. "Aidan had put the usual sort of message on it—who he was, when he'd be back, what to do in an emergency, how the caller should leave his own phone number or address, and so on.

"Well, the first message we played back was one of the old farmers, who probably wasn't even certain of how the phone worked. Anyway, when he heard Aidan's voice, he apparently started telling what was wrong with his cow, because he seemed to be in the middle of the long explanation of a bovine malady. Then, he was apparently cut off when the tape ran out. So he called back. 'I'm talking to the vet,' he said. 'Don't be talking back at me now, I'm tellin' ya, I'm talking to the vet.' And again, he went on at this, sounding more and more frustrated about already talking to the vet. He called back a couple more times, with the same routine, until, on his final one, he said a few resounding words and apparently slammed down the receiver."

At that point, the Whelans had decided the time was probably not yet right for an answering machine in rural County Cavan.

With me and Drogheda, it was love at first sight. The town itself is somewhat grimy compared to many small Irish cities. And it seems to know instinctively that it is less important than Dundalk to the north or Dublin to the south. It is, in that trio, the middle child. And, like many middle children, it has been neglected, and worse. The "worse" consists of times it would have been better off neglected, during the Cromwellian era for example, and even further back than that.

In 1348–49, when the Black Death ravaged Europe, both Dublin and Drogheda were almost completely depopulated in the space of a few weeks, despite the fact that Richard FitzRalph, a great scholar and finally Archbishop of Armagh, preached on March 25, 1349, in Drogheda's Carmelite church, that praying to Mary would relieve the populace of its distress.

Later, in 1649, Drogheda would again be subjected to a form of depopulation, on a smaller, but much more pointedly brutal, scale. In that year, Oliver Cromwell brought his Puritan army to Dublin. In his efforts to root out Royalists wherever they lurked, he took especially brutal revenge on the Royalist garrison at Drogheda, and many of the townspeople as well. He chopped off heads with abandon, whether Catholic or Protestant, so long as they were Royalist, and displayed them on pikes around St. Peter's Church for weeks. I'm not superstitious, but if there is such a thing as vibrations from hallowed ground, then Drogheda has them. I passed the church many times, even before knowing about Cromwell's atrocities, and each time my skin crept.

But Drogheda is not all history and horrors. In fact, modern Drogheda is, for an aging industrial and seaport town, quite pleasant. It boasts several department stores and many other smaller shops, a lovely beach, and an Irish-style hotel that, while not grand, has supplied this weary traveler with a multitude of comforts generally called by the name of tea and biscuits. It was, in fact, in the White Horse Hotel that I first understood the restorative powers of a good cup of milky tea.

It was on the day I visited St. Peter's. Still somewhat shaky after my immersion in the less savory parts of history, I was on the lookout for a change of pace. Always a sucker for animals, the drawing of the white horse's head on the hotel marquee was enough for me, and in I went. I was directed to the lounge on the second floor to wait for my tea. It was a sunny, comfortable room with a TV in one corner. No one was in the room that fine August day (there was full sun and it was a Saturday, so what Irish person would waste it?) but me and my husband.

When the tea came, I began to fill my cup, milk to follow. The waitress, seeing my intent, offered to "pour out" for me. This she did: first the milk, then the tea. The brew was much lighter in color than anything I'd ever seen at home. Despite the load of milk, it was still too hot to drink, as the Irish boil the water for tea for many minutes. She added two good-sized lumps of sugar and departed, telling me to be sure to call if we needed more hot water; in Ireland, the tea leaves are left in the pot, and you can add more hot water to them for at least one more tasty pot. And you can do it for free.

There are also monuments in County Cavan and the surrounding area that are not Christian but wildly pre-Christian. Ireland has experienced several waves of immigration, often in the form of subjugation, both before and after the Celts. The first people of Ireland were not the Celts. In fact, the early Irish were a prehistoric band, but they nonetheless seem to have built a substantial civilization.

The first of these people were those who lived in ring forts and crannogs, like those I visited in County Clare. These were a hunter-gatherer people who eventually disappeared from the landscape, archaeologists believe. They had come about 10,000 B.C. By 5,000 B.C., they had begun a munitions factory, Stone-Age style, and were exporting axes to England. By 3,000 B.C., they had built what are generally referred to as megalithic tombs. But this I do not believe they were.

I visited several of these "tombs," huge mounds of earth rising almost like natural hillocks except for their uncanny symmetry.

The Irish government has made some of them, like the extensive one at Newgrange, into permanent guided attractions for the public. Inside Newgrange, which is reached by climbing down a ladder into the chamber, there are several radial hallways and a large central chamber. In the center of the central chamber, there is a very large (more than a meter across) concave stone. Some archaeologists think this was probably an altar; only the chiefs, they say, or other important personages would have rated a burial mound like this one. I do not believe they are tombs. Although charred bones have been found in the chambers in large numbers, I believe that it was a later people who used them for burial sites. I believe they served a dual purpose earlier, or perhaps a triple one, and were used as astrological/religious observatories, astronomical observatories, or defense lookouts.

I've drawn these conclusions because of what I saw in person. For instance, each of the mounds I've been in contained a concave stone, which, fitted with a shiny metal surface—which they knew how to make—would reflect the heavens. It is argued that the mounds are covered now by earth ramparts. But were they always?

Each one had the same symbols on the walls, a sort of double whorl that looks to me very much like a graphic rendering of a spiral nebula, like the Milky Way, for example. It has been suggested that these are actually stylized drawings of a human figure, representing the ancient world's death goddess. That people who could engineer the mounds and learn to plant and harvest by seasons and engage in intercontinental commerce could do no better than two squiggly circles for a human face seems difficult to believe.

Each mound has emplaced about its outside huge boulders, scored deeply in one geographical direction or another, depending on whether the stone is at the north, south, east, or west of the area.

Later people discovered that from each mound, save the ones nearest the ocean, you can see another mound in each compass direction; later people used them as signaling mounts. When the castles were constructed in medieval times, their owners borrowed the principle: each chieftain could see, from his parapets, the castles of his friends or enemies.

The mounds literally cover the central part of the Irish island from shore to shore, basically on a north-northwest to south-

southwest axis. This may have had to do with weather patterns or the tilt of the earth itself.

You can feel the history riding through the valley of the River Boyne, possibly because it cuts through the key to Ireland's past. In a wedge-shaped area bounded by Dundalk, Dublin on the sea, and Mullingar inland, most of the country's invaders, from early continental Celts to Vikings and Danes to Anglo-Saxons and the British, have landed. That is the most hospitable area on the east coast, allowing landing. The wedge itself is one of the few nonmountainous and scarcely boggy areas in the country, allowing easy movement overland. And there are two major rivers, the Boyne and the Liffey, to speed invaders throughout the land.

Aside from military history, however, this area also produced some of the greatest of Ireland's civil heritage, from the Book of Kells to the High Crosses, the highest being at Monasterboice, to the earliest great Irish monastery at Mellifont.

While you'll find no proselytizing in Ireland today, at one time it was, both incoming and outgoing, a grand Irish pastime. Mellifont Abbey, now a stand and rubble of gray stones, was the first outpost, although a grand one, of the Cistercian missionaries from Europe. With them, they brought new ideas of architecture, replacing the small dank churches of the land with huge, airy buildings more fitting for a religion ever more allied, mainly through the efforts of Saint Malachy, with the teachings of Rome. Today, Mellifont is a grand place for a picnic.

Just a bit down the road is the entrance to a national forest, with trails for hiking. And there's the greensward, sheep-dotted, that surrounds the grand home of one of Ireland's best-known scientists and writers. Townley Hall, Dr. Frank Mitchell's home, is a perfectly restored Georgian manor. In it, Mitchell lives with his family and a wonderful Labrador retriever. He writes factual and popular books, such as *The Irish Landscape,* and is the grand old man of Irish scientific letters. He very kindly invited me to tea there, to have a chat about one of Ireland's other legendary beasts, the Irish Elk.

We were served tea in his large, light study, the dog naturally hanging around for a tidbit off the tea tray, if he could get one. Mitchell's study overlooks huge, rolling fields that are among the most historic sites in Ireland. Fields such as these were treasure troves for hunters of antlers. They were probably prized early. In the medieval period, Irish nobles and chieftains hung the huge antlers in the great halls of their castles. Today, splendid examples of the giant deer antlers are on display at the library of Trinity College, where Dr. Mitchell is a professor, and at the Irish Museum of Natural History. Or you can go look for your own antlers and bones. You'd be most likely to find them in huge peat bogs in Counties Limerick and Dublin, about three feet deep below the peat and just above a layer of limestone marl. More likely, you can find antlers in roadside antique stores or in farmyards.

To me, it's no secret why the deer grew so large. Looking out the tall Georgian six-over-six windows across the fields, we saw, as we saw all over the country, herds of monstrous cows, much larger than the same breeds in the United States, grazing contentedly on the rich, succulent grass, cousin to the grass, presumably, that nourished the giant Irish deer.

The evening found us dining with Mrs. McDonnell and headed toward some advertised Irish traditional music in a pub in Ballinagh, a small town nestled north of Virginia, deeper in the Cavan hills and closer to Ulster. When we'd invited her to come along, Mrs. McDonnell told us, with a knowing glance, that she'd pass.

When we reached Ballinagh, it seemed as if the town was battened down for the night. Of all the Irish towns I've been in, at any time of day or night, this one looked most as if someone had hung out a Closed sign. There was no one at all walking about, hardly a car on any street we drove down or crossed, and few lights showing in town-center row-house windows. There was only the faintest smell of turf fires, though it was a chilly night. And it was only by chance that we found the pub, darkened almost totally on the outside. But there were several cars in front of it, and, eventually, we saw two people go in. We did, too.

Once inside, having bought tickets from the most taciturn Irish man I'd met, we did see a room full of people. In fact, we had to cross to the far wall to find two seats together on a bench. Before us was a small, round table—these are everywhere in Ireland—that hadn't been cleaned in a while. The band that had been playing was finished, and the next players, it seemed, had not yet arrived. This was a group effort.

We ordered drinks from the waitress who eventually arrived, just as the band was finally in place and tuning up. Were we imagining things, or were we getting unfriendly stares from the two brawny men at the bar across the room? Must have been imagining it.

We got immersed in the music, played by two young boys and an older man. But between sets, we again had the feeling that we were the recipients of hostile glances from the direction of the bar. Still, we stayed, amused by the antics of a raucous group of French soccer players who had come blundering and blustering in to fill a long table right in front of us. They had apparently lost the match to the local Irish team, for the French were standing the Irish drinks.

A new band played on, and it began to get quite late. This was my last night at the Park, and I wanted to get an early start the next morning. But when I got up to leave, I noticed the brawny men were eyeing me strangely. No, it was not my imagination. They now looked deadly serious about being hostile.

We decided to sit back down, order another drink, and decide whether or not we were going to be followed out and . . . well, who knew what? And why? But then we took a good look at each other. We were dressed not like Americans, in blue jeans or polyester pants suits, but in tweeds, like English tourists. We had, neither of us, an accent broad enough, of any sort, to be taken for Yanks on that account. Clearly, that was it. They thought we were Brits, and, in this touchy border area, had decided to give us a bit of a fright.

When the waitress came, we not only ordered, we asked her if she had ever been to New York, making up some tale about having seen a young woman who looked like her near our house. We thought she might report this at the bar. And indeed she did. When she returned with our drinks, we noticed "the boys" were no longer staring at us, so shortly we left.

This was the first time I'd had the least unfriendly feeling in Ireland. But this was a border town; it was hard to know who your friends were, I suppose, and that might explain the extreme wariness to welcome strangers, especially those who look like a former adversary—or current adversary, to some. And it was a rough sort of a pub, not the kind of place most British or American tourists, or any other tourists, might go. It was not, probably, even a place a well-bred, upper-class Irish Catholic like Mrs. McDonnell would be likely to go. It was, in short, a haven for what my Irish-Yank friend back home calls the "begrudgers," those few Irish who are, like a few everywhere, ne'er-do-wells with a yen to pin it on someone.

The greatest danger in County Cavan is from something far smaller and far simpler than "the boys" or adolescent bulls. The greatest danger is Cavan disease.

This disease is likely to strike susceptible people within half a day of their arrival in Cavan. The first time I stayed there, I spent the Sunday morning after my arrival in the Church of Ireland across the road, praying, first, that I would somehow live through the sermon and, second, that I would live through the rest of the trip.

Mind you, I wasn't deathly ill; Cavan disease is not a pox or a plague, and if I had a fever, it wasn't much. No, Cavan disease is the Irish version of "tourista." But, like everything Irish, it has its own vagaries. For example, it lays me low for a day or two, then passes. It never hits my husband at all. My mother developed a touch of it, though she had, I think, been practicing the precautions I had developed to cope with it. If she hadn't, it might have been worse.

What are these precautions? Let's just say they're typically Irish preventive medicine. I refuse to take any water to which a healthy dose of spirits has not been added. I won't even brush my teeth in the clear stuff. Of course, mint-flavored toothpaste isn't the biggest taste treat rinsed with weak Jameson's water. But it's effective. The tea and coffee are all right, too, because the Irish boil the water so hot for it.

Mental research has finally led me to a conclusion about Cavan disease. I recalled that several years ago, I caught a similar malady after having a glass of water at a friend's new house—built on a floodplain near Boulder, Colorado. The plain had until recently been a dairy farm. Aha! *E coli.* bacteria, a famed by-product of cows.

Now, it is true that all of Ireland is a cow pasture, very near. But in Cavan, specifically in Virginia, there is a large lake—Lough Ramor—draining the farms around it and, for all I know, used for drinking water in the neighborhood. Or, if it's not, by now the bacteria have thoroughly infested the groundwater, I should think, as they had in Colorado. I could just imagine all those little whip-tailed thingies happily swimming in the cold clear water, munching on the highly nutritious diet all those cows provide.

But Cavan disease is, as I said, manageable. And many never get it at all. I certainly haven't seen it written up in the medical journals. But it's no figment of my imagination, either, of that I am absolutely, abundantly sure. Nonetheless, Cavan is a fine and wondrous place, and a few microbes will hardly stop me from returning. But, rest assured, I'll have a flask along.

11. Ulster

I enter Northern Ireland, still England's only frontier. I learn more of Saint Patrick, see prosperous farms and bombed-out cities. I meet a soldier, and a woman writer long dead. I satisfy a longing in Carrickfergus.

The road from the safety of County Cavan and the fastness of Cavan Town, with its auto dealerships, its farm market days, its many well-trained gards, took me quickly to the border of the Republic of Ireland and its neighbor/cousin/enemy, the North. Also called Ulster, the six counties that make up the British territory of Northern Ireland are merely part of what was, throughout history, the ancient Irish province of Ulster. When partition arrived in 1922, Counties Donegal, Cavan, and Monaghan elected to join the Republic (actually, its forerunner, the Irish Free State). Fermanagh, Tyrone, Derry, Antrim, Down, and Armagh elected to remain allied to Great Britain. But there are Gaels there, and there are places dear to the hearts of Celtophiles. And it is impossible to write about the Republic of Ireland without also discussing the North. So, I had to go.

I wasn't frightened. I knew that the danger existed only in circumscribed locations, for all that American TV and print journalism blew it out of proportion. I would not be dodging bullets or putting life and limb in the way of any plastic explosives—or even a crude car bomb—as long as I simply followed the rules.

What were the rules? These rules were given to me by an Irishman with family and business in the North, although he spent most of his time in the Republic. And, they seemed to me as reasonable and sensible as the rules followed by New Yorkers or Chicagoans or experienced inhabitants of any major—and therefore troubled—city in the United States. The first and foremost rule is: Don't go into downtown Belfast—or Derry or Newry—at night. Second, when stopping for food and petrol, I was to make sure I or my companion stayed with the car. Sometimes extremists of either side, seeing the Republic's license plates and the rental status of a car, will steal it and then blow it up either for practice or to stop the "other side" from getting new supplies; such supplies often travel with mock tourists in rented cars.

With that in mind, I entered Fermanagh from Clones. I had a full tank of gas, but I stopped in the first grocery store I found for some food for lunch—cheese, an apple, a Cadbury bar, and a "mineral," or soda. For the next few miles, I was back and forth across the border several times. I knew this from the bright yellow lines painted on the roads. And then I was firmly back in the Republic again, coming into Monaghan. Beyond it, at Middletown, I crossed the border for once and all on my way to Armagh.

As Kilkenny is black and gray, Armagh is red. It, too, is built of local marble. Armagh is the rock on which Saint Patrick built his Christian church in Ireland. Unfortunately, its Catholic cathedral is as ugly today as when Morton found it. Its Protestant one, small and of red sandstone, is nonetheless a spiritual home of much repute, holding a special place in the heart of he who is Archbishop of Canterbury. The city itself still boasts the peacefulness Morton found there.

It is a shame this heritage is not better recalled now. On every spare wall in the meaner parts of Irish cities, both north and south, the single graffito "Provos Rule" is splashed in yellow spray paint. The Provos were formed in January 1970, after a split in the Irish Republican Army (which is not *Ireland's* army, but a radical paramilitary group that has dedicated itself to uniting Ireland; it is banned in both the North and the South). The "Official" IRA, as the original band was subsequently called, favored emphasis on political agitation. The Provos (short for Provisionals) favor terrorism. Indeed, I believe I had a run-in with them—or their fellow travelers—during the late 1970s during a business stopover in Dublin on my way to the continent.

I was staying at Jury's in Ballsbridge, a very upscale part of the city. The hotel itself caters both to business people and tourists. One evening after dinner, I was summoned by a knock on the door; the "girl" asked me to please come as quickly as I could to the main lobby. The hotel had had a bomb threat.

I did as I was bidden, joining other guests, soon joined by still more. We sat and waited. Next to me on the sofa were two rather scruffy young men. As the hours passed, for the hotel was being searched rather thoroughly by the Army (*the* army of the Republic) and the Garda Siochana, we began to chat. The two were a bit tipsy and launched into a diatribe about how awful the hotel was, making us all wait like that. But I had begun to suspect they were not hotel guests. They were Irish, for one thing, and all the other Irish people staying there were business types. These men, little more than boys, were too young—and too badly dressed. They spoke like laborers.

Finally, there was an announcement that we could return to our rooms. As I got up to leave, one of the boys handed me a postcard, an antique one of pre-Revolutionary Dublin. I had the sense, instantly and overpoweringly, that the two boys had had something to do with the bomb scare. Maybe they were trying out for the Provos. Maybe they just had big ideas. Maybe they were drunk or crazy, or all of the above. I no longer have the postcard. Indeed, no one does. When I got back, trembling, to my room, I destroyed it and threw the tiny pieces out the window. Possibly, I later thought, I should have given it to the police. Possibly, I should have made better note of what the two youths looked like and discussed the whole thing with an official of some sort. But the denouement had happened in a flash, and I was a weary traveler who wasn't thinking quite straight. Until the moment he handed me the card, I had assumed the two boys had just been having a pint in the hotel's pub and had toddled along to the lobby so as not to miss the excitement.

Armagh did not offer me any similar excitement; nor did my next stop, Newry. I didn't linger long enough to find out. Of all the border towns in Northern Ireland, during my visit Newry was the Duke of Devastation. People I spoke with in Dundalk reported that they could often hear firing at night; there were constant skirmishes reported in the newspapers. No, indeed, I decided to go on, through Belfast as fast as possible, to the single place in Ulster I really wanted to see—Carrickfergus.

Carrickfergus was, before the Protestant Plantation, the only real town in Ulster, and thus has the longest inhabited history. It is also the subject of a beautiful piece of music by the Chieftains. It was that piece of music that made me want to explore Carrickfergus at all. In "Carrickfergus," the harp is ascendant, conjuring up the human voice better than a human could. The harp is played by Derek Bell, the only member of the Chieftains, fittingly, from Ulster.

Morton pointed out that Ulster is very Scottish. How could it be otherwise? For the Protestant Plantation was the planned migration of Protestant Scots to Irish soil, a "plantation" of King James readers in a papist field. They flowered and flourished. But in Carrickfergus, the connection is taken even further back. (Mind, now, all the current commotion is a matter of religion alone, or almost; both ancient Scots and ancient Irish were Gaels, and the ancient tongues are similar.) Carrickfergus takes its name from Fergus, who foundered off this point on one of his journeys between Antrim and Scotland. The ancient kings of Scotland were descended from his line. As they have long been subsumed into the royal line of England, it might fairly be said that Queen Elizabeth could trace her forebears to Ireland, and thus she is a product of it, and not it a product of the English royal house. There is today in Westminster Abbey, in fact, a red marble stone said to have been brought by Fergus from Ireland for his coronation. All this connection and counterconnection makes one wonder about the troublemakers. Today's political separation is significant, but not mortal unless it is made so. It is hard to understand how people who are one under the skin, no matter what is written on parchment, can make so much trouble for each other.

Since Morton's visit, right after the creation of the Irish Free State, north and south have diverged more sharply, obviously and sadly, especially in the years since the Cold War, when, it can be reasonably argued, provocateurs from the Eastern bloc began to foster unrest. What makes it all the more devastating is that the years have given the population even more time to meld into one.

The Ulsterman is Irish, but not, perhaps, the same sort of Irish as his half-brothers to the south. I don't think, for example, that the United States and Canada should be a single nation—but then, we never were. Nor was Ireland, except under British domination. The six provinces were sovereign throughout history, except when briefly united by a forceful and charismatic leader like Brian Boru. There is nothing that makes me think the north and south of Ireland should be united again. The Roman Catholics are a minority in Northern Ireland, to be sure. And there's little doubt they've been oppressed. I was shocked, driving through the cities, to see Catholic areas cordoned off with wire fences, although this is now as much for their protection as internment, it is said. But other countries have accepted partition: we no longer own parts of Mexico, though there are certainly Spanish descendants on both sides of the border. And in Ireland, the dispute isn't so much a national one as a religious one, with the Protestants stiff-necked and Calvinist about it all, the Catholics claiming a divine right to be united with the south.

But things change, given time. Today, there are reconciliation centers in the Republic of Ireland meant to teach the young people that living peaceably together is possible. It may be too little and much too late. But swords have been turned to plowshares before.

Carrickfergus Castle, militarily occupied for seven and a half centuries since it was built in 1180, is one such, having turned the other cheek and become a museum in 1928.

I stayed that night in a good hotel near Carrickfergus. And I found two things. The breakfast menu on the morn was larger than those common in the Republic, and more English. And the people were not as friendly.

In Doolin's little art shop, I had picked up a book to read as I went along: *Penelope's Irish Experiences.* Its author, Kate Douglas Wiggin, was an oddity for 1901 when the book was published—a travel writer of some international repute. She had also written *Penelope's Experiences in Scotland, Penelope's English Experiences,* and *A Summer in a Canyon,* about California. She wrote novels as well. And she had found, as I had, an extensive breakfast menu, although hers was in Belfast. In fact, it was almost exactly the copy of mine—eighty-four years later.

> How the long breakfast bill at an up-to-date Belfast hostelry awed us, after weeks of bacon and eggs! The viands on the menu swam together before our dazed eyes.
>
> Porridge
> Fillets of Plaice
> Whiting
> Fried Sole
> Savoury Omelet
> Kidneys and Bacon
> Cold Meats.
>
> I looked at this array like one in a dream, realising that I had lost the power of selection, and remembering the scientific fact that

> unused faculties perish for want of exercise. The man who was serving us rattled his tray, shifted his weight wearily from one foot to the other and cleared his throat suggestively; until at last I said hastily, "Bacon and eggs, please," and Salemina, the most critical person in the party, murmured, "The same."

Unlike Mrs. Wiggin, I found the extensive menu presented me no problem. Of course I would have bacon and eggs! There is no bacon like Irish bacon; the rest of the menu I could have anywhere. Fortified, I set off for Derry, around the far northern coast of Ireland, long considered through historical experience by the Anglo-Irish Protestants to be the last outpost against the Gael, and today a troubled city on the border. This promised a long day's drive, and I intended to be in Donegal by bedtime.

The Coast Road follows a series of bays, but ones so wide that the view is really to the North Channel. In summer, it is not too gray and nasty. And I did have another sunny day. They were becoming prized.

I decided on only two stops on the way, one to eat lunch and view Rathlin Island and one at the Giant's Causeway, which Morton had thoroughly enjoyed. The coast along this road gives the feeling much more than most of Ireland's volcanic geology. There is, not far off the road, a volcanic plug, the earth that once surrounded it all worn away. The Celts believed it was a fairy mound, and I can't say I disagree. The glens around it glowed magically in the sunlight as I passed.

Further on, I paused at Torr Head, a commanding promontory into the North Channel with a view directly toward Scotland. Hereabouts, until sixty-five years ago or so, the inhabitants spoke Gaelic, like so many coastal people in the south. But it was Scots Gaelic they uttered, not Irish.

The next headland, Fair Head, offered me a view of Rathlin Island, and a car park where I could break my bread, cleave my cheese, and shatter my block of chocolate. In legend, the island was a stepping-stone created by the mother of Finn MacCool as she crossed to Scotland to bring her son some whiskey. Later, a real-life knight, Robert the Bruce, took refuge in one of its caves. I can't imagine how so many people, real and imaginary, reached the place. A boat to it leaves only every hour or so, if you're lucky and the water is calm.

The Giant's Causeway is far easier to see. In Morton's day, photos of it were probably the most common Irish photos around. Today, I'd say that honor goes to Bunratty Castle. So I hadn't the fear of the mundane to cope with the way Morton had. And, though small in area, the Causeway is magnificent in its oddity.

The Giant's Causeway appeared to me like surrealist cubes, stood on end as if they were models for a giant city of skyscrapers. Gray, steely, and basaltic, these rocks are further evidence of the vulcanism that created this greenest of all lands from the reddest of all substances, molten lava.

Starting from here is the "Armada" coast, all the way round the eastern part of Ireland and south to Cork. The "black Irish"—the blue-eyed Irish with black hair and freckles, not the brown-haired, brown-eyed, light-skinned Irish—are said to be descended from Spaniards who landed on the shores when the storm broke up the Armada fleet in 1588.

I had not spent nearly as much time in Ulster as Morton had. And I had found it a lot less charming. But then, he was English and Ulster then was more English and less war-torn than it is now. I was glad to be headed toward Derry and then back into the Republic.

Near Derry, the countryside looks very English indeed, with the whitewash of the Irish farms giving way to the red or gray paint of the English, even more so than in the Cork area, which I think—at least in the rural places—looks quite annoyingly English. Perhaps that is why tourists like it; it looks like movie films they've seen of "the British Isles." But back to Derry.

The land looked prosperous, certainly more so than around the coast, and more so than much of the Republic. But I was in for a shock in Derry.

The road led me to the first roadblock I had ever seen. The first, that is, surrounded by gun turrets and bunkers. Such exist also in Belfast, Newry, and Strabane, but I had avoided them by traveling the rural roads and visiting smaller towns. But Derry was a seat of some great degree of unrest.

The soldier manning the gate could not have been more than nineteen or twenty years old. He had the pink, fresh skin of a teenager, and he was very polite and smiling. But the rest of him, covered in camouflage khaki, was, unfortunately, all military, as was the automatic weapon he carried.

At the direction of the soldier manning the gate, I stopped my car. "Open the bonnet [hood] and the boot [trunk] please," he commanded.

I handed him the keys, which he passed to another soldier, to open the boot. They rifled only lightly through my luggage.

I looked and looked inside the car, and couldn't find the bonnet latch. The soldier looked impatient. So did the driver of the car behind me; I had glanced at him in the mirror.

"I'm sorry. It's a rented car and I haven't had to open the bonnet yet. I can't find the latch," I told him. I had turned in my previous rented car in favor of something larger.

"Right then," he said. "Would you mind moving over to the passenger side a moment."

Although it was phrased politely, as a question, the soldier was making a statement. I complied, and quickly. I slid ungracefully over the gearshift. And the soldier, automatic rifle and all, got in beside me.

He simply reached under the dash and pulled the bonnet latch—which was exactly opposite where I'd expected it to be. Left-side driving, right-side latch. Simple. There were no sticks of dynamite taped to my engine. Shortly, I was waved on.

Once in Derry, I knew what Dresden must have looked like after the war. Whole streets contained nothing but blackened hulls of houses and shops. Other streets had gaping black holes between still-used houses, like ugly cavities in a row of teeth. Few people walked about, although I passed a priest walking his dog. I was on the route through the city, though, not into it, so I didn't expect to see the main shopping thoroughfare or the nicer neighborhoods.

My map directed me up one street I couldn't use. There was a policeman inexplicably guiding people away from entering it. "I don't know my way around," I shouted to him. "How can I get back on the route to Rathmullan?"

"I don't know," he snapped. "But you can't drive through here."

Great. Lost in an erupting metropolis. I would have to find my own way, and it was getting dark. Logically, I should be able to drive parallel to the way I wanted to go, and eventually cross the road I wanted to turn onto anyway. But this was—sort of—Ireland, where little is as it seems and there's no such thing as a straight line, let alone a parallel street. Ah, but this was Ulster. And there *was* a parallel street.

I crossed over the River Foyle at a very famous site. There, the Irish Catholics, fighting to restore James to the throne of England, laid siege to the Derry Protestants (who still label Derry as *Londonderry* on their maps), and stretched enormous chains and booms across the river to prevent a relief fleet from sailing up the river and rescuing the beleaguered walled city.

The Siege of Derry in early 1690 was a terrible experience for the Ulster Protestants. They had offered resistance to James's armies in the north, and the Irish army had encircled Derry, cutting off all food and supplies. At the time, most of the city was on an island in the river. The siege dragged on for three months. The food supplies were quickly exhausted and the inhabitants ate anything they could find—domestic pets, rats, birds, and so forth. And the besieging army kept up a steady barrage of cannons against the walls, killing and wounding many, and starting fires around the city. But the Ulster Protestants held on, and an English fleet relieved them, finally, driving away the Irish army.

The Ulstermen soon thereafter also defeated the Irish army at the Battle of Enniskillen, once and for all destroying the Catholic Irish domination of the province of Ulster. Of course, in battles at Aughrim and at the Protestant siege of Limerick, William and Mary's armies defeated James again, destroying the freedom of the Catholic Irish until the emancipation laws of the mid-nineteenth century and, more basically, until the founding of the Irish Free State in 1922.

I tell the story of the Siege of Derry not for its importance as a battle but for its importance as a modern symbol. The "Orangemen" of Derry still celebrate—seriously, not exuberantly as we celebrate St. Patrick's Day—their victory at Derry, and the victory of William and Mary over James. This is hard for Americans to understand—the incredibly long and often bitter memories carried in the Irish bosom, both North and South. It's far different from our feelings about Yankees and Rebels of the Civil War.

Derry is also where the most recent Troubles began in 1972. According to the Catholic viewpoint, the trouble was caused because of a Protestant refusal to enfranchise the Catholics in Derry. It appears that since William's victory, the Protestants had gerrymandered voting privileges in Derry to favor themselves and disenfranchise Catholics. Or, at least, they had so weighted the Catholics' voting power that they could never gain even proportional representation on the Derry Town Council. During the late

1960s and early 1970s, a Catholic drive to gain full voting rights and rescind the seventeenth-century voting method was undercut. After this, violence broke out, and the situation has worsened continually to this day.

Truly, in Ireland's case, the sins of the fathers are visited upon their sons and their sons' sons many generations later. Nor are the sons themselves blameless.

Today these events seem to me to be modern excuses to overturn a separation between North and South that not many people, except the Catholics in Northern Ireland, really want to end. I told a prominent and well-informed person in the Republic that I thought no political leader in the South could possibly want to reunify the North and the South. Consider the situation: The Republic's population of 3.5 million people, almost 99 percent of whom are Catholic, is a homogenous group hard for an American, used to the melting pot, to imagine. Why, I pondered, would political leaders in the South want to disturb this status quo by mixing more than 1.1 million Protestants into the situation? Even today, more than sixty years after the establishment of the Irish Free State, the few Protestants in the South still tend to hold the best jobs, control the most businesses, graduate from the best schools, etc. Yet they have little political power. But, adding a million Protestants to the population of the Republic would give the Protestants at least one-quarter representation in the Irish Dail (or parliament) and dramatically increase their influence on national social, economic, and political policy—beyond the influence they have now as well-heeled and industrious inheritors of the Ascendancy, the Anglo-Irish aristocracy. These influences are exactly what the leaders in the South have been trying to reduce or avoid since Irish independence. It would seem to me the Republic's leadership has a strong vested interest in maintaining the division between the two. It is a division of religious and economic interests that have had ample time and space to solidify since they emerged clearly in 1690.

The authority with whom I spoke at first disagreed with me, but ended our conversation by saying, in different terms, what I had maintained all along: there is little for the Republic to gain by an actual, political reunification, but much to be gained by *seeming* to want it.

The demand for Irish unification, the violence, the political maneuvers, and the involvement of ill-informed and naive Americans continue. These same "patriots," who would be the first to cry foul if they believed outside agents were fomenting riots in their home, feel free to send arms and money to buy arms to factions in Northern Ireland. Despite them—and more bitterly because of them—the division between North and South, for all the diverse reasons, is likely to continue for many years to come. But, it can be sincerely hoped, a peaceful solution, perhaps in the form of a confederation, can be found.

With these serious thoughts in mind, and only minutes lost, I was back on my way out of Derry. Shortly, I was on the far side of the River Foyle. From the top of one of the many hills that surround Derry, I looked back at the city. I saw the modern bridge that links Catholic Derry—on the west side—and Protestant Londonderry—on the east side. I saw the walls of Derry, and it seemed still to look like the fortified town that James and William had fought over so long ago. The palpable taste and feel of history that pervades Ireland was never so firmly lodged in me as then. Nor was the intense sadness wrung from a thousand million tears. As I turned to seek happiness again in the Republic—in the form of a good dinner and a warm hotel, and maybe some good "crack" (fun) with its irrepressible natives—I wished them all equal fortune in finding a comforting solution to their problems, ones so much greater than my own.

12. Donegal

I meet an old woman and find the home of my forebears. I walk on the ocean floor. I find out much about the pace of life in the far north of the Republic of Ireland. I spend time in the IRA's reputed holiday haunt and learn about the Irish viewpoint from a student.

When you enter Donegal in the Republic of Ireland from Ulster, you owe it to yourself to go the long way round Lough Swilly if you intend, as I did, to make the whole circuit of Donegal. In any case, Lough Swilly is not a place you'd want to miss. For starters, there are the hayricks. While the rest of Ireland's farmers stack their hay in the familiar round-topped piles, those on Lough Swilly build conical shapes with tufted heads, looking almost like straw tepees. Why? No reason, except that's the way they've always done it, I was told. Or it may have to do with the character of Lough Swilly itself. While Ireland consists of rolling hills, and even the "bens" do not sport the ragged peaks of European mountains, Lough Swilly is, properly speaking, a fjord.

Like its Scandinavian cousins, it boasts the wild differences between low and high tides. In Gaelic, its name is Loch Suilagh, which translates to "Lake of the Eddies." Of course, as a finger of the ocean, it is not a lake at all. The lough cuts into the coast of Donegal for a good thirty miles or more, and has been the site of a good bit of the world's history, despite its location at the top of the inhabitable world. It was, in 1607, the place from which the Earls of Tyrconnell and Tyrone began their Flight of the Earls to France. During World War I, it harbored modern fighting fleets. Today, it is the site, say local people, of much coming and going of both smugglers and "the boys," the IRA, to and from Ulster, and points east. The lough has been called the Lake of the Shadows, and indeed, that's an apt description on two counts. The shadows of war have fallen, and still fall, over its becalmed waters. And the Knockalla Mountains, which border the lough on the west, keep much of its depths in shadow; the sun, veiled by scudding clouds looking for dockage over the sheltered plain at the lough's head, provides an ever-changing pattern of light and shade.

I entered the Lough Swilly region after lunchtime, through the sizable town of Letterkenny. Not wanting to get involved with city streets, I followed the signs through it to Ramelton. There, on the shores of Lough Swilly, perched on an arm that reaches a couple of miles inland from the major lough, is a perfectly sleepy, perfectly Georgian village. Coming down into it from the hills, I passed a number of in-town farms, a modern Catholic school, and several suburban houses before reaching the town center. Taking a right turn, down farther toward the water, I spied a hand-lettered sign for "Teas" placed between the steps and the curb in front of a Georgian row house.

Ramelton is still much as it was in Stewart times, when it was built as a plantation; the residents of the town supplied the fighting men to keep the native Irish at bay.

On entering the main floor of the row house, up a small flight of steps, I saw nothing but empty rooms. But I heard voices coming from below, and headed toward the interior stairs. When I'd got my bearings, I smelled, in any case, a turf fire and freshly baked pastry.

Belowstairs were two small rooms, looking on the back garden of the house and over the black mud flats of the lough; it was low tide. The two rooms contained perhaps a dozen mixed (round and square, large and small) tables, all covered with oil cloth in different patterns. There was no one there but me, and a girl who was tending the turf fire and was not very practiced at it. In fact, as I sat down, I was aware of the chill in the room; the doors and windows were all open, to clear the smoke.

"I'm sorry for the smoke," the girl told me when she took my order for a jam tart and tea. "I'm not used to this chimney. But when Mary gets back, she'll get it working right, and then we can shut things up again and take the chill off."

Until that moment, I'd honestly never noticed a chilly Irish person, although, by our standards, all Irish buildings are chilly. But that girl was cold—bare-legged and blue, in fact. The bare-legged part was not unusual: except in the cities, young Irish women often go about without hosiery. In the days when H. V. Morton visited Ireland, he often found the women entirely barefoot, trotting behind their livestock on a summer's morning. Remember that in Ireland, a summer's morning is likely to be no more than 60°F, and, since the ground has not been truly and deeply warmed in historic times, the tender feet are contacting an age-old coldness. Of course, Ireland was still quite a poor country during Morton's time. Today, it's not because they can't afford hosiery that the girls don't wear it. It's either adherence to long tradition or the Irish habit of paring things to their most simple. These same girls were bare-legged, with white socks only, while they were in school, and may see no practical reason to cover their legs now. Still, the whole practice has made me decidedly chilly just to look at them.

Shortly, Mary returned, fixed the fire, and apologized to me, in case I'd been uncomfortable. We fell into conversation, and she told me that the tea shop had been opened to fund some of the restoration of the house, one of the only remaining Georgian row houses in all of Donegal. The undertaking had local roots, but was sponsored in part by the Irish Georgian Society. Hearing that I was both an overseas member of the Society and a friend of its founder, the Honourable Desmond Guinness, Mary offered to take me on a tour of the uncompleted restoration, and I gleefully accepted.

We went first to the topmost floor. Here, the rooms had sloping ceilings, following the pitch of the roof, and tiny windows. They would have been for servants, said Mary. None of these rooms had a fireplace.

On the floor below, there were the family bedrooms, of pleasant proportions and with large six-over-six windows. Although there would not have been indoor plumbing as we know it, there had been a room for bathing; this was not being restored, but rather refurbished as a modern lavatory for site workers and visitors to the house. The bedrooms, of course, would be restored, as would the landing, which had a charming and, said Mary, unusual octagonal window looking out on the harbor.

The main floor was to be restored partially, and partially used as an art gallery and gift shop. The ground floor, now the tea room, would still be a tea room, although it would be fitted out as the Georgian kitchen it once was, with the modern cooking facilities and so on in an alcove.

An historic home in the United States would not be opened, as this one was, before it was complete. We would think it unseemly, wanting everything to be presented to us in a Madison Avenue gloss condition. This may be because we are so new, as a people, and even our oldest buildings are newer than a great portion of Ireland's housing stock. But I found the tea shop, smoky turf and all, charming. And I can't think when I've been more interested in an historic house tour than I was when Mary took me around the Georgian house in Ramelton. It had been a very personal visit. She had seen my interest in the house, more than she'd perhaps seen from other visitors, and responded to it in a typically personal, typically Irish way. She hadn't planned to interest me. She had no set patter to give me. She had instead her intelligence, her enthusiasm, and the polite ways so native to the Irish.

In Ireland, one often gets filled up spiritually along with the tea and scones. In a previous chapter, I explored the Irish attitude toward dieting. I think, now, I left something out. All the American diet advice I have read lately advises paying attention to one's food, savoring the experience of eating in and of itself, leaving the TV and books and magazines aside while dining. In Ireland, there is an abundance of natural spirit fodder, it seems to me, that goes with eating. The restaurant, or the view, or the conversation you have with a new acquaintance (or friend) in the lounge beforehand, or the smell of the turf fire, or the sea air, or the cheap and good and ample serving of sherry, or the fresh beauty of the waitress—any of these may restore the soul as well as the bloodstream.

We went on to Rathmullen, to the Rathmullen House, a fine hotel in the European tradition, and one of only four in Ireland listed in the French guide *Hotel et Relais*. But it is indeed justly listed. Sitting on a bluff overlooking Lough Swilly, it is a thoroughly modernized late-Georgian structure. Each bedroom is decorated differently. Mine was papered in light yellow and had a charming entryway, with multitudes of closets, and a huge windowed bathroom, with the ubiquitous KangoLine. Found in almost any good Irish hotel, KangoLines are spring-wound lines tucked in a box above the tub. At the far end of the tub is a hook. By stretching the line, you can rig a perfectly useful instant clothesline and wash out your "personals" if you've not time to wait for the hotel laundry, or just if you want to.

Another prevalent Irish hotel amenity is the heated towel bar. I'm not sure if these were invented in the name of luxury or self-defense in a cold, wet climate. But either way, I learned to love them. These towel bars are nothing more than chrome piping fitted to the hot water system. When you turn on the hot-water tap in the tub, it runs first through the towel bar, heating it and the towels on it. When you've used the towel, the remaining heat in the metal helps it dry. This seems like a minor thing, but when one is traveling, the delight of the experience, I have often found, is built on a series of small miracles like these.

The following morning, I decided it was time to cash another draft, and thought the best place would be at the bank in Letterkenny. So we drove back down the road.

The night before, I had again been reading, with growing pleasure, the quaint book I had picked up in the strange little shop in Doolin, the book called *Penelope's Irish Experience*, by Kate Douglas Wiggin. Published in 1901 by Gay and Bird, London, it is the chronicle of an English upper-middle-class woman's travels. At that time, before Ireland's independence, it was common for the English to look upon the Irish as slightly quaint; today, some English, particularly those landed in America and influenced by our press, look upon at least some of the Irish as highly dangerous. Neither case is, or was, true.

Nonetheless, "Penelope" did make some observations about the Irish character, though she misinterpreted them, that are as true today as they were then. One of these is what she calls "the precise moment of working." Particularly, she had been discussing road-repair crews, which, then as now, tend to follow this routine:

9:30 A.M.—arrival at job site
9:35 to 11 A.M.—discuss how best to perform job
11 A.M.—have tea
11:45 A.M.—call engineer to approve plan for doing job
12:00—the Precise Moment of Working
12:10 P.M.—find a problem and discuss progress until lunch
1 P.M.—Lunch
2:15 P.M.—discuss solution to problem
3 P.M.—the Precise Moment of Working
3:15 P.M.—stop in order to plan tomorrow's progress

4 P.M.—have tea
4:45 P.M.—begin putting up tools in order to leave on time
5:30 P.M.—go home

In all my traveling around the country, I had indeed seen road crews adhering to many parts of this schedule. Of course, this also applies to road crews in the United States, with the specific times altered to fit our Protestant work ethic of "early to rise" and so forth. But, I had never seen the Precise Moment of Working in Ireland until Letterkenny. And what a thrill. Another small miracle.

The bank in Letterkenny was a small miracle itself, as well. While Irish banks are used to cashing traveler's checks for Americans, they are not used to doing what I requested: I wanted to write a check on my bank in New York and have them convert the dollars to pounds, giving me the cash.

I truly believe there is not another foreign country in the world where such a risky transaction would even be considered. But the Irish have their own ways to accommodate, and to minimize the risk as well.

I was sent by the teller to see the branch manager. We sat down in his spacious office, my husband and I, and he instructed his "girl" to hold his calls. Whereupon we began to talk about anything and everything except our business with the bank. How long had we been in the country? Where had we gone? Whom had we met? What were we here for? Whom did we know in New York? It developed that we knew several people he knew in New York—merchants, bankers, members of the Irish government agencies operating in New York, and so on. Having thus established, in a polite and enjoyable way, our bona fides, he cashed the check and, further, invited us to a musical entertainment taking place that very afternoon at a "castle" out on a lake near Letterkenny. We had nothing planned, and said we'd see him there.

It would begin about 2 P.M., he advised, so we went in search of lunch first. The bank manager himself, it seemed, would shortly leave for his own lunch before riding out to the castle, where he was involved in running the festival.

We got on what we thought was the road to the festival. And the "short" of this story is: We found it at great length, after going obviously the wrong way round a mountain—over it, in fact—on a dirt road with huge pointy boulders as the entertainment factor. And when we found it, we knew we were there mainly because the army was directing, by walkie-talkie, a traffic jam of cars backed up in two directions on a less-than-single-lane road leading round a lake to the castle.

I'm sure the festival was enjoyable: all the youthful singers and dancers I saw getting on their buses to leave looked completely drained—and there were several hours' worth yet to come. Still, the sun was going down and we were a long way from Rathmullen and our dinner. So we made a two-hundred-point turn in a jam-packed courtyard and, finding the bank manager looking for a lift out to the army outpost and his own car home, we took him on and just barely talked the army into getting us a clear way through and out. And we never heard a note.

It was too late for tea when we got back to the Rathmullen House, and too early for dinner. Nonetheless, I needed a restorative of some sort. We had noticed earlier the sign for the lounge bar, which was in the basement and done up as a wine cellar, so we went there. The barkeep was just arriving and, while we waited for him to set up his bottles and glassware, we were joined at the bar by a young couple with a baby from Ulster, on holiday, who also looked as if they had had a trying day. We didn't know if they were Catholics or Protestants, but it didn't matter.

At least it didn't until the barkeep began telling jokes. "Did you hear the one about Ian Paisley? He was on a visit to the Republic, and he wanted to send some postcards home. So he went into the post office and asked for the stamps, and the girl thought she'd seen the last of him. But he was back in a sec. 'There's something wrong with these Pope John commemorative stamps you gave me,' he said. She looked at them.

" 'Sure, then, there's nothing wrong with the stamps,' she said. 'It's you're spittin' on the wrong side.' "

Neither of us knew whether or not to laugh. But the tense moment passed and, in fact, the barkeep had broken the ice. We didn't, after all, know if he was Catholic or Protestant, and, especially in these parts, a person could be either. And in any case, life goes on. He told us some of the local gossip, most of which I cannot recall because I had no reason to, and no reinforcement. But I do remember about the accident that killed the lawyer's wife and her two children.

It was a sad story, all by itself. But the next day or two, I walked down into town (the Rathmullen House sits on a hillock overlooking it) to buy some sundries—a notebook, some chocolates, some tissues for the car. I passed a small shop showing handmade pottery and tried to go in. A sign said to knock at the house next door for service, so I did. A young married woman (as opposed to a girl) answered, and said she'd get the key and be right over.

As I chose some small gifts to take home (Ireland abounds in small gifts, and not the tacky sort either—saying "Gift From Ireland"—although you can get those, too), we chatted. The store owner was not there, she explained, because of the accident—assuming I'd know what accident, and indeed I did, as there are so few. The owner was a close relative of the family; she herself was a sort of cousin. But she didn't feel she was so close as to go straight into deep mourning—and life had to go on. Though it was (she clucked and drew in her breath in a peculiarly Irish manner) a sad thing indeed for the man to be left without a family.

And this, too, displayed to me something of the Irish character. In the United States, we'd be weeping for the mother and especially for the two young lives snuffed out too soon. But we'd be glad that the father wouldn't be left with children to raise alone. The individual, to us, is paramount. In Ireland, it's the family. And there's no doubt that if he had been left wifeless with children, these same cousins, and others, would have helped in the raising of them. And the help would not be seen as a sacrifice.

It seemed, finally, to be time to find the distant relatives I'd been told I had in Ireland, so we set out early one morning to take the Coast Road to Bunbeg, a tiny seacoast village halfway round the wide peninsula that is Donegal. When we got to Carrigart, we stopped to buy some woven blankets and got quickly back on the road. It was a long way to Bunbeg.

It had begun to drizzle. As we rounded a curve outside Carrigart, in what I am now certain is the only extensive wooded area in Donegal, we passed an elderly woman trotting at a good clip along the tarmac. "We can't just let her walk wherever she's going in this," my husband said. We backed up. Gratefully, she got in. She was on her way home to Downings, after having finished her day's work as a housekeeper at a hotel in Carrigart.

"I waited for the bus for about an hour," she said. "But then I thought I could walk home faster than he was likely to come; they get caught up sometimes," she explained.

Downings was not originally on our route, taking us off the main road on a several-mile loop around the head it was on. But we were in Ireland to discover it, and all adventures were gratefully accepted.

Downings is a fishing village on the Rosguil Peninsula. Interspersed with the fishing fleet are the holiday makers, many using the windswept golf course, not "greened" exactly, but tufted with hardy littoral grasses. Donkeys graze on it and around it; in fact, it was in Downings that I began to think there might be as many donkeys, all apparently at their "aise," as people in Donegal—though I am assured this population imbalance is actually between sheep and man. From Downings, you can sail to Tory Island or Inishbofin.

Inishbofin is a culture unto itself. Lying actually out of sight of Downings, across from the peninsula to the south called Bloody Foreland, Inishbofin has been home to a band of Irish having a culture significantly different from that of the mainland and one that, in recent years, has come under attack. The people of Inishbofin, while Catholic, have a marriage rite that no church on earth would condone. The young people will not marry until their parents have died; needless to say, this would lead to the birth of darned few children. So, the children are had and reared in the mother's house, without benefit of marriage. When the father's parents die, the couple marries and moves in together.

The marriage itself often takes place by proxy. Because there is no resident clergy, and the waters are often too rough for crossing, when a marriage is to happen, the priest stands on a bluff and does it all by smoke signal. Now, this may not have happened in a hundred years, or it may have happened again yesterday. But one thing is certain: the people of Inishbofin are a world unto themselves, and they want to keep it that way. In that interest, the Irish government had supplied a teacher for the island's children, at some great expense (because who, not of the tribe, would want to live there?) and at, thought some government pundits, the sacrifice of educational quality. Thus, there was a plan afoot several years ago to bring school-age children to the mainland, to live with temporary families and be educated. But a member of the Dail, Denis McGinley (whom we were to meet that very afternoon, by happenstance), put at least a temporary stop to it.

When we got to Downings, we dropped the woman at her house; the trip, by car, had taken almost half an hour. Walking, or even trotting as she was, would surely have taken up a good part of the day. After we left her, we saw parked in the town center a bus labeled "Carrigart." The bus driver was deep in conversation with the driver of a car parked next to him; he may have been there for hours and might, we realized, be there for hours yet. We stopped in the McNutt factory in Downings, as long as we were there.

McNutt makes tweed fabrics of the best quality. Mr. McNutt demonstrated how the fabric was woven and lamented that he was unable to export it to what he saw as a prime market, the United States. "You've got quotas for sheep products," he explained, "and tweed fabric—but not tweed garments—comes under it." He thought, he said, there was a way around it, and that was to add a percentage of silk to the cloth so that it wouldn't be an agricultural product. (Since I spoke with him, two things have happened: he has added the silk, and the U. S. import regulations and quotas have been changed, and, as regards tweed fabric at least, relaxed.)

Reluctantly, I left McNutt. But it was getting on for lunchtime, and I still had a very long way to go to Bunbeg.

Bunbeg is in the middle of that vast seaward area of Donegal shore called Bloody Foreland. As we entered Bloody Foreland, looking to the right, there was a steep hill down to the shoreline farms and pastures. Halfway out of sight below the roadbed was an unused thatched shepherd's hut, grown over with brilliant red fuschia. The photo opportunity was more than I could bear, and the results show an almost abstract geometric pattern of yellow thatch, red billows, green stripes, and the azure oval of the bay, all backed by a tourmaline sky. The day had, in Irish tradition, turned fine.

In Gweedore parish, where Bunbeg is located, I took out what meager notes I had gathered from aunts and cousins at home about the possible whereabouts of distant Irish relations in Bunbeg. I had one name, Con Doherty, and if I could find him, I had the key to the rest, they had assured me.

Lo and behold, at the far end of town was a hardware store

named Con Doherty's. I inquired, but it wasn't the right Con Doherty. I was told that Doherty was the most common name in Bunbeg and there were at least two others. At least. But if I was looking, as I said I was, for the house of a woman who had emigrated to the States before 1920, then I'd best go see Mary Gallagher at the hotel; she was of that age and doubtless would remember.

She would, indeed. She recalled a young girlfriend of hers going to America, but the name wasn't Anna McBride, she didn't think. Still, she did know Con Doherty, and he was related to some McBrides. And she told me where to find him. He was retired himself, she said.

We headed out in the same direction as the wrong Con Doherty's store and, very near it, took a turning down toward the water. The whole coast along there was full of indentations forming tiny peninsulas not a mile across, and often containing one or more roads, winding past huge boulders, tiny fields, weather-worn cottages, and a few brand-new homes with some of the best scenic water views in the world. Finally, we found a still smaller road and, thinking it was the one in Mrs. Gallagher's instructions, took it. But it dead-ended at a farm where a woman was working in her garden and her preteenage son was riding in on his bike just then.

"Could you tell us where to find Con Doherty's house?" we asked.

"Sure, I could, then. But you might not find it. My son will ride with you up to it and show you the way," she offered. And the boy agreed.

It was quite close and, when we were at the drive, the boy hopped out and walked back down the road, though we told him we'd be glad to drive him back, now that we knew the way. He wouldn't hear of it; in fact, he couldn't, as he was halfway across a field before we had the words out.

We knocked on the door, identified ourselves as best we could to the man who answered (he was Con Doherty, the right one), and no sooner explained our mission of finding Anna McBride's house than he was leading us off to the car. "I think we'd best drive to where I think you want to go," he explained. "Though I'm not sure myself who Anna McBride was, although I know a Maurice McBride. But we'll see."

Shortly, we came to a rise in the road, and there was a good-looking young man, hacking at his front yard (impossible to say lawn) with a pick. "This is Denis McGinley. He used to be the schoolteacher in Bunbeg; now he's a member of the Dail," Mr. Doherty told us, probably because I told him Anna McBride's parents had been schoolteachers.

"Now, you know, the name Anna McBride doesn't ring a bell," said Mr. McGinley. "But would she have had any other name? You know, in Gaelic, the name Anna can also be Nora. Was she called Nora, do you know?"

I had never heard her called that, but then she has been dead almost twenty years. "She married a man named Box," I added

"Ah, Mrs. Box. Sure, she used to write to my own mother at least once a month and send pictures. And I'm almost certain the house up right behind my own is her family home. Some people from Glasgow use it now in the summer.

"I'll tell you how to find out," he added. "Go to the bottom of the hill and ask for a woman there named Maureen Greene. She keeps the keys to it, and so she'd know who uses it, and if they're any relation to you or no."

We went, we found Mrs. Greene, explained our mission—the three of us, I, my husband, and Con Doherty—and she went inside for some keys. As we walked back up, she asked if I knew a pretty blond-haired woman in New York who had married a dark-haired man and was wearing a very full lace wedding gown and all this occurred about 1960. And I said I did: my cousin, Maureen Donlon Robinson. Maureen Greene had received such a photo and never knew who it was, though she assumed it was a relative and therefore kept it. I knew we were on the right track.

I must add here that, although millions of Americans can trace their roots to Ireland, that had never been my purpose. My father had kept his two children far from associations with the Irish in Brooklyn, where he grew up, and I saw my relatives on his side of the family at little more than wakes and weddings. He had been completely adopted by, and had adopted in turn, my mother's highly New England, highly Protestant relations. In truth, I am no more than one-quarter Irish—and the Mr. Box my grandmother married was of an old Long Island Tory family. But I am convinced the Celt rises in the blood, and sooner or later, willfully or not, is reclaimed. I think I would eventually have discovered Ireland, had work not taken me there.

Mrs. Greene left us, the three of us, at the cottage. It was once a thatch that had since been roofed with slate. She said we could drop off the keys whenever we were ready.

I opened up the door and found myself in the main room of the cottage. A traditional Irish cottage has walls over a foot thick, as this one did. Often, except for word of mouth or parish records, there's no telling when they were built, as the materials and styles did not change for hundreds of years. These cottages consist of one large central room and two other rooms, one at each end. Often, there are sleeping lofts built up under the roof above these rooms and reached by a ladder. Usually, too, one of these end rooms is larger than the other, being the master bedroom, and may have a fireplace backing on the main fireplace and thus economizing through use of the same chimney. The smaller bedroom will have no fireplace.

The main room was furnished scantily, with a table and chairs, a couple of easy chairs, and an iron standing on a window ledge, no doubt where the most recent summer guests had left it to cool when they departed. A vestibule and extra outer door had been added to this room, leading, I imagine, to the outdoor plumbing. In this alcove, also, an electric cooker had been installed. On the walls were some religious prints, and on the mantel, unbelievably, a pair of Victorian pug dogs that I am sure had been there since my great-grandparents moved in.

My husband went through to the larger bedroom and, for unexplained reasons (but much in Ireland happens inexplicably), drew the door shut behind him. When he did, he let out a yelp of shock—not because of the door but what was behind it. A copy of my parents' wedding picture.

He ran with it into the room where I was. "Is it truly your father and mother, then?" Mr. Doherty asked. "I guess we've found the right house for you after all. And that means you're related to Maurice McBride—I can take you by his house—and to Mary McFadden. In fact, let's go to see her."

So, after taking pictures of all and sundry—including half a dozen pictures of the picture—we three piled back into the car for a ride out on another winding road. We waved good-bye to Denis McGinley; he was still at work with a pick, making, he said, a bona fide lawn from the boulder that constituted his front yard.

Mary McFadden is a very old lady, and I'm not sure what relation she is to me, even after meeting her. But Mr. Doherty had a grand visit with her, while her son, visiting from Birmingham, England, where he works, took me on a tour of the area. Standing on a windswept hill looking out to sea, he explained to me how things were, still, in Donegal.

"My mother has had electricity for a number of years, and she uses it," he said. "Did you see the new big stove in the kitchen? It is fired with turf or wood, and has a tank at the side which keeps water warm for bathing—and goes right into the tub through pipes. This is new to this area in Donegal, at least among the older people in the older houses. I bet your gran's house had no amenities, did it?"

Indeed not.

"There's one old woman who hasn't turned on a light since electricity was first installed in her house in 1959," Mr. McFadden related. "She's afraid it will kill her."

I don't know, still, whether these are tall tales. Certainly the young people are like young people everywhere; Gweedore parish even has its share of computer games installed in shops for them to play.

But it was still true, McFadden said, that many younger people who wanted a family or wanted to get ahead had to emigrate to the United States or at least part-time to England, as he had, to find work that paid decently. In that respect, Donegal is the slowest of the counties to prosper. And the Industrial Development people say it is so, although Mayo, too, is lagging a bit behind the rest of the nation in grabbing a share of Ireland's new prosperity. The problems in Donegal are, of course, many. For one, it is the northernmost county in the Republic of Ireland, and the coldest and rockiest. Its ports are more likely to be victims of severe weather and less attractive than those in the more populous south of the country to international trade. While virtually all of Donegal's people are literate in Gaelic, many are not skilled in English even now; indeed, many of the older people speak Gaelic only. Con Doherty himself told me he considered English to be his second language. And he wasn't perfectly comfortable with it; his wife was less so. Even his dog was trained in Gaelic. All this sets Donegal apart from the rest of the country. And, too, there is the persistent rumor, possibly fact, that Donegal is where the IRA goes on holiday. August is holiday month in Ireland, and it was in August that Lord Mountbatten's boat was blown up in Donegal waters.

Finally, we decided it was time to leave, especially as we had at least a two-hour ride, not stopping and moving fast, to get back to our hotel.

Before we dropped Con Doherty at his house, we were invited to return the next day for afternoon tea and a trip to Burtonport, from which, he said, my grandmother had emigrated.

I was in culture shock, to say the least, but my husband was less so, since they weren't his relatives. Still, the O'Shields were a Donegal clan, as well, and he had a quarter of his ancestry among them, though so far back and so processed through the American South that it is probable all of and none of the O'Shields are related to him.

I decided, in any case, to have champagne for dinner, whether to celebrate the linkage of my roots or to assure myself that, yes, I was still a cosmopolitan New Yorker, I am not sure.

The following day, we picked up a young man who was hitch-hiking to Bunbeg. Surprised that he was headed for so small a town, I asked why. "To see Denis McGinley," he said. "At school, I am a member of his party, and I do work for it in the elections. At the moment, I'm up here at the Colaiste Uladh in Gortahork taking the summer Gaelic course, and I thought I'd stop by to see Mr. McGinley." The Colaiste Uladh offers intensive training in Gaelic. For a period of six weeks, the students live with a Gaelic-speaking family and speak nothing else. This young man was a Dubliner, and previously had known little more Gaelic than "Erin go bragh." With him and his peers, he said, learning Gaelic is immensely popular, though they don't expect it to help them in the professions they plan to enter.

We stayed easily on the subject of politics, and the youth asked us how we liked our President Reagan. "The students here don't like him," he said. "It's the way he comes across in the press." We then talked about the press, its responsibility and its distortions. The student was surprised to know that many Americans think Ireland is a dangerous place, mainly because of the wide and intense reporting of such IRA incidents as happen. The summer of Bobby Sands's death, for instance, droves of Americans had stayed away from Ireland, fearing the worst. And yet, there was nary a dustup, save in the same sorts of neighborhoods tourists would avoid in Ireland, or anywhere else in the world, for that matter.

The young man didn't plan on either politics or journalism as a career, but rather medicine. But he did, as almost all the Irish do, read a newspaper every day. And he was willing to discuss the news from all angles at all times—again, a trait the Irish seem to get with their first taste of mother's milk. While the French seem to be congenitally interested in food, the Americans in the dollar, the Italians in their wine—the Irish are interested in politics. And who can blame them? After a thousand years of subjugation, first by the Vikings and later the English, they now have control over their own politics, and thus, in addition to their natural inclination, have still the ardor of new lovers about it.

It has, in fact, been little over sixty years since they've been a nation. Next even to our young government, the Irish one is a baby. And yet, it has back of it the strength of thousands of years of unbroken civilization. Once again, the Irish are melding opposites, and in a uniquely workable way, for their government is one of the most stable in Europe.

When we reached Bunbeg, we went our separate ways, and I didn't see the student again. I assume he found Mr. McGinley at home.

We sat down in Con Doherty's comfortable cottage, a twin of my grandmother's, except that his furniture was better and newer. His great shaggy dog lay at my feet. Mrs. Doherty came into the room with a tray laden with things she had baked for our coming. We had tea and a long sit and a bit of talk. And more tea. And finally, Con suggested a ride to Burtonport before the light faded. (This doesn't happen until about 10 P.M. in summer.) However, as we learned, personal cars are still somewhat rare in that section of Donegal, and Con, having worked all his life at road repair, rather missed riding around. His wife, however, chose not to go.

It was the trip to Burtonport that brought home to me two separate thoughts in painful detail. One is that Irish time is never what it seems. The other? Never pass up a lavatory when you have the chance.

"It's only about ten minutes to Burtonport," Mr. Doherty assured us as we drove off. Maybe as the crow flies. But taking winding roads around the sea, it was much farther. In fact, it took forty-five minutes, and I'd had a lot of tea. I badly wanted a "Mna," a ladies' room. While Mr. Doherty and my husband looked at and photographed the fishing fleet that still uses Burtonport, I went to the pub in search of facilities. No such luck. This was a male pub in a male town, and so there were "Firs" (men's rooms) only to be had.

Back in Bunbeg, luckily, there are two hotels. After we had dropped Mr. Doherty at his home we raced to one of them, both of us by now needing relief. The Ostan Gweedore, the one we chose, is a modern hotel built right on the beach. The tide was out, and we could see people driving over the hard-packed sand of what was, at least half the time, seabed. We weren't adventurous enough to do that. And besides, we thought there might be a trick to it, maybe knowing how to skirt quicksand or something. But we were willing to walk over it, and we did. We climbed a craggy, slippery boulder and sat on its top, knowing that when the sea raced back in, even if the top were above the tide, it would be impossible to sit on it, nor probably even hold on to it for dear life. It was an odd sensation, to say the least, knowing that we were treading on King Neptune's domain with impunity, like creatures transformed through a charm for a short time, only to regain their humanity or mermaidhood or other form at the gods' whim.

But as had happened before, the wind shifted and we began to get chilled. It was time to trek back to our hotel and dinner again. This time, we decided to take an inland route past Mount Errigal rather than the beautiful Coast Road.

Mount Errigal is a long-dormant volcano and is the salient feature of the Donegal landscape for miles and miles. At its base is what is known as Poison Glen, with a lake rumored to contain poisoned water due to poisonous plants growing at the water's edge. This, however, is a tall story. The name supposedly truly arose because some Frenchmen, having had an abundant catch in it, named it "Poisson" (fish) Glen, which the locals then corrupted.

The Irish are very fond of French names. They call *cakes gateaus,* after the French, rather than using the English word. *Zucchini* are *courgettes, eggplants* are *aubergines,* and not just on Frenchified menus in fancy restaurants either, as would happen in America. This is the way the woman in the street speaks of them, and it may have to do with a long, if only mildly fruitful, alliance between the French and the Irish—understandable in view of the antipathy of both, at times, toward the English.

The French, you may recall, sent seven thousand seasoned troops to help the Irish and James against William of Orange at the Battle of the Boyne. Later, in 1794, Irish patriot Theobald Wolfe Tone is reputed to have delivered to a French agent in

Belfast the information that the Irish would welcome a French invasion of the country, as a step toward getting the English out. In fact, in 1796, France did send an expedition to land in Ireland. But it had been delayed in the shipyards at Brest and set out in winter storms. Some ships were driven out to sea, and those that reached Bantry Bay were not able to land due to the weather. Naturally, this was bad news to the rebels Tone led. But the government of Ireland at that time, which was, naturally, British, was overjoyed; it followed up its jubilance by enacting further oppressive measures against the Irish. But, despite the failure of the action, the Irish seem to have remembered with fondness the efforts of the French on their behalf. They forget, as well, that as many as three hundred and fifty thousand Irish expatriate troops serving the French died between the Flight of the Earls and the First World War. But that, too, seems a continuing facet of the Irish character: the land lays full claim to its citizens while they're in it, but denies them if ever they leave. Many an eloquent Dubliner, from Oscar Wilde to Brendan Behan, would say that it was true.

It's so rare that a really sizable town is inland in Donegal—in fact, that any town is, so filled with rock mountains and untillable plains is much of it—that Stranorlar and Ballybofey, on the inland road from Letterkenny to Donegal Town, are a surprise.

The most amazing thing about the two of them is that they grew up so close together, and they both have very attractive shops. But the most attractive shop in the whole of Donegal, to my mind, is Magees. Nominally a department store, it carries only fabric goods, from bolts of tweeds to ready-made clothing (made in their own factory) for men, women, and children. There's linen, too, of course, and smaller, "less dear" goods such as tea towels and curtains. And on the second floor is a café, serving light snacks or full lunches, cafeteria-style.

It is a pleasant place to shop: lots of fun finding what you want, and competent help. And there are always bevies of tourists to watch, as well.

Donegal is an old city, and, as such, is intrinsically interesting. It is more interesting still on a "soft day" as you approach its gray roofs and rookeries out of the gray mist. Walking along its gray streets, in the gray northern light, it's easy to catch the twinkle of the gold crosses in the jeweler's window, reminding you that of all places in the world you might reach rainbow's end, it is in County Donegal. Outside the gray town, the stony reaches, softened by a thin layer of heather and gorse over scrabble, are wide, vast, unpeopled, and lying endward and sideward to the bowl of sky. When the weather clears, you imagine, there will be a rainbow. Ireland has more than its share of them because of its northerly position on the sphere and the refraction of the sun's rays over its curve and through the lens of its watery veil. And you imagine that, with a fast enough car, you could reach it and claim the pot of gold.

And then you're brought back to here and now as suddenly as you left it. A huge, jovially painted green-and-white CIE tour bus pulls into the town center, flinging its catch upon the slick stone sidewalks. Like exotic fish, the gaily colored newcomers flounder about the almost mossy sidewalk, out of their depth for a minute in a completely alien world. And then they drift off in twos or threes to investigate their surroundings and maybe bring away something to wear or eat, or something less tangible and more lasting still—as I had.

epilogue

I have been home now for quite some time since my most recent trip to Ireland. I have written a book about it and I hope it expresses the affection I feel for the country and its people.

But what do I think of the Irish, now that I am home?

To begin with, they can be maddening. I have thought of the Irish and their country that way many times before. But that didn't prevent me from returning to Ireland, again and again. And it never will. When we travel, we are children. Like children, we long to be taken care of, we long for familiar comforts. This is not likely to occur. And so we get annoyed. We want the Irish, or any other nationality at home in their own land, to be more like us. Stupidly we want this. Intelligently, we who travel recognize it before long and let it go. One cannot, after all, take a lover unless there is something *different,* even opposite one's own being, about the beloved—or else it would not be love at all, but simply narcissism.

The Irish are also charming. Responding to that charm permits me to shake off their contrariness and crumble when I see an impish grin on a clear-eyed lass enjoying a rare sunny day. It is this response to their charm that lets me grow fond of a grown man so shy in the company of women that the simple playful raising of a skirt can turn him red and giggly.

The Irish are fundamentally polite. How else could they welcome strangers to their door, as they have done so many times to me? The vet's wife. The woman whose husband helped me with my car in Connemara. The landed gentry feeding me, not a put-up fancy dinner, but a homey Sunday night supper with left-over birthday cake, no less.

They are helpful in the extreme. I have rarely asked for something that was not provided.

They are fun-loving. They are warm-hearted. They are no fools, however, and can bargain with the best. Their lateral thinking doubtless helps them compartmentalize sentiment and business.

They are fond of children, and not so fond of dogs as I might wish. In fact, even the English are not so fond of dogs as I might wish. (I find it is Parisians who really regard dogs in the proper light. But that is another trip entirely.)

They seem to like underdogs, though. The island nation was one itself for so long that it's not hard to see why. This attitude expresses itself in, I think, their seemingly endless willingness to give anyone the benefit of the doubt for any reason at all. In fact, this very attitude may have kept them bound to England longer than need have been. On the other hand, perhaps it will save them the terrors some pundits are forecasting in the wake of the accords between the Ulster government and the Republic of Ireland.

All this is merely to describe a few of my reflections about a few of the Irish people, however. Certainly, no one has ever asked me about Ireland and not gotten at least one long anecdote about at least one of the country's people. (I'm less keen on "things.") But even so, often the people and the things are inextricable. How, for instance, could one separate Sean O'Driscoll from Castle Matrix?

I guess I feel about Ireland as I feel about life! I can hardly explain either one in a few short pages, though I've made a good stab at Ireland in this book. The only way I could better tell you how I feel about Ireland would be, in fact, to tell you about it in person. I would begin with the parts I like best (the people, obviously) and would continue in that vein if I saw you were interested. I'd tempt you further with a few bits about the most magnificent landscapes. Then, I'd dazzle you with the history. And the architecture. And the flora and fauna. And, yes, even the food. And when I had completed recounting all of Ireland's glories, we'd raise our glasses together in a toast to that magical land and plan our next trip back.

index

T

U

V

W